A WEALTH OF COMEDY

An Autobiography

Richard Digance

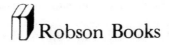 Robson Books

First published in Great Britain in 1999 by Robson Books,
10 Blenheim Court, Brewery Road, London N7 9NT

A member of the Chrysalis Group plc

British Library Cataloguing in Publication Data
A catalogue record for this title is available from the British Library

ISBN 186105 301 0

Printed and bound by Creative Print and Design (Wales), Ebbw Vale

Contents

Foreword

I first met Richard Digance in a departure lounge at Heathrow, where I was bound for the Middle East with Richard as my supporting artiste. Little did I know that this gangly rather shy Eastender would end up being my mate for life – so far.

What impressed me with Richard was his ability to hold an audience and take them on a ride through several different emotions during his set, from the rip roaring 'Drinking with Rosie' to 'The Beautiful Washerwoman', a song written by him and dedicated to a mother that he loved.

I soon realised that Richard had a few dodgy habits, for instance, he never ever buys cigarettes, but smokes twenty a day. He also has a devilish sense of humour. Once when we were entertaining the troops in the Falkland Islands, I put some shaving foam on his pillow. He got his own back by standing on my bed and weeing on it, fortunately I had gone for a walk. Once when playing golf, I was within half an inch of getting a hole in one and, instead of congratulating me, he sulked for a week.

Richard Digance is not only a unique performer, but one of the few people I could turn to if ever I was in trouble and I am sure one day that I will.

I hope by reading this book, you will become a little better acquainted with Richard Digance, the man I know and love.

JIM DAVIDSON

Chapter One

In Memory of Captain Blaney

Captain Michael Flood Blaney died a Second World War hero. He was hardly known by name, but his unselfish and dangerous work was appreciated by many thousands of working class folk who never knew him. He worked with the No 64 Bomb Disposal Section of the Royal Engineers, in the East End of London. He had defused bombs in Park Avenue and East Ham Manor Way, very much my neck of the woods, in September 1940. He was killed on 13th December of the same year, dismantling a particularly awkward beast with an anti-disturbance fuse. Whilst hoisting the bomb to allow transportation to the safety zone on the Wanstead Flats, a large green area of the East End, the UXB (the term for an unexploded bomb) unexpectedly went off and that was the end of Michael Flood Blaney, together with nine of his fellow bomb disposal comrades. Gone, but as they say, not forgotten. Indeed, I for one have his name etched in my memory forever.

At the East London Crematorium, he was laid to rest in the same Gardens of Remembrance as my mother and father, adjacent to the green playing fields of Wanstead. Laid to rest where the nasty bomb should have been laid to rest. That's how strange life and death can be.

There are dangerous jobs and dangerous jobs. During and after the Second World War in the blitzed areas of the East End of London, bomb disposal really had to take the biscuit. In that part of London, which was my part of London, there could never have been a more dangerous occupation than Blaney's, perhaps with the exception of keeping goal for Leyton Orient. The bombs had rained down on the East End during the war, killing thousands, including many of my own relatives. If your name was on it your time was up. That's what everyone said. We all felt particularly sorry for Mr and Mrs Doodlebug

1

of Manor Park! A very old gag, that one, but worthy of mention for its aptness at this particular point. They say if you could hear them overhead you were safe, but if the droning stopped then you were in trouble. Being born in 1949, I never heard them overhead. I used to nearly shit myself every night as I went to bed in such eerie silence.

My dad hated the Germans. Probably for the same reason he hated me too when I bought a Mercedes.

'Couldn't build tanks, let alone cars. Get a Ford, son.'

Any car not made at the Ford factory in Dagenham was a hostile enemy vehicle in disguise according to dad. In fact, come to think of it, I think my dad hated everyone except the man who invented Golden Virginia. Oh yes, my dad did enjoy a good shag, as he innocently would say each Christmas at my Auntie May's when offered a cigar. He won some medals during the war but he slung them away because it had taken away five years of his life. He was never to forgive until the day they laid him to rest near Blaney. My dad praised the partisans, the Yugoslavians and the like. God knows what he would have made of Milosevic. Oh yes, and he hated the French as well, but fair dos on that one, who doesn't?

Michael Blaney received the George Cross, Britain's highest award for gallantry, though he was sadly never to know he'd been honoured for such bravery. A further tribute was to be bestowed upon him too. A new council housing estate had been built near the Barking by-pass towards the end of the 1940s. It was to be known as the Gooseley Housing Estate and comprised of three storey council flats and a few houses for the upper crust. They would all be built around a green, in a sort of crescent shape, opposite the Beckton gas works. The bomb damage had been immense around the London Docks, and Gooseley was yet another completed rehousing scheme some two miles north of the River Thames docking areas. Some reckon when parts of the East End were bombed that the Germans did millions of pounds worth of improvements. In a sadistic way, it was a truism. The flattening of our area caused the authorities to get on with redevelopment at greater speed.

In 1949, the year of my birth, East Ham Housing Committee allowed a street to be named after the brave Michael Blaney. Overjoyed with the council recognition, the Old Comrades Association dedicated a plaque to their fallen hero, which read:

Dedicated to the memory of Michael Flood Blaney, GC RE and comrades of the 64 Bomb Disposal Section who were killed in this district on the 13th December 1940, whilst engaged in removing an unexploded bomb.

I remember the war memorial well.

I lived at 39 Blaney Crescent for sixteen of my earliest years and the memorial played a significant part in my growing up. It consisted of two pillars and a pole across which housed the sacred plaque, and it was positioned on a triangular green. Sadly, the memorial just so happened to be the approximate size and shape of a goal and the grass was the same colour as any world famous football stadium. Need I say more? Michael Flood Blaney did more than bomb disposal, he built me my very own Wembley Stadium. On this very subject I was to write one of my first personal songs, 'Back Street International'. It was to become a song adopted by Wolverhampton Wanderers and England centre forward, Steve Bull, whose biography bore the same name and quoted my lyrics. Bully was the sort of guy I'd have let play on my sacred turf, a working class hero with lots of guts and determination. My dad would have appreciated him for that. None of that poncy blond stuff as portrayed by the occasional French international.

Steve announced his retirement in July 1999, as I worked on the final pages of this book. An end of a true legend and wonderful servant to his club, Wolves. Loyalty, that's a word that becomes less important by the day and nowhere more so than in the world of football, the world I wanted to savour more than anything.

Every Friday evening I would wait there, in Blaney Crescent, in the shadows of the war memorial, for Mr Jackson, the milkman from the United Dairies, to turn into the crescent from Folkestone Road in his bright red electric milk float. That night each week he would collect the milk bills and I had the job of defending his stock from marauding hooligans in search of third pint bottles of orange juice. I loved the stuff. He seemed to spend a lot of time in various housewives' houses on Fridays, obviously doing a hard sell of the dairy products he carried on the float.

'How would you like your eggs in the morning?'

'Unfertilised thank you.'

An old gag worthy of a mention.

The equally old gag of the East End being so rough I rode shotgun on a milk float was almost true in my case. His stock was safe ...

except for the orange juice which I sold to my mates at half price without him ever knowing.

Mr Jackson never paid me, but every so often he bought me a tin soldier for my hard work and my diligence. I collected knights that resembled Ivanhoe at the time, and they all had different shields, coats of arms and coloured cockades on their head armour. They were quite expensive, the equivalent of forty pence in today's money, so I only had a few in my collection. Mr Jackson never bought me any of those though. The miserable bastard only ever bought me a tin London policeman or a Yankee commando with a green helmet. I risked my life for him, guarding his milk float. Just as well I did make a few bob flogging cheap third pint bottles of contraband to my mates in Blaney Crescent. None of my friends objected to paying for the liquor, I was after all the regular supplier of new Frido red plastic footballs when the knackered ones burst.

I never did get the knight with the yellow chevron on white background. I think he was from abroad somewhere. Dad would have hated him too.

'A poof with a feather in his hat, he's not coming in our living room, I'll tell you that for nothing. Go and get yourself a set of spanners and grow up.'

All my soldiers were timeless and inconsequential. I recall one military parade in the front garden of 39, when I amassed the ranks for briefing and was quite surprised myself by the assortment of regiments and occupations. I had Montgomery with binoculars hanging round his neck, standing beside Sitting Bull on a rubber horse. I had three American airmen standing to attention beside an AA patrolman who had bandy legs because I'd lost his motorbike, and behind them were two stretcher-bearers, a few Household Cavalry bandsmen and a police frogman who'd somehow escaped from my bathroom. What a motley crew, but I tell you this, those men would have died for me. In their own ways, they were all as brave as Michael Flood Blaney.

Some did die actually. In evil ways. It can't be pleasant being squashed by the paw of a cat three hundred times the size of yourself. Brave buggers the lot of them. Until, that is, the day they all decided to desert. Well, I assume they deserted because I don't seem to have any of them today. One minute they were all nestled happily in their metal biscuit tin barracks, and then they'd upped and gone. It happened some time between 1958 and 1999, but I can't really be more accurate than that except that I think it was at night.

The Co-op baker had an electric float as well, very much like the United Dairies wagon. His was British racing green, a bit like Mike Hawthorne's speedy car. A lookout? Never! He never entrusted anyone with such a job; he carried too many cream cakes for comfort. He knew the score. One step too near his travelling goody shop and we got thumped around the ear. Mickey Gent, who lived at 37, once let his tyres down and as the poor bloke went off for assistance this was, let us not forget, the days before phones – the Blaney boys stripped his van like a shoal of piranhas fighting over a wounded haddock. Mickey Gent was a biker and he once stabbed one of the Lane family from Gooseley Lane but he was always very polite to my mum. Then he bought a really big motor bike and I never saw him again. It must have had tremendous petrol consumption.

My life began on 24th February 1949 at Howard's Road Maternity Hospital, Plaistow, London E13. It isn't there any more. Neither am I!

I moved from London when my parents were rehoused from that council flat in Blaney Crescent to a tower block, Austin Court, situated behind the north stand of West Ham United football ground. To return with my memories through the many pages of this book is a visit I had to make, to remember when and how it was. Maybe to pay my long overdue respects to Captain Michael Flood Blaney after so many years. I had shown no respect to that memorial as will become evident, but now I take the opportunity to remember one of the many brave men who gave their lives in protecting others during the Second World War. During the first six months of the war, over four thousand unexploded bombs had to be dealt with in the East End alone. Poor Captain Blaney just happened to dabble with one of the less secure ones. I'd have had him next to Sitting Bull and the AA patrolman any day. I had little connection with the military during my life. Nearly a quarter of a century spanned the erection of the Captain Blaney memorial and my trip to the Falkland Islands with Jim Davidson in 1984 entertaining the British troops.

That year I stood beside the Governor of the Falklands, Sir Rex Hunt, and Jim Davidson, in Port Stanley, the capital of the Falkland Islands, the day of the unveiling of the war memorial to those who fell in action during the South Atlantic campaign. It was a cold day and we had a drink in Government House after the event, where I discovered Sir Rex's wife, Mavis, came from Ilford, not a million miles from myself. Ironically, Captain Blaney had defused two bombs in Little Ilford Lane. I think of the two contrasting war memorials in East Ham and the Falklands and am stunned by their far removed levels of importance. It's hard to imagine young Falkland Islanders playing football against such a sacred and respected monument and one can't help thinking poor old Michael Flood Blaney got a bit of a raw deal. That was the big difference, the Blaney boys all wanted to be professional footballers, the Falklands kids were already wealthy oil magnates of millionaire proportions. My dad always said the rich didn't know what they were missing. Things like impetigo, tuberculosis and never going away on holiday. It must have been shit being rich as a kid. We had a rent man with impetigo. Someone at the hospital had smothered his boat race (boat race: face) in purple paint. He looked like a blackcurrant spangle on legs. There was also a rumour that someone had tied him to a pram shed and covered him in red ink. When asked where he was, someone said he was marooned!! I doubt if that was true but it was funny anyway.

The cockney East End has changed now and I've changed with it. Yet my brain is still cluttered with the bags of sherbet lemons that had stuck together in the school desk, causing the owners to spit pieces of the paper bag out of their mouths as they sucked their sweets on the way home from school. The painful Chinese burns which weren't so bad on your arm but rather nasty in other places. Red scooters with stupid brakes on the back you could never find before you split your head open on a wall, bikes with stupid clicking things that pointlessly told you how many miles you had cycled. They're all filed away in the sad grey filing cabinet in my head. And it all began at Howard's Road Maternity Hospital, which they pulled down. I think David Essex was born there too, and Dame Vera Lynn. Bloody hell, how could they pull it down, it should have become a shrine.

The years between my modest entrance onto the world's stage in Plaistow, and leaving the East End behind in 1976 were times I shall never forget, nor wish to. Indeed, they created the backbone of my career in entertainment for over a quarter of a century. Most of my true stories have started out in East Ham and gone along with me, as my faithful literary companions. My birth must have been as sad as the Bambi film, because I cried all the way through it. Some say I was an ugly child and that my mum never showed me off to the neighbours until 5th November, when she collected twelve quid.

> Plaistow through the bars of a cot
> Plaistow through the eyes of a tot
> Council houses leaning into each other
> Like whispering grans or teenage lovers
> National health orange juice and cod liver oil
> Milk for Ovaltine just on the boil
> Plaistow this little world was mine
> My wardrobe dangling on the line.

My first home was at 14 Denbigh Road, off Hatherley Gardens, also in the shadows of West Ham's sacred pitch. I remember nothing about the place because we were moved, when I had reached the grand age of one, to Blaney Crescent. Compared to other areas of the war-torn East End, Blaney was a class manor with lots of green bits and open spaces where we could take our homemade track bikes, and break our arms in peace. I reckon I signed more plaster casts in my early days than I ever did album sleeves in later life. Every friend I had broke their arm at some time or other on the dirt tracks we called West Ham Dumps.

Poor old Blaney. Even if he'd been a deserter or a Japanese sniper he deserved better really. While we played football on the memorial green the girls did handstands against the inscription of his bravery, revealing their grubby knickers. Well, they called it handstands – we boys called it 'money boxes'. And the Captain gave his life for a better and more peaceful future. Some of those schoolgirls should be downright ashamed of themselves, except for Kathy, nothing wrong with her.

Blaney Crescent still stands to this day, but is now dangerously adjacent to the M25 motorway that surrounds London. It's a legacy, a monument in its own right, of how the East End used to be. It's a reminder of how poor kids can grow big and strong on stolen United Dairies orange juice and Co-op cheese cakes. Those council flats still stand like a dodgy set of teeth, some leaning, some cracked and filled in, but all still in relatively decent working order. Sometimes those council flats were cowboy saloons; sometimes they were changing rooms at Wembley Stadium. At other times they were boring bedrooms to rest up in until the next beautiful summer's day arrived during the school holidays.

Some things have changed though. The garden allotments where we nicked rhubarb and sold it round the streets are gone now. There was barrow-loads of the stuff and myself, Margaret Duly and Richard Cole made a few quid selling the contraband back to the unsuspecting neighbours who'd grown it on their own allotments in the first place. It was my very first business venture, and quite enterprising it proved to be, constructing a barrow with four pram wheels, which strangely had white tyres I recall, and two Jaffa orange boxes. We nicked tons of the stuff.

Now all the rhubarb plants are beneath that motorway that surrounds London. I wouldn't be at all surprised to see rhubarb creep through the six lanes of that God forsaken motorway in years to come as a remarkable legacy to the by-gone gardeners and young business entrepreneurs of East London. Perhaps when the first truck collides with a huge green leaf and maroon stem, Margaret Duly, Richard Cole and myself should have an allotment association reunion. Just the three of us. I kissed Margaret Duly on the lips once, which is more than can be said for Richard Cole.

Where did all those pram wheels ever come from? I imagine the East End to be full of screaming kids who couldn't get home for their rusks because their prams had been immobilised by gangs of kids in search of 'jigger' wheels. Yes, that's what we called them, jiggers. Other towns called them go-karts or karts, we called them jiggers. The only problem was the dumps emptied out onto the Barking by-pass and so it was a dangerous place to race a jigger down a steep gradient. It wasn't too difficult to end up under a Tate and Lyle's sugar lorry. My mate Francis Honey's dad was a carpenter. He had a jigger with a door that opened by brass hinges. No Jaffa orange box for him. No-one ever went in Francis's jigger, it was too poofy. If you got out of a jigger it was over the top of the box, head first, because you collided with something. You didn't open a door and climb out like the Queen.

What do you call those stupid things you get on sticks at a party? Yes, pensioners. I've just realised that most people mentioned within these pages are at that level or beyond by now. Subject matter of another of my songs: 'Life Is A One Way Street'. There ain't no turning back to where you've been.

These days, leaving the London Docklands, along the Southend Road in an easterly direction, it is easy to pinpoint the flats of Blaney Crescent, standing as proud as pensioners on those sticks. They are situated by the main traffic lights, where East Ham High Street South crosses the Barking by-pass, just before the M25 link road which we called the Rushing Waters, because there was a shitty river called the Roding cascading down to the even shittier River Thames. By the lights stands the Norman church of St Mary Magdalene, a very significant building in my life for so many reasons. Beyond the church and the run-down graveyard where I saw my first fox and took down my first puff of cigarette smoke on my way home from choir practice, are the Gooseley Lane playing fields where I scored so many goals for England and Brazil. Just by St Mary's Church where I sang at so many weddings as a choirboy and where I said my final farewells to my mother, stands the Beckton ski slope, just visible from the M25 motorway, though it's probably safer to keep your eyes on the road. It used to be a slagheap where we raced our track bikes and learned about birds and bees. I took my second puff of cigarette smoke down there. I had more confidence and I think it went down a lot further. It was a Senior Service and I had yellow gob for the first time. I wouldn't allow any member of my family to ski down that slope knowing what's underneath. There's more French letters propping that thing up than you'll find in a Paris post office. A slag heap indeed!

The mile or so between the Beckton ski slope and the M25 motorway doesn't look much, but that was my patch. It was the site of the largest gas works in the world, and the aforementioned Gooseley Park where Bobby Moore, captain of England and recipient of the World Cup, once gave me some football tips with my red Frido plastic football. Bobby Moore died on my birthday. I met him many times in later life and he knew he was my hero. He didn't say a lot, I think he was a little on the shy side, but on the football field he was a genius. He had claret and blue blood. He wouldn't have pissed off to Manchester United for fifty grand a week. Not Bobby, he was ours. Claret and blue all the way through like a stick of rock. He wouldn't have left us in a million years. Mind you, I would have done given half the chance. Come to think of it, Bobby Moore ended up playing for Fulham. He must have had a black and white blood transfusion at some time. My mate Tony Gale started his career at Fulham and actually cleaned Bobby Moore's boots. Hard to comprehend they may well have been the same boots that he made grubby by kicking my red Frido plastic football over Gooseley Park.

Along the Barking Road and down towards the by-pass
Everything is still the same, but somehow things are strange
I haven't been round here for oh I don't know how long

It must be twenty years or so and nothing much has changed
Kiss chase I played here, getting caught on purpose
Hopscotch when the girls would tuck their dresses in their drawers
I remember thinking then they looked just like Sir Walter Raleigh
No wonder no-one liked him when he came home from the wars.

So early into my life and we have already mentioned two of the most important men of my youth. Captain Michael Flood Blaney whose bravery gave me somewhere nice to live, and Robert Moore, one of the greatest footballers who have ever lived. Maybe this is the beginning of a kind of roll of honour for those who are no longer here. If it is so, we should give star billing to my mother and father. Someone sang 'only the good die young'. As true a word as was ever written. Blaney and Moore met untimely deaths, as did my mum, Doris, a mature art student sixty-eight years old who died of an undiscovered stone that had disintegrated into her bloodstream. Nothing wrong with her apart from that. Rotten luck. Doris Ivy Davis, born in Botha Road, East London on 27th February 1917.

Doris Ivy Davis and Leonard Digance were neighbours in Mortlake Road, in an area known as Custom House. The Second World War loomed and dad had to go. It was a big move for dad, all he'd ever done up to that time was sleep in an armchair every evening and all of a sudden he was off to Africa. Not a good move for dad, who, you may recall, hated everybody from every nation if they weren't born on the even number side of Mortlake Road. Dad thought that even people born in Blaney Crescent should be on the side of marmalade jars. Suddenly he was off to the grubby mud huts where non-Londoners lived. It must have been hard for him to take. I'm not sure what he did, he never kept any war memorabilia, apart from a huge grudge. He hated them all.

Mum, on the other hand, loved everybody and everything, especially stray cats I seem to remember, and even more especially those ginger ones that always stank of piss. We had three of our own, Monty, Sooty and Fluffy, but this ginger thing called Mickey strayed onto our windowsill one day and was rehoused with little fuss. She belonged to our neighbour Iris Wickham who cheaply wore make-up at fourteen and was therefore in no mental frame of balanced mind to look after a cat like Mickey. While she was out in her best clobber, sometimes until eight or nine o'clock at night, Mickey had made his way through the fanlight window, to the warmth of our fireplace.

I never knew my grandparents. My mum's dad, a carpenter called Jack Davis, was hit by a train at Barking Station and my grandmother died from something or other that caused her to have both her legs whipped off. It was obviously something more threatening than athlete's foot. I have the only family heirloom, an oak coalscuttle grandad made with amazing brass hinges, far superior to the ones on Francis Honey's jigger. He went to the first cup final at Wembley, the real Wembley, when West Ham were beaten by Bolton Wanderers, and he told my mum it was so crowded his feet never touched the ground. We lost 2-0 which goes to prove that referees were shit in those days too. I have a photo of that West Ham team of so many years ago in my billiard room at home. I bought it for my dad and when he died it was one of the very few things I rehoused in Hampshire.

My dad never, ever told me about his parents. To this day I know very little about them other than my other grandad, his dad, loved a drink to the extreme and my gran was named Mary. Oh yes, and they had a son who had a nasty knack of sticking new piston rings into the engine of an Austin Ten on our kitchen table. My dad and I seldom spoke. He was always asleep and when he woke up he went to bed! He wasn't nasty in any way, he just wasn't really interested in his children.

He worked for the Essex Ambulance Service at Barking during my earlier years and encouraged me to do the same, which I did – one of my last proper jobs entailed driving an animal ambulance for the PDSA. There must have been one evening in his early twenties when he stayed awake long enough to chat my mum up. His cousin Harry was going out with my mum's sister, my Auntie May, so he obviously had a bit of help, even with that. They played doubles at tennis. And they all lived in Mortlake Road, so the lazy sod didn't even have to walk mum home. Doris was the greatest friend I ever had. She died the very week my first television special was transmitted in 1985. Doris Ivy Digance (1917-1985). Again, gone but not forgotten.

They got married, an unlikely pairing really, at St Cedd's Church, Beckton, before dad sailed off to the distant lands where those funny people were born. Yet he must have come back from the fray at some time or other because my brother Len was born in 1943, although I can't work out the answer to that one.

Auntie May and Uncle Harry Cater lived at 42 Acacia Drive, Upminster and we spent most of our Christmases there. It was a time of 45rpm singles, Craig Douglas, and Del Shannon singing with a voice that suggested he'd left part of his anatomy dangling on a barbed wire fence somewhere. They had a half size snooker table, which I wasn't allowed to play on, and a splendid piano, which surprisingly I was. My cousins still to this day tell me I was the only child ever allowed to tickle the sacred ivories that were Harry's escape. I think he was my longest living relative of that generation, surviving in a Southend rest home until 1997.

I attended his funeral at Southend Crematorium in December of that year, and for me, on that sad day, the whole generation of my early Christmases had passed on. It moved me. All my Cater cousins were there and I saw them all together for the first time in a quarter of a century. Mary who's always kept in touch. John who lives in South Africa and is the same age as my brother. Andrew who lived a lot of his life as a high ranking police officer in Hong Kong, and Margaret, who married Mick, the same Mick who taught me my first chords on the guitar. We were all there together, and everyone looked older and more tired than they used to be.

On Uncle Harry's piano in Acacia Drive, began my musical career. We would take a tube train and struggle, armed with Christmas presents and clothes, along the steep climb up Bridge Avenue, past Hornchurch football ground, to no 42. What a bloody journey! Walk to the Barking by-pass, 106 or 147 bus to Barking Station, train from there to Upminster Bridge and then the walk. I remember the broken black gate bearing the name 'Auld Reekie', apparently the Celtic name for Edinburgh. Don't ask! Then, the day after Boxing Day, we'd get a lift home from my cousin John in a green Zephyr, registration FEE 146, back home to Blaney. I'd spend the next few days banging a football against the Michael Blaney memorial in my new West Ham strip which mum and dad seemed to buy me most Christmases.

May and Harry had an enormous back garden, at least forty feet long, which contained two apple trees. Oh no, goalposts again, as my cousin Andrew and I soon discovered. He was always Bobby Charlton. Upminster was middle class so I always felt Andy was entitled to be Manchester United, a snobby bunch of eleven individuals if ever there was. Whatever we did he was Manchester United. Things sadly changed after the Munich air disaster when so many of our heroes on the Subbuteo field were killed on that snowy German runway. Duncan Edwards? Manchester United and England? He was indestructible. He would never die. Andrew was

Bobby Charlton until we were both too old to be anyone other than ourselves, a rather sad time that seemed to be interlinked with the realisation that Father Christmas was dad in drag. I loved to boast about spending Christmas there when I went back to school after the holidays.

It had its perks too. I'd made it to the school football team as a goalkeeper but couldn't play because I didn't have a green jersey. Auntie May gave me Andrew's and so began what I thought would be an illustrious football career.

It's easy to see how we Digances ended up in the East End of London if you study the family shrub. We came over from France to escape some unfair persecution during the seventeenth century and we landed in Chichester, Sussex. We deserved persecution really, after all, we were French. It served us right. I don't think my dad ever knew he was a Frog, or he would have stabbed himself. The Digances were a French Huguenot family consisting mainly of market traders so it seemed only natural to eventually settle in the area that boasted the country's most famous fish, vegetable and meat markets, good old London Town.

Yet, still to this day, in Aldborough Church, near Chichester, there are documents that prove my distant relations were well-meaning churchwardens or similar. Henry Digance donated the Ten Commandments stone by the altar, but knowing the Digances he probably offered them just nine for cash. Another distant relative, John Digance, donated the Lord's Prayer. I have never visited the church but probably will some day. At a concert at the Chichester Theatre in October 1998, it transpired the St John's Ambulance lady in attendance was a Digance, as were two of the audience who dropped me a line, so at least a few of the Digances stayed put when they landed from France.

By the time I came along, the Digances were firmly entrenched in the East End. Mum and dad's Mortlake Road in particular and Custom House in general was an area near the London Docks, where most of the inhabitants worked at Ford Motor Company, Tate and Lyle Sugar Factory in Silvertown or Standard Telephone and Cables. Of course, many didn't work at all. It was a time of union power. The Ford mob were always on strike and so were the dockers. It was more a case of who you struck with rather than who you worked for. There were a few Digances knocking around those murky backstreets. In the London telephone directory there were two other Digance families I knew nothing about. We were a bit like mouth ulcers, we weren't spreading wildly like a herpes epidemic but we were there, hovering annoyingly in the background.

At the end of Mortlake Road, by the Northumberland Arms, a pub owned by legendary BBC disc jockey Pete Murray's mum and dad, stood West Ham Stadium, a venue even larger than Wembley with its one hundred and twenty thousand capacity. This wasn't the football ground. Dad went there every Tuesday night to watch the speedway. It's a housing estate now; years ago West Ham United tried to buy the place but they couldn't afford it. I always thought it strange that the Hammers never owned their own ground. They only rented Upton Park from a Catholic school. I only went to the stadium once, to see stock car racing, but I couldn't believe some of the cars were classier than the ones the dodgy geezers were flogging in East Ham High Street. I remember my dad telling me they all chased the gold top. I expected to see a dozen cars in pursuit of a bottle of milk, but the gold top was the top boy. At West Ham Stadium it was Aubrey Leighton.

Being brought up on Bobby Moore, Geoff Hurst and Martin Peters as well as cod liver oil and stolen National Health orange juice, there was little choice. I just had to be a professional footballer when I grew up, or, alternatively, work in a stinking orange orchard that reeked of cod's livers. Many who have heard me sing, wish I had done either, and others who have heard me play the guitar think I probably did!!

The move from Mortlake Road to Denbigh Road for my parents was short-lived. New council flats were built to replace the prefabs and terraced rows that were damaged during the Second World War, and so it was that we took up residence at 39 Blaney, by Captain Michael's war memorial. I loved the place. It literally was a crescent, with a big green outside for playing football and breaking windows as a result of some wayward penalties. The flats were divided into six, two each side of a lobby on three levels. We were bottom right and had a small garden where I played war games with my army Dinky toys. And I mean a small garden. Any fat woman's tits would never have fitted into our garden without lacerations from the fence.

Oh yes, back to the military parade, I've just recalled the lead stretcher-bearer in my army whose head had broken off and was therefore held in place by a matchstick. He had three hundred and sixty-degree vision and was as brave, in his own little way, as any other stretcher-bearer in any other war. He was the one flattened in our garden by a kitten over three hundred times his own body weight. He didn't even flinch. Mind you, he never encountered the huge pair of tits I just mentioned. They would have seen him off.

Funny how grannies of years ago had such huge breasts. My mate Joe reckoned, as a baby, he had to share the left one with his grandad, and he smoked Old Holborn. When dairies run out of milk they go out of business and close down. When mums become grannies, their milk churns flop down like a pair of spaniel's ears and expand as if Richard Branson were attempting to fly around the world in them. On ambulance duty I saw women's breasts that should have been donated to the starving children of India.

Next to us lived Mr Gent the dustman, as they were known then before they moved above their station and became refuse resettlement engineers or whatever they call themselves these days. He was the father of Mickey the biker who disappeared. Mr Gent was the first dead body I ever saw. I stood at the door as they carried him out. They could well have been his workmates but they weren't, it was a Saturday after all. Upstairs to the right the Dulys, and to the left the Coles. At the top were the Potters and the Sierces. The families didn't come and go as much as they do these days, everyone seemed to stay put until they died like Mr Gent. Funerals were commonplace. The hard-working East End fraternity seemed to frequently work themselves into early graves.

The next block of flats, at right angles to our own, housed a far more interesting collection of people. Mr Hoskins was top left, Iris Wickham and her mum were bottom right. Mr Hoskins had a nasty war. He'd served in the Royal Navy and something happened to the poor old chap. He staggered home from the Perseverance in Vicarage Lane every night, singing his bollocks off. In between him and the Wickhams lived the Snow Family, who strangely we only seemed to see in wintertime. Mr Snow, who dared to call one of his children Rupert, owned most of the rhubarb we stole from the allotments. Beneath the Snows lived the Catchpoles, an endless gathering of children, I think four or five of whom were great friends of mine. Making up the collection were the Clatworthys. Dawn looked and acted like Marilyn Monroe and her dad, a grey haired man in a white bri-nylon polo neck jumper, drove a white MGB with the roof down, and had white hair to match his white driving gloves.

Our school summer holidays were spent at Gooseley Park playing football from first thing in the morning until last thing at night, seven days a week for six weeks. The only change in timetable was if one of those commonplace funerals took place, then we had to show our respects by peering at the coffin through a pair of net curtains. When the parky blew his whistle our games stopped until he had gone. Then we'd climb between two bent railings and continue our matches. Occasionally he'd come back on his bike, after we'd smuggled ourselves back into the football stadium, and tell us to sling our hooks before he called the police. Sad bastard! While he was having a go, one of us gobbed on his saddle, a moral victory in a sad way.

So every summer holiday, John Lacey and I made the draw for the first round of the cup. Every football team in Britain was included and we, just the two of us, for six weeks, painstakingly played every game until the final, which strangely was always West Ham against Tottenham. There were quite a few internationals involved so they deserved the very best. For the final we always used a brand new tennis ball as a mark of respect. Then we switched to cricket, rubbing knackered tennis balls up and down our groins to provoke movement in the air. We'd seen Freddie Trueman do that in Test matches so we emulated him. We also brushed our cascading hair from out of our eyes, just like Freddie did, a strange and difficult task for both Johnny Lacey and myself as we both had crew-cuts at the time. Then we'd wear our whites and re-enact the Wimbledon All England Tennis Championships, grunting and bouncing the tennis ball three times before each service. Lying endlessly about balls that were over the base line.

Then it was September and we went back to school. So basically, we got as much football in as we could in the first few weeks.

On rainy days we played on regardless. The only thing, other than funerals, that prevented a cup-tie getting under way was when twenty-two grown ups wanted to show off on the Gooseley Park football pitch and play for real. Then we cycled down to the Woolwich Ferry. Now we are talking majestic moments. Those ferries began service in 1889 and continued, as a free service, until ugly diesel monstrosities replaced them in 1963.

We all went on the ferry a few times a year. Our dream was to touch our first female breasts in the engine room. This manoeuvre was known as 'going for top' and was something I was sadly never to accomplish at sea. There was Squire and General Gordon and I think John Benn. Three outstanding examples of Victorian marine engineering. We sat on the top deck as we passed from north to south of the Thames, popping down to the engine rooms to find the brass pistons throbbing away and to see if there were any tits hanging out and then back on deck to collect our bikes before disembarking. Every girl in East Ham knew it was a pulling venue so we never saw a single girl on any trip.

It never stopped us though. Stupid girls couldn't dilute our dreams of a bit of top afloat. I still sense the smell of that engine oil up my nostrils. The smell of detergent in the Thames as we waited by the jetty for the return journey. The ferries were sold to the Far East, I think in 1964, and another chapter of our East End days had passed forever. I bet the tits are much smaller over there.

I started at Vicarage Lane Primary School in September 1955, just a few hundred yards from Blaney Crescent. It was the year of my earliest recollections – I remember little of the years before. Newcastle were playing Manchester City in the FA Cup Final at Wembley and my mum sent me to Woods Bakeries in Brighton Road, the next road along to Eastbourne Road, for some crusty bread. I kicked a tennis ball against the wall all the way there and all the way back. I must have been a dozen different players and scored a dozen brilliant goals on my way to Woods'. Mum gave me threepence for going and I bought my first ever Wagon Wheel, and what a big bastard it was. Wagon Wheels in those days fitted wagons and you needed a couple of mates to carry it home. I listened to the Cup Final on the radio. Vic Keeble scored and West Ham signed him. I remember it so well, but not a thing before it.

I recall the shops on the way to school, all in Vicarage Lane. Colletts where I bought my bubble gum to collect football cards, including Brian Clough who I'd never bloody heard of! The Victoria Laundry where I took mum's 'big washing' once a month in a white sack. Bill the Barber who cut my hair like a crazed sheep-shearer for a shilling (5p), which probably explains a lot. There was a grocery shop that sold records, but only by the Shadows and Mike Sarne. There was a fish and chip shop that wrapped fish in newspaper. The number of times I read the football results on the arse of a chunky cod. Vicarage Lane I walked twice a day for years. I knew it like the back of my hand.

Of all those shops, Colletts sweet shop had to be the most significant one by far. The material I gathered for my comedy act over the years, it all stood on display in that shop. Great big jars with arrowroot biscuits the size of dustbin lids. Ridiculous things, I never saw a single kid ever walk down the street eating an arrowroot biscuit. They would have resembled those tribal chappies who had things shoved in their bottom lips by their parents, purely to ensure they never took up the mouth organ. A fucking good idea if you ask me! The fruit salads and the black jacks, two of each for a penny. Liquorice wood that made your teeth turn yellow. Tubes of Pepsodent that made you wonder where that yellow stuff disappeared to. Everlasting Strips that were toffees made from sheep's gut. Impossible to bite. Impossible to finish. Impossible to even think of resucking on the way home from school. The sports bars, the tuppenny wafers, or the palm toffees if you were brassy that day. Oh, those flavours in the middle of a palm toffee, I can still taste them now. Banana, strawberry, dark chocolate (poof's sweets) and so on.

Colletts had literally shelves and shelves of confectionery items that would one day provide me with my longest and most durable comedy routine which I titled the 200 Remembers. I cannot possibly estimate the number of penny bubble gums I bought there in the vain hope of completing my set of football cards.

There was Jones the Chemist who combed his hair in Latin, Stock's the grocers, and the Perseverance pub that Mr Hoskins frequented.

At Vicarage Lane School I learnt the art of negotiating school dinners. It was there I discovered that school stew had skin on the top so dinner monitors could divide it into eight. There I discovered pink custard. I never realised at such a tender age it would be the only time in my whole life I would ever encounter pink custard. Yellow stuff, lumpy stuff, but pink? Never again would I come across it. I should have regurgitated some and revealed all on the 'Antiques Roadshow'. The bent forks, hundreds of the bloody things, and in that disgusting dinner hall I also developed the art of finding a shiny spoon and licking it so nobody else stole it from you. School bread that tasted and felt like used nappies, and margarine that reminded me of dad's hair. The dinner hall was a former air raid shelter. It cost two shillings a week (10p) to stay but the overall cost was higher. The rotten teeth and fat kids who'd grown on beef gristle and cheese pie, which we called groundsman's feet. We were being kind as our groundsman was the smelliest, dirtiest person you'd ever meet. I was one of the lucky ones as my teeth remained in good nick throughout my childhood and I put on very little excess weight throughout my life.

We ate our dinners as quickly as we could and shot into the playground for more football. Playing for England with a gut full of grey mashed potato with lumps in wasn't easy but we managed it five times a week.

The marvellous Mr Percy Stitson, to dubbin footballs and pack the kit for the school game on Saturday often excused me lessons. Mr Stitson was a wonderful man who believed in me, and I met his son at a concert in 1995. He was proud of what I achieved by all accounts. I could never repay the joy he gave me when he told me I'd been picked for East Ham Schools. We played in the Crisp Shield and I actually played in front of a crowd at the Flanders Road ground where admission was by ticket only. There were a few talent scouts around but nothing materialised.

I looked after the rounders and netball kit too. There were a few opportunities there to do wicked aromatic things, but I was far too young and innocent to do anything more than fold the vests and shorts away in a large coal sack as neatly as I could. A classroom had been designated the sports equipment store and I was in charge of that. I enjoyed it so much, being on my own, devising kit storage systems and making the footballs look in good condition.

Safety Sam visited our school playground one day and showed us how a policeman on a motor bike could fall off and injure himself. I know at least two classmates who used that useful knowledge in later life, scarpering from the odd post office with the boys in blue in hot pursuit (Scapa Flow: go). What a complete waste of time, being told that was what happened when you walked across a road without looking. You caused a policeman to kill himself. Not a clever admission in the East End of London where most unlawful abiding citizens spent hours and hours trying to work out how to dispense with the law.

I failed my eleven plus at Vicarage Lane, rather easily I thought, and from that primary school I limped rather than progressed to Thomas Lethaby Secondary Modern, which became Langton Comprehensive in later years. I didn't progress to long trousers until the second year, as my Vicarage kit hadn't quite worn out. I never knew who Thomas Lethaby was but he had a school named after him so he must have been some grovelling, portly councillor with a big ego problem.

It was probably the first crisis point of my life. I missed Vicarage, the mixed classroom, and the accolades on the football pitch. I'd also become school chess champion, around the same time strange bodily movements were manifesting themselves under my desk. I knew I would grow bigger, but never quite understood it would be so immediate and involve only a certain part of my body at one time. Lots of my friends had made the grade to grammar school. I felt exposed although I knew I'd never passed. My maths stretched only to the number of penalties I'd saved that season. My geography took me no further than that snow-ridden Munich runway where Manchester United and Andrew's Subbuteo team were cut down in their prime. I never saw Duncan Edwards, but I very nearly did. If only my dad had taken me to Wembley to see the Hungarians instead of snoring and farting in the armchair. Then I would have seen my fallen idol. Other than that, I recall little more of Vicarage other than the fact I formed a skiffle group called The Happy Outlaws. Without question this was my first dabble into the music business.

We were originally The Outlaws, but John Lacey's mum, Pat, decided it was a rotten name that made us out to be hooligans and muggers, so she made us put 'happy' at the front. It was poncy, especially for an East End band of rogues, but we reluctantly agreed as it was her husband Les who was painting the name on the tea chest. Kevin Sullivan of Blaney Crescent – 65 rings a bell – played a real guitar, but only with his right hand to be honest. I played John's plastic Beatles guitar, only about eighteen inches long in old money. Keith Williams, another Blaney resident, possibly 28, played washboard. Strange really, because he always had a tidemark round his neck. And John, from the flats in nearby Folkestone Road, played the tea chest and sang. I never wanted to play that bloody thing. The very thought of lugging it around to various flats for rehearsal was enough to blow it for me. Sod that for a game of soldiers, I was perfectly happy playing the Beatles guitar with the gut strings you couldn't tune.

Our repertoire was predictable. Most songs came from Lonnie Donegan. 'Does Your Chewing Gum Lose Its Flavour On The Bedpost Overnight', 'The Battle of New Orleans'. I loved that song. I visited the actual battle scene down the mighty Mississippi on two occasions, once in 1994 and again in 1999 as part of my fiftieth birthday celebrations with my friend Rod. And of course we had our own song, written by John and his mum Pat:

We are the Happy Outlaws and this is our new song
We are the Happy Outlaws, we won't detain you long.
We are the Happy Outlaws and just before you go
We'd like to sing a song for you, we hope you enjoy our show.

Bloody hell, they don't write 'em like that anymore. I wasn't even bright enough to know what 'detain' meant, let alone sing a song about it. It was bollocks anyway, nobody enjoyed our show.

Keith Williams had a nasty brother, Colin, who used to beat everyone up and steal things. He wore National Health glasses with the pink plaster on one eye. No wonder he was humpy. He became a prison warder. He really did! He once tried to stab me with a penknife but some Henry Kissinger type must have intervened. He played football for Vicarage but was always dropped the week before the team photograph was taken.

John's stepdad was special. While my dad slept, he taught me to fish at Eagle Ponds near Wanstead. He landed my first specimen fish for me, a two-inch gudgeon on the Thames at Walton on Thames. Many of my weekends were spent fishing. I made a rod from a tank aerial and it weighed a ton. I eventually joined Woolwich Postal Angling Society, cycling every Thursday, across the Woolwich Ferry, to the Lord Raglan in Raglan Road, Plumstead, where I had my first ever drink, a bottle of brown ale. I then joined Newham Angling Society, which was far more convenient as the coach picked us up at Whitfield Road, East Ham.

My fishing memories are plentiful but probably the story that remains foremost in my brain is the time I fished the River Medway at Baring in Kent. I caught a pike that was ten feet long. It only weighed five and a half pounds but it seemed ten feet long to someone so tiny. I didn't have a gag to open its mouth and take out the hooks, so one of the club members shoved a two-ounce Golden Virginia tin between its jaws. The pike bit straight through the tin and nearly had the bloke's hand. I still say to this day it's probably the only pike ever to die of lung cancer.

We formed an angling club of our own, just four of us, called Leander Angling Club. Full membership comprised Richard Cole, Michael Walker, John Lacey and myself. I started to see less and less of John at Thomas Lethaby. We'd been the biggest of pals through primary school, done everything together, but then we started to make our own friends and directions. He seldom came fishing, but nonetheless we had a fortnightly club meeting in my mum's kitchen. We'd plan the weekend trip to Aveley gravel pits and I'd show Mike and Richard all the trade leaflets I'd received from *Angling Times* adverts that week. Leander Angling Club closed due to lack of support and nobody was ever to know except me.

Les, John's dad, often came to watch us play football for Vicarage Lane too and when John and I made the East Ham Schools team he ferried us around in an old cream Zephyr Zodiac. We were a brilliant school team. Kevin Sullivan played left back for the district team. George Hilsdon made it at centre-half. His grandad was the Chelsea footballer they dedicated and named the weather vane after on top of the main stand at Stamford Bridge. John played left wing and I played in goal.

Four district players from one school wasn't bad. Yet we never won a thing in all the years I was there. Being broke, I had little kit of my own. I wore Kevin's boxing shorts, black things with a thick white stripe, and my cousin Andrew's jersey. I never wore boots due to the fact I was born with spastic toes that curled under which necessitated weekly trips to Great Ormond Street Hospital with my mum. I believe it could well have been me who set the pattern for goalkeepers to wear different clobber to those who played in the outfield.

Two of our district side reached professional status: Roger Cross for Fulham, he came from Shaftesbury Road School, and defender Bob Glozier joined West Ham from Latham Road. I had a trial for Leyton Orient, broke my big toe by inadvertently kicking a goalpost and gave up. I seem to recall Bob Marley did a similar thing so I consider myself in great company. I remember well the Orient trial at Brisbane Road. Another kid from our district team, Raymond Tucker, whose dad, Ken, played on the left wing for West Ham, smacked his nose and played the whole trials with a plaster on his nose, just like Robbie Fowler does these days. Ken Tucker had a sweet shop by West Ham footy ground. He sold penny bottles of drink. They were all different colours but they all tasted of piss.

The Vicarage boys and Tucker from Latham Road gathered by the players' tunnel after the first trial which was nothing more than a bunch of kids kicking a ball about. A man by the name of Eddie Lewis asked me if I could take constructive criticism. When I replied that I could, he told me I was shit. So were Leyton Orient, perhaps we were made for each other after all. I never fully recovered from various foot injuries and inherited ailments and I began to lose interest.

The trips to Great Ormond Street were difficult and expensive for mum who had to keep taking days off work. I resigned myself to my spastic toes and stopped receiving treatment.

At Vicarage I played in goal from the age of seven to eleven, with the same yellow string gloves my brother used on his paper round, and I became house captain of the yellow team on school sports days. I hated the yellows. They were all fat sniffers. The fattest kid in our school represented us in the high jump. Jumbo Tonbridge never stood a chance. They didn't even put a bar across; they simply let him jump into the sand, where half of him disappeared. School sports days always fascinated me, watching the fattest kids running their guts out for a tube of Rolos, which would make them even fatter. Yellows were called Tudor. Totally stupid. I've seen loads of Tudor houses in my time and none of them have ever been painted yellow.

I gave up competitive football for a while when my mum took a job at Alf Jinks's butcher's shop in Silvertown. Through no fault of my own I was unavailable on Saturday mornings. Instead, I played with a tennis ball on an adjacent bombsite while my mum put in the hours in the run-down shop beneath the shadows of Tate and Lyle's sugar factory. My mum introduced me to Harry Hooper whose dad she worked with. Harry played on the right wing for West Ham, the opposite wing to Ken Tucker. I think he moved to Chelsea and played once for England. My dad said he was the fastest winger in England. I don't know about that but he was quicker than me . . . and three times bigger. If my dad said he was the quickest winger in England it simply meant he wasn't German.

My mum left Jinks's, I don't know why, which meant on Saturdays I remained on duty as my sister Jill and I took a bus to Leytonstone to collect a carrier bag of meat from Auntie Winnie and Uncle Dick's butcher's shop outside the Church Road entrance to Leytonstone tube station. So still no football. Winnie and Dick weren't really our relatives. Mum worked with Winnie at Marks and Spencer's when she was a teenager before the Second World War and they were best friends. I also think my mum had a soft spot for Uncle Dick, or vice versa. Good luck to them. Times were hard and they deserved any fun that passed their way.

Dad didn't really get close to anyone, so very little fun passed his way. We never saw any of his friends. Maybe he didn't have any, except for Bill Elliot who cycled to see dad once every six months from Dagenham. They were together in the war. He had a large grey mac and that purple paint on his face like the rent man. None of our Blaney Crescent neighbours befriended dad either. He just went to work, came home, slept, and that was that. Even in later life he had very few friends, and his small funeral turnout confirmed this. I think back on him as a solitary man. He died at the age of eight-two.

It strikes once more how often one must mention death in a book such as this. My parents, Bobby Moore, Auntie Winnie and Uncle Dick. The chap with the dodgy purple boat race. They're all in that great pie and mash shop in the sky. Oh yes, and of course, let us not forget Captain Michael Flood Blaney, without whose war memorial I would never have become a goalkeeper. My thoughts are with them all at this moment.

If I wasn't fishing I was playing football and if I wasn't playing football I was fishing. There was little time for anything else other than watching West Ham at Upton Park. I first went there at the age of five to watch Sir Stanley Matthews play for Blackpool in the FA Cup. The Hammers won 5–0. I had a claret and blue bobble hat my mum knitted me, and I collected star badges with photos of the players in the middle. The Leyton British Legion band played before kick off and then, to the sound of the 'Post Horn Gallop', out ran my heroes in claret and blue. At floodlit games they played in white with a claret and blue band. And they often played continental teams like Sparta Rotterdam and Spartak of Russia.

Dad and I saw them play Liverpool in 1957. A free kick from John Bond put us into the First Division and our first home game of the season was against the mighty Wolves. So many internationals on show that night. Billy Wright, Ron Flowers, Norman Deeley, Bert Williams, I'd seen them all in my football annuals and there they were in real life in their old gold and black kit. They looked bloody frightening.

I collected the Tiger league tables and every Saturday night I put the teams in their league positions before going to bed. It's all so different now. Kids today want to look like David Beckham or Ryan Giggs. I never wanted to look like any of my football heroes, they were all ugly bastards, and I certainly didn't envy the fifteen quid a week wages. If I'd become a professional footballer as planned, I would have retired a couple of decades ago with some injury or other. No thanks. My football memories don't stretch a lot further than the cup finals I played by the memorial for Captain Michael Flood Blaney.

And so this was how the life of Richard Digance began. Fishing and football. From such humble beginnings in the East End of London he became a live performer extraordinary, one of Britain's most popular stage and television entertainers throughout the 1980s.

On his fiftieth birthday party on 24th February 1999, whilst among his closest friends at his local pub, Richard decided he'd done enough touring and confirmed he would close the diary at the end of the twentieth century, sit down and write this book. It was a live performance career spanning thirty-one years from 1968 to 1999. Richard actually turned professional in the early 1970s but his endless crusade around the stages of the world began with 543 folk festival and club appearances in Great Britain, Canada, the United States of America, Belgium and Holland.

As a major theatre headline act Richard performed in public concert on 2,646 occasions in Great Britain, Hong Kong, Sweden, Indonesia, Morocco, China, Germany, Holland, Belgium, the Falkland Islands and Ascension Island, Belize, Cyprus, and the United Arab Emirates. Never once did Richard make a headline concert of his own in America, Australia or Canada.

He entertained at 309 corporate cabaret events in Great Britain, Thailand, the United States, Tunisia, France, Austria and Switzerland and on two cruise ships probably in international waters!

He began the long haul to success as a support act during the 1970s, giving 744 support performances in all, almost a third the number of headline shows. That is testimony to how long the show business apprenticeship can be. The supports and their memorable occasions are as follows:
304 with Jim Davidson, the only solo act in music or comedy to employ Richard in Great Britain
105 with Elkie Brooks, four years of touring including the Royal Albert Hall in London
72 with Chas and Dave, getting booed off in Margate
48 with Jethro Tull, including a week at London's Apollo Theatre, Hammersmith
43 with Steeleye Span, the first act ever to book Richard for a tour
37 with Joan Armatrading, getting booed off at Belle Vue, Manchester
24 with Tom Jones, including the Channel Islands and the Royal Albert Hall. Getting booed off just about everywhere
28 with Steve Martin in the United States of America
21 with Richard Thompson, where RD got his first support act standing ovation at the Brighton Dome
20 with Dana, a tour Richard remembers little about
16 with Hale and Pace as a once-a-month support act at the Tramshed Theatre in Woolwich
4 each with Supertramp, The Chieftains and Fairport Convention
2 each with the Kinks and Stomu Yamashta

And finally, for one night only, Richard supported the following at the following venues:

The Beach Boys at Knebworth; Eric Clapton at the Victoria Palace Theatre, London in aid of the Ethiopia Appeal; Elton John and Robin Williams at a Prince's Trust Concert at the London Palladium; the Allman Brothers in Atlanta, Georgia; T. Rex at Rush Green College, Dagenham, Essex; Billy Swann, once again at the Great South East Music Hall, Atlanta, Georgia; the Nitty Gritty Dirt Band and Esther Phillips in Denver, Colorado. He also worked on the same bill as Crystal Gayle and Roy Orbison at the London Palladium.

Richard Digance has walked onto a stage, somewhere in the world, and performed to an audience nearly four thousand times. That's over nine years of his life he's stood with a guitar round his neck in front of someone, somewhere.

But let us not forget the television and radio performances too. The longest continual series of one hour television specials in the history of British television; from the Old Grey Whistle Test at the beginning to the Jim Davidson BBC show towards the end, television appearances far too numerous to mention but probably in excess of four hundred and fifty performances. The five years at London's Capital Radio as a disc jockey and a folk music presenter and the endless radio appearances for the BBC.

No-one can deny that Digance served a fair apprenticeship. In all, placing together the stage and media appearances, the man has spent nearly eleven years, almost a quarter of his life, on stage. Literally thousands of nights on stage or in a recording studio. One night in three for thirty-one years he was there, making them laugh and sing along. So the decision was not a hard one on that fiftieth birthday on 24th February 1999, to enter the new thousand years with the memory of such a workload. The sore hip, the blistered fingers and round shoulders from stooping down at audiences, had taken their toll on the modern day troubadour. In the words of Richard Digance himself, he was fucked!

And it all began at Blaney Crescent when his classmate and neighbour, Jimmy Sarling, brought the Beatles' Please Please Me *album round to 39 for the Digances to listen to. The long and winding road indeed. Paul McCartney could well have been describing Richard Digance's life on the road.*

Chapter Two

Blaney, Breaks from Blaney and Lethaby

I eventually enjoyed my years at Thomas Lethaby Secondary Modern. Things certainly picked up considerably when my mum let me wear long trousers. I went there in 1960 and was nearly expelled a year later for slinging a milk carton at a girl in a neighbouring playground. We had a great form master called Vic Wernham, who taught technical drawing, and our art and pottery teacher, Trevor Sowden, was a big mate of my brother Len. Mr Jones taught us English, even though he was decidedly Welsh, most weeks making us read from a book called *With The Eagles*, which was about as boring as watching paint dry. More importantly though, I was regular goalkeeper in the school team and I hadn't excluded the possibility of rekindling my early ambitions in football. Now I was older and starting to grow a bit taller, an important requisite for a goalkeeper. Various scouts had been watching John and me, together with George Hilsdon and Kevin Sullivan from Blaney, and I hoped that the Hammers would make their move. They never did.

> I'm just eleven but I ain't stupid
> My feet are firm on the ground
> I was born on the wrong side of London
> To see the Sun shining down
> But at least I have my dreams
> And some people don't know what that means
> Don't pity my bashed about shoes
> For I can be anyone that I choose.
> I'm an international and that's all I want to be
> An international, and that's good enough for me
> I'm a back street international.

I'd made the cricket team too. It took a while because I never had a white shirt. I had to wait until my dad joined the Barking Ambulance Service. I wore my football shorts and a pair of my sister's white socks and felt rather aware of myself. I was the only cricketer in the school team with a white shirt that had black epaulettes on the shoulders. Never mind, it didn't look as poncy as all that sunblock stuff they splash over their faces these days, especially those Australian chappies. What's wrong with a bit of sunburn anyway? Yes I know, skin cancer, but hypothermia isn't too clever either if you get a rather bad dose of it. It seems a no-win situation to me, which makes me think that some scientists are too clever for their own good at times. I burnt my arms, right up to the tee shirt line, every first week in August for twelve years and my arms never died of skin cancer.

Speaking of the sun, we seldom went away on holiday. We sometimes went out for days. Just two days. A rip off, one day visiting an ailing old relative and the next getting a 101 bus to some park or other. Standing at the bus stop in East Ham High Street with a rubber innertube round my waist was total humiliation. We didn't even expect to go on holiday so it never mattered. As a child, holidays were rare. I remember all of them as if I'd just returned. Most years we just went to Canvey Island and looked after our auntie's house and dogs, Tiny and Scamp, while they went further afield. No 4 Ash Road. I recall the journey well, a steam train from Barking station to Benfleet, over a level crossing and a green bus to the Haystack, and from there we walked. She wasn't our real aunt, she was a friend of my mum's friend, Auntie Winnie with the butcher's shop, but we called her Auntie Elsie, although we never met her because she was never bloody there. If she had been there, we'd never have gone to her house in the first place.

Another ingredient of the 'going out for days' deal was visiting grandparents who never spoke to the young ones and probably didn't remember who you were anyway. Terrible thing, old age. I can't remember who it was we visited but she had a crocheted table cloth full of biscuit crumbs and always gave me a packet of Olde English Spangles that used to taste like bloody grow-bags. I hated the things. I was trying to be one of the lads, sucking three Victory V's at a time. Spangles were cissy sweets, only one up from Parma Violets. We called her Nan but like Elsie, she wasn't related in any way as I lost all my grandparents before I was born.

Our first self contained, non-helping, non-visiting family holiday was in Cornwall, in 1956, when dad borrowed Mr Morgan's Austin Ten. It took three days to get to the West Country, and we started a day late anyway because dad wanted to check out the tappets or some other bit of the car I can't spell. Mr Morgan ran our local grocer's on the junction of Gooseley Lane and Eastbourne Road. The latter resembled Coronation Street, and paradoxically, I visited its terraced houses every Monday and Wednesday through my paper round. Mondays was *Sunny Stories, Jack and Jill, Soccer Star, the Eagle, Charles Buchan's Football Monthly*, and *Woman's Realm*.

Stop for a Digance gag that did the rounds over the years:

The difference between *Cosmopolitan* and *Woman's Realm* was *Cosmopolitan* told you how to have an orgasm and *Woman's Realm* told you how to knit one.

Wednesdays was *Angling Times, Radio Times, New Hotspur and Victor*, and *Exchange and Mart*, all in all a bloody heavy bag to hang on your shoulders. I hated Wednesday's round, especially when it rained. The *Radio Times* turned into tons of papier maché in no time at all.

The second holiday I recall was to St Osyth in Essex, a small caravan site near Clacton. We stayed in a crumpled, cream coloured, hand-built pile of compressed cardboard called 'Leswick', which slept one comfortably and five very uncomfortably. It was the shittiest caravan on the site, and even at the age of seven I was starting to get a bit of a complex. I only sneaked out to the beach at night. I saw a show there in a small green metal hut. It featured a magician by the name of Val Duval. He was marvellous. I went twice. It was his summer season. Having survived and learnt about show business as much as I have over the years, there's no getting away from it, he must have been crap, or certainly his agent was. Nine weeks in St Osyth, in a green metal hut, that was only just better than delivering Wednesday's pile of mags down Eastbourne Road.

We went to North Wales two years running, 1958 and 59, staying at a farm in Fourcrosses, near Pwllheli. We went in our own Austin Ten, HTW 466, this time, in convoy with our upstairs neighbours the Dulys, in their sky blue and white Hillman Minx, KHV 543. They arrived three days before us because dad wanted to check the piston rings before we travelled such a distance, so again the engine came out onto the kitchen table, thus causing another cancellation of Leander Angling Club's fortnightly meeting. We stopped at Swallow Falls on the way, sat on the beach in the pissing rain for four days and then we drove home. North Wales was a long way before the advent of motorways.

In terms of holidays that was about it, the rest of the time was 'going out for days' visiting and playing by the war memorial in Blaney Crescent.

The blocked up drains are my swimming pool
The overflow is like a pretty waterfall
The bonfire is a barbecue
And the compost in the corner
Steams and steams and steams
And so we use it as a sauna.
Sand in the barrow, our seagull is a sparrow
Dad doesn't have the cash to go away
So I just hang around the house and dream all day.

Thomas Lethaby School had thrown a spanner in the works as regards my plans to become a professional footballer. A new sports master arrived, a nasty shit called Alan King whom I hated more than school custard with lumps in. We didn't get on at all, the arrogant track-suited bastard, and I wasn't the least bit surprised when he subsequently dropped me from the first team. John Window became first choice. John's dad had taken over Mr. Morgan's shop at Eastbourne Road and we got on well as mates, but he couldn't tip shots over the bar like Ron Springett or me. It was all quite ridiculous really as I'd been playing at district level for East Ham and had trialled for Leyton Orient. I gave up football in protest and disgust, not that difficult as I wasn't actually being picked to play anyway, and decided to concentrate on those troublesome GCEs and a bit more fishing. As my last years of school neared I even considered becoming a professional match angler, but it was a thing unique to the north of England, and I didn't really fancy moving to Chesterfield or Newark at the ripe old age of sixteen.

On one occasion, King made me cycle all the way home from school, just before an important after-school football game, to ask my mum the developments of the Krushchev and Kennedy crisis in Cuba. I cycled all the way back again with the news that the Russians had backed down, and I was completely shagged out. Then I never got picked. Hardly surprising. John Window hadn't cycled anywhere. World War Three hadn't arisen after all, but in my mind, it was raging. Alan King had to go. Not picked for the team, I had to be linesman, running up and down the touchline like a demented gazelle while King pranced about like a crazed dying swan, blowing his whistle whenever he felt the attention was being diverted from him to the football match.

No doubt about it, Alan King and me hated each other's guts. If he lived long enough to read this I would be somewhat surprised. I would be even more surprised if I gave a toss. He was probably the first person in my life I really, really hated. I so much wanted to be a footballer and I think I had every chance, but he took away the tiniest glimmer of hope I had. I concentrated on cricket but was never very good. I kept wicket in my uncle's motor cycle gauntlets once and wouldn't have looked too bad if I hadn't worn his goggles as well. I may also have been the first cricketer ever to wear a helmet, a crash helmet!

My elder brother Len, by this time, was already at Goldsmith's School of Art in South London and a viola player of some note. My sister Jill also played violin in the youth orchestra and drew plants and shrubs as competently as Beatrix Potter. She became a nurse. My brother married and became a Jew. I had a lot to follow musically and artistically, but somehow I knew I was destined to let the side down with my lack of interest in the arts and the academics. The time had come to do something about it. I bought a new briefcase and paid David Howard the equivalent of five pence for doing my homework for me. He was small and easy to beat up. I scraped O level passes in English, art, technical drawing and my favourite subject, modern British history. I read endless books about the Industrial Revolution, about Jethro Tull, Hargreaves's Spinning Jenny and Kay's Flying Shuttle. I knew I'd pass and I did, just as I knew I'd fail my metalwork when my steam engine resembled a Hepworth abstract, and I achieved that too.

I actually left school with four O level passes, nine RSA stages one and two, and my National Cycling Proficiency certificate. It didn't look that good.

My metalwork partner at Lethaby was Graham Morse who only owned one jumper, a large, red crew neck, obviously knitted up a ladder by his mum. He always had the sleeves rolled up. The Beatles fashion never took hold on Graham. The Mersey Beat was not Morsey's beat. He runs a pub now, the Queens, in Haverhill, Suffolk and I saw him this year, by chance, at the National Angling Exhibition in Birmingham. I bought him lunch, pie and baked beans, we swapped phone numbers and went our separate ways. I liked

Morsey. We promised to meet up some day and have a fishing trip together. That would be nice. Unlike Graham, I was into the Beatles straight away, from their first hit single 'Love Me Do'. I saw them at East Ham Granada with my sister and her friend Gillian Snow, she whose dad grew the contraband rhubarb. Everybody screamed and I never heard a note but I still marvel at the fact I saw John Lennon in real life. All the girls loved Paul and his childish good looks. We East End geezers went for Lennon. He was weird. We liked that. He was cool. We liked that too. The album Jimmy Sarling had lent to us had come alive, all except for George Harrison who didn't really seem to move much. They only played for twenty minutes, incredible really, and they used Vox AC30 amps at full blast in large cinemas. No wonder we never heard them too well. I tried to brush my hair forward but it was too curly and it ended up looking like a windy day on the Thames.

In 1977, I visited the Beatles Museum in Liverpool. It was a miracle of nostalgia, seeing the very poster on the wall for the concert at East Ham Granada.

'I was there!' I gasped.

Nobody seemed particularly interested.

Mind you, most of the other visitors were Japanese.

Like Chris Evans, I would very much love to have met John Lennon. From humble beginnings like the rest of us, he became a legend. A lyricist with a soul, and a singer with a character vocal. He would probably cringe now at some of his anarchic early radio and television comments, but there again I wasn't too impressed with my first appearance on the Old Grey Whistle Test when I saw it fifteen years later. Strangely, I visited the Beatles Museum whilst touring with Elkie Brooks. She'd been an important part of those early music days in the north, being born in nearby Salford. She'd actually supported the Beatles. Imagine that! My friend actually supported the Beatles.

Mum and dad seldom let us buy records, they were far too expensive, but I simply had to get the first Beatles album. Jimmy Sarling's was returned and we missed the Fab Four's music. We had a dog called Ringo, a tortoise called Paul, so mum just had to Let it Be. So *Please Please Me* was the first album our family ever owned. That was followed by the Rolling Stones, who my parents never listened to because the band had long hair and pissed in West Ham garage forecourts. I saw them at East Ham Granada too. It was becoming a regular tour venue on band itineraries.

The new band thing was a cultural shock for Jill and myself who'd, up until then, only bought silly singles by Adam Faith and Michael Holliday. Believe me, there were some silly records around in those days too. Barry McGuire singing about the 'Eve of Destruction'. He had a voice that sounded like he'd eaten a ton of gravel and washed it down with a pint of Swarfega. Then he went and sang a load of crap called 'Three Wheels On My Wagon' and his credibility was shot away I'm afraid. It might have been the other way round but he lost me anyway. He was a member of the New Christy Minstrels and you probably won't find that information in any discography book.

Tommy Steele sang about a ridiculous 'Little White Bull' and as for Mike Sarne, I say nothing. Charlie Drake's fucking boomerang wouldn't come back and people were finding mice in windmills in old Amsterdam. Bloody hell.

But suddenly, we had joined the Sixties revolution. We had a ticket to ride and Jill had fallen in love with Paul McCartney. I think she wrote to him once, but no reply followed. You just couldn't trust the post, even in those days. Every time they released a new single we queued at the Co-op in East Ham High Street for that familiar black Parlophone label in the dark green sleeve. Then we both raced home to play the song they'd sung the previous night on 'Ready Steady Go'.

When my youth club band, the Small Faces, made it onto that show singing 'Watcha Gonna Do 'Bout It' I was so proud of them it could have been me. The same went for Brian Poole and the Tremeloes. One moment my mum's buying a pound of mince in his butcher's shop, and the next he's twisting and shouting on the telly. There was definitely a small pocket of East End resistance against the Mersey sound that was engulfing the world. Bloody hell, I nearly forgot the Honeycombs! The female drummer. Honey Lantree. Their singer Denis Dell did a duet with me in 1979 in the Swan at Thaxted in Essex. He wasn't a bad blues guitarist. What happened to Honey of the Honeycombs? I didn't really like to ask, to be honest.

I met Kenny Jones, the Small Faces drummer and later with the Who, at a do at the Grosvenor Hotel in London on 25th May 1999. We laughed like drains as we reminded ourselves of the times in that run-down youth club in Manor Park. Kenny reminded me of their rival band, the Outcasts, who were visually far straighter than the Small Faces. My brain recalled the name and their faces immediately, even though I'd forgotten about them for thirty-five years. Bloody hell, the Outcasts. Nice one Kenny.

I was in the studio audience once on 'Ready Steady Go'. My mate at school, Bob Crockford of Langdon Crescent, wrote away for some tickets and off we went. I wore a red casual shirt, buttoned down at the back, you may well remember me! I danced, best I could for a div, to the Kinks singing 'You Really Got Me'. Herman's Hermits sang 'I'm Into Something Good' and I nearly tripped over the singer's wisdom teeth as I strutted my stuff camera left. Yes, that was me. Didn't use autocue then either.

The Small Faces had made the big time and the gigs at the Kensington became sparser. Proportionally, the package concerts increased and we popped along more frequently to the Granada to see the Stones, Gerry and the Pacemakers, Billy J. Kramer. We even cycled to Woolwich, knowing the route from our earlier searches for bits of female top, to see Chuck Berry and Bo Diddley. My brother Len was a beatnik, an arty farty chappie, into jazz musicians like J. J. Johnson and Andre Previn. He made no comment about the Beatles, or any other chart band of the era. He felt cool splattering around on his grey moped, registration ULL 588, and then his BSA Bantam, RVX 876. All I remember my brother doing was smoking Bristol tipped cigarettes, bringing female art students home for the week-end, which meant a reshuffling of beds, normally with me slung on the settee in the living room, and riding around on old two wheeled contraptions.

But despite his disinterest the music revolution was accelerating. Steve Marriott left the Small Faces and became involved with supergroups. America called with Humble Pie and our local singer made good was gone from us forever. He died in a house fire after returning from America. His wife was at my manager Brian Shaw's house in Ongar, Essex, and it was there she received the news he'd burned to death. It was a sad loss.

At Thomas Lethaby we had a maths teacher called Mr DeBell (ding dong) who collapsed and died in assembly one morning. He was my brother's housemaster. It was a blessing for me. I was supposed to see him after school that day for cheating at algebra. Many lads clapped him out of the hall as he disappeared from sight between two ambulance drivers. My maths book would never be the same. It had more red ink than blue until his untimely departure. He was the loudest and hardest cane whacker in Europe. Nobody knew what he died of, we just assumed, being our maths master, it was something geometric as he stumbled from the perpendicular to the horizontal.

Nobody famous went to Thomas Lethaby, apart from a couple of burglars that made it into the big time, although I think it was Adolf Hitler who took us for religious instruction. Pilky, the miserable bastard, walked around while we read the Bible out loud. He had a flattened nose which some say happened in a Japanese prisoner of war camp. I think he was simply unfortunate at birth. Had he been of a different generation, there could be no doubt his nickname would have been Concorde. The most boring half-hour of the week, reading about that bloke with the boat and the animals whose name escapes me. Mr Pilkington wore a double-breasted suit and he was so thin it buttoned up at the back. I hated his lessons. I never read the Bible. I never saw the point. Eight hundred pages and I knew what happened at the end, he died and you get an egg with Smarties in it.

Actually Brian Phelps was famous. But only for a short while. He won a gold medal at the Rome Olympics in 1960 for high diving. We had to clap him in assembly when he stood waving this gold thing on a ribbon. To mark his success the school bought him a trampoline to practise diving, which none of us were allowed to use. Oh yes, Alan King was a shit all right. This was a skint school and there were the Parent Teachers Association coughing up for a trampoline because some little boy wonder had won a medal at diving. King was the first nasty bastard, and this was the first case of unfair dealing I had ever encountered in my life. And it was all interconnected. Strange, that's the way big business seems to be, as I was later to find out!

Every summer Thomas Lethaby School had a fete in the playground and my mum always ran the white elephant stand. One year it was opened by Ronnie Carroll who had a hit with 'Roses Are Red, Violets Are Blue'. He was as tall as one of the third formers and most of the second formers. He was lucky he wasn't beaten up! Then it would have been more a case of Noses are Red! Not so the following year when a cowboy by the name of Cal McCord turned up on a horse. Nobody had ever heard of him but it cost me threepence for his poxy autograph just the same. Most cowboys in that area went on to sell cars or build houses, very few in East Ham rode horses and wore suede jackets with tassels dangling from the sleeves. He was a ponce. Probably a wealthy one at that with all those threepenny bits tucked in his saddle bags. I think he came from abroad. He certainly spoke with a mild and unfamiliar twang.

Just before leaving Thomas Lethaby School I'd become a mod. The whole class were mods with centre partings except for one brave soul by the name of David Matthews of Charlemont Road. He wore a leather jacket covered in studs and hair covered in shiny stuff. He got away with it because he could drink a bottle of blue-black Stephen's ink straight down until Bic biros put him out of business. He had a Viking bike that was the bollocks. A biker in the making.

Then something strange happened. I became an academic. Micky Walker, Michael Cave and myself were taken out of class due to our excellent progress, and instead of being transferred to the grammar school, we were given our own room next to headmaster George Lees's office. We were never disturbed, a lucky thing as the room stank of Senior Service tipped. With Micky, from Claremont Close, North Woolwich, a founder member of the aforementioned Leander Angling Club in the same class, we spoke incessantly of fishing. We had fishing matches every week at Moor Hall gravel pits in Aveley, near Dagenham, and every week I either won or came second unless third club member Richard Cole cycled along. Richard Cole, 41 Blaney Crescent, who later still became my first ever roadie when I bought a J4 van for fifteen quid. It seemed peculiar to divide my interests the way I'd chosen. Fishing one minute and then desperately trying to be interested in girls who weren't the slightest bit interested in me the next. Something had to give and I started to lose interest in dangling my worm in the hope of dangling my worm.

My new best friend at the time, John Kitson, originally of Beckett Road, who left school early to work for the Norwich Union, had bought a gleaming blue and white Vespa GS for £185. He drove it like a maniac. It was a strange but fashionable time. I was trying to brush my curly hair forward, a thankless task. John's mum used to let him smoke at weekends, so every Friday night I went to his house at Laburnum Drive in Elm Park, Essex. We'd become big Sandie Shaw fans for some unaccountable reason and we talked about her incessantly between puffs of Ariel tipped, a strange and highly unsuccessful brand of cigarette. No Senior Service tipped at John's house. We walked around Elm Park looking for girls. I remember once John and I encountered a couple in Barking Park and I was terrified.

I'd had a few after-school and Saturday jobs to help sponsor my various pastimes. What was I doing the day Kennedy was shot? 1963? I was packing shelves in Brown's the Grocers in East Ham High Street South. Anchor butter to be precise. I earned three half crowns for Friday night and Saturday, the equivalent of about 35p today. The shop's still there to this day. It's obviously changed hands, but it still stands, though now overshadowed by a huge BP petrol station where Vicarage Lane meets the High Street. I had a snog on that corner once, on my way home from fishing club. No tongues, so no need to elaborate on that one. Definitely a female though.

I then went to the new Safeways store in the main High Street on Saturdays only. They treated us like shit, made us wear bow-ties and searched us when we went in and out. I spent most of my time stacking pink and white marshmallow biscuits and hiding in the loo, stuffing my face. Every night I went home feeling sick and bloated.

Our school captain, Brian Peart, a decent kid who smoked Piccadilly tipped, marked my card that True Form were looking for a Saturday shoe salesman. It was adjacent to Safeways too. The manager was Charles Sodeau and I liked him very much. I worked myself stupid for him, made a few quid on commission and played it totally straight with him because he trusted me with the till. I loved that job. How would I ever have known that Hush Puppies, plimsolls with elastic across the front and sensible shoes that didn't bend would become such a significant part of my stage act in those days. Charles allowed me my first real taste of responsibility and I shall never forget him for that.

Music seemed to be creeping more and more into my life and I would soon say goodbye to my early friends when my life took a sharp turn away from the East End of London. Our youth club in Manor Park, East London, had boasted regular performances by the Small Faces, who lived nearby and rehearsed in the Ruskin Arms, just down the road. I passed on the table tennis to watch Steve Marriott and Ronnie Lane go through their paces. Kenny Jones, who joined the Who, was on drums and Jimmy Winston, who left the Faces to form Winston's Thumbs, was on keyboards, pre Ian McLagan. Kitson once told me how he could tell how much I'd love to be up there with them. I never knew how he could tell but he was absolutely right. We started going further afield, searching out the rhythm and blues clubs in the West End. We'd hang out at Tiles in Oxford Street. We were growing up and starting to leave the fold. John had a girlfriend, Jackie Carnaby, and I made up a foursome with her mate Rosie Smith, who lived in the Hameway, just by the new Beckton ski slope, and we all went to see the Swinging Blue Jeans and Freddie and the Dreamers at the Granada. I worked with the

Dreamers at Lyme Regis Marine Theatre thirty years later and told them they were instrumental in me gaining my first potential snog. They just looked at me as if I'd been let out for the day. Who cares, I never got the snog anyway. It's just that 'If You've Gotta Make a Fool of Somebody' I'd have preferred it wasn't me, that much 'I'm Telling You Now'.

I walked Rosie Smith home and bravely asked her for a kiss at her garden gate. This was my first attempt and I felt very embarrassed and shy. I felt my toes curl up in my green Hush Puppies and my mouth went very dry. I had entered uncharted territory and didn't feel at all comfortable. But I knew that's what boys did so I went for it, just like I'd been told I had to. When she refused I was so embarrassed I called her a wanker and she packed me up. I never ate for two days. I think I hyperventilated – something strange definitely happened but it may not have been as long a word as that. She had a blue PVC mac, long hair and all the other requirements. I couldn't believe I'd blown it. Christine Lawrence would have kissed me. Who was Christine Lawrence? She lived in Sandford Road. She always won the hundred yards at school sports days and was much quieter than the other girls from East Ham. How did she become part of my life? Or not? All will be revealed in a short while!

I never spoke to Rosie Smith again, although I often saw her walking down Flanders Road on her way to school. She blanked me and crossed the road. I didn't blame her, as I wouldn't have gone out of my way to collide with a sad individual wearing a duffel coat, attached idiot mittens and National Health glasses. How could the National Health ever make such crap glasses and such wonderful orange juice for the same generation of youngsters?

This is a good time for you, dear reader, to take a rest, as I'm about to travel abroad for the very first time. Mum paid weekly into the school travel club and I was on my way, my first expedition to foreign soil. Dad made many such trips, all in army uniform, and therefore didn't think it was a good idea for his son to visit the lands where those filthy rotten non-Brits lived. Mum told him to grow up. I'm not too sure he ever did. My sister once went to Lake Garda in Italy with the school and brought me back a pencil case with an Italian map on the outside. He bloody hated that as well. I wouldn't mind, but I don't think he ever met a single solitary German in his whole life.

Gag: Old Man, ex RAF, meets German and German says to ex RAF man:

'Have you ever been to Germany?'
'Only at night.'

We'd all taken our GCEs and as we awaited results a bunch of us went on a school trip to Switzerland. It was my first trip abroad, ten days at Hotel Rigi by the banks of Lake Lucerne. I'd already secured the promise of a job at Babcock and Wilcox, an engineering company, and also in the drawing office at Ford Motor Company. I hadn't decided which to go for. The Ford job depended on my results but I plumped for them because my dad, various cousins and uncles and neighbours worked there and it seemed the thing to do, plus the fact I'd get a lift to work every morning. It was the most embarrassing of moments when my exam results came through and I had to leave the Dagenham offices because I was an O level short. That failed GCE was without question the first major turning point of my whole life. I packed up my geometry set, ate humble pie, and settled for an engineering apprenticeship with Babcocks.

Their London offices were on the corner of Euston Road and Gower Street. From my fourth floor window I enjoyed watching the excavations for the new Euston underpass during the mid-sixties. Each lunchtime I strolled down to study the old Roman pipes and vases they had found. There were hundreds of them. It was obviously a settlement of old and it was far more interesting than drawing steam valves and boilers for power stations.

How strange it turned out that I eventually worked on the adjacent corner of the Euston underpass, in Euston Tower, the home of Capital Radio, where I spent endless hours staring out of the window at the fourth floor of Babcock's building opposite. My life had certainly changed around, and yet I used the same sandwich bar through both occupations, and took the same lunchtime walks, some twenty years apart. Only the crisps had changed. The little blue bags had gone. The underpass was completed in 1968 and it seems hard to believe it was once an important Roman settlement as now the cars, buses and lorries rattle through with little consideration for the history of London which once lay beneath them in the soil. Truly fascinating, and didn't those Romans smoke a lot? Bloody pipes everywhere.

During the trip to Switzerland I'd met my first proper girlfriend, Margaret Mole. Having learnt my lesson with Rosie Smith I decided not to even try to kiss her, but Margaret played an important role in my life. My schoolmate Steve Clarke was sniffing around her but was a tall gangly git and I fancied my chances if I kept myself to myself and made the move when appropriate. I fell in love with this folk music fanatic from Seahouses in Northumberland and the following year, after many letters to and fro, I went to see her during my holidays. Until I met Margaret I'd loved no-one but Christine Lawrence of Sandford Road, oh yes and possibly Rosie Smith from The Hameway, even though Christine never knew and Rosie never cared.

When I think back to Christine's blonde hair and school uniform I can't help admitting I still love her now. I kissed her just the once, on a coach to Bexleyheath, Kent, where the school football and netball teams played a school called Beadonwell or similar. Christine and I were to be married. Such a shame she never knew that either. I never, ever plucked up the courage to ask her out and now I'm too old. Sod's Law.

One of my old classmates at Vicarage Road Primary, Barbara Summers, came to see my show at a holiday camp in Great Yarmouth in 1997, and she kindly sent me the class photograph, which I'd lost before decimal currency came in. They were all there. Christine, John Lacey and Kevin Sullivan and numerous others. Out of the forty-three kids in our class, forty years later I named thirty-seven. You never forget the friends you had at school. Just keep away from reunions, that's all. That's when you realise that everyone looks an ageing relic except for yourself.

A year had passed since the trip to Switzerland and Margaret from Seahouses had gone off me and thinking back, I can't blame her an inch. Every night on the harbour wall, she and her friends would play acoustic guitars and mouth organs and sing songs from the *100 Favourite Folk Songs* book. This silly little mod felt well out of it, and yet I loved the songs they sang. Bob Dylan and Donovan had become big time and it was an era of PVC coats, faded jeans and jumpers. There was me with maroon suits and button down collared Ben Shermans. No wonder it went pear-shaped. Through it all and despite the mismatch, Margaret's dad was brilliant. He took me sea fishing for cod most days and I had a great time, even though I'd lost Margaret's affections. I didn't really mind.

Her mum wrote to me thirty years later via Yorkshire Television, where I was filming at the time, and I wrote back saying I had nothing but brilliant memories. It's with the greatest pleasure and fondness that I declare had I never met Margaret Mole of Seahouses, I'd probably never have become the folk singer I eventually became, so credit where it is due, and Margaret, wherever you are, thanks! If my failed GCEs were a significant turning point in my life, then my trip to Seahouses was certainly another. So many times on the road, as I travelled up the mighty A1, I saw the signs for the small Northumbrian fishing village and smiled. I never went back there but I remember the place with great affection.

What my guitar-playing acquaintances in Seahouses didn't really know was that I had developed a natural aptitude for music some years previously, the same as my brother and my sister, but I hadn't really bothered to apply myself to my inherited skills. My brother was into the classical stuff and the jazz, and a certain Bob Dylan who promised all that the times they were a-changing. And changing they certainly were. Some of the songs they sang on the harbour wall I already knew from early Dylan albums, but I didn't join in, I felt stupid enough as it was with my mod gear and ridiculous centre parting. For me the times were about to change even more, and perhaps my small dose of musical education would come in handy!

I'd had four years of piano lessons from Mrs Tinham in Charlemont Road and played violin in the East Ham junior orchestra. Me and nineteen other herberts played 'Three Blind Mice' at East Ham Baths, all totally paranoid the stage would collapse and we'd all go straight into the deep end. I could play violin a little, but I couldn't swim at all. I didn't have a ribbon on my trunks for swimming a width. Oh my god, those woollen trunks. Who would imagine any of us would have thought about those things ever again in our lives? They expanded when you climbed from the water. Sometimes you had to drag your arse to the shore, some ten feet behind you, leaving a wet trail as you tugged away. Maroon woolly trunks. Mum! Why?

Anyway, on the train home from Seahouses, via Newcastle, all those years ago I decided I would learn to play the guitar and sing 'The Wild Colonial Boy'. It was my favourite song from their harbour wall repertoire. I even bought an album by Tommy Makem and the Clancy Brothers to learn it correctly. I could easily have joined them in that one on the harbour wall and played mouth organ, but enough was enough. Thanks, Tommy and your sister too. I have never forgotten you nor how you inspired me!

I was asking around at work for a cheap guitar. One of the mechanical draughtsmen at Babcocks was named John Mulland. He was a fat bloke who played left back in the firm's football team and he told me to visit his house in Chingford, Essex and he would sell me a guitar for £3. My mum lent me the money and I travelled home on the bus with this dusty thing without a case. I was a mod and felt really uncool. It was a Chamberlain jazz guitar and the first stupid thing I did was wood-stain it. Yes, it did exactly what it said on the tin. But at least I was playing the guitar. I took a tube train to Tottenham Court Road station and walked along Charing Cross Road in search of *100 Favourite Folk Songs* which I found at Francis Day and Hunter's sheet music shop. I was ecstatic. There it was, the very book I leafed through on that Seahouses harbour wall. For the next few months I did nothing but go to work and come home to practise my guitar playing. Sadly I wasn't getting on too well. I purchased a Bert Weedon (also born in East Ham) guitar book with chords but none of the tabulated chords were in my repertoire.

I loved my trips on the London Underground to Charing Cross Road and Denmark Street, the original Tin Pan Alley. It was in this small side turning off the main drag where the music publishers of yesteryear would leave tapes running for the office cleaners, known as 'old greys' because of their grey overalls. They would listen to the songs all night as they went about their duties. If the cleaners were whistling the song in the morning it proved the melody was commercial enough to release. This became known as the Old Grey Whistle Test, and became the title for a long-running music programme on BBC 2, featuring Bob Harris.

On that programme I made my first ever television appearance, singing 'Drag Queen Blues' and being interviewed by Anne Nightingale. I remember the next day I walked around Romford Market craving to be recognised. Bloody hell. I'd appeared in front of millions, surely someone somewhere would cop the face. I felt totally demoralised as I stood at the bus stop on my way back to Gidea Park, where I lived at the time. Then it happened. A lad rushed up to me and asked me to sign his scrap of paper. I was so made up, but not so when he looked down, tore it up, and apologised for mistaking me for Leo Sayer.

Most of my trips to the West End were made on Wednesdays so I could be the first to pick up a *Melody Maker* and see who was playing at what folk clubs. To have the paper before others was a major coup. I plotted my following week on Wednesday nights when Roger Moss would come round my house for guitar practice. Most of what I play even today was taught to me by Roger, a brilliant guitar player. The technique is based around a conventional clawhammer style, which was originated in the Deep South American penitentiaries by great players like Leadbelly and Big Bill Broonzy as they languished in jail for whatever reasons. A collector by the name of Alan Lomax tabulated the technique and the first time I saw the style played here was by Bert Jansch of Pentangle fame. Roger Moss taught it to me and I've played around that style of the perpetual bass and rhythm fingerwork ever since.

In a matter of just twelve months my career in the drawing office seemed to be getting in the way of my love for music. It had all moved on so quickly from the time when my cousin Mick Cook had taught me three new chords on the Chamberlain guitar. From E, A and D, I had developed to the clawhammer technique and was playing at least three or four hours a day on my new Levin. In 1966, my sister had married Rob Tungate at my old choirboy venue, St Mary's. Jill had the reception at home. I made my public debut singing 'Not Fade Away' and teaming up with Midge, Rob's sister, to sing 'I Got You Babe'. I seem to recall I was paid a bowl of peanuts. One can argue I've been paid peanuts ever since but luckily for me that argument hasn't really stood up. Thank heavens!

Rob rode a Vespa 150 at high speed and had a friend called Terry Wilkinson of Strone Road who worked at the same engineering company as myself. I only met Wilky once though. He was a swot and I was quickly becoming a disenchanted lazy bastard. He studied his Chapman workshop technology books, volumes one and two, whilst I was getting into the songbooks of Paul Simon and of course the Freewheelin' Bob Dylan. Those who've never understood Bob Dylan have never realised what went before him. Not much! He wrote words that made us think when we were sick and tired of 'Windmills In Old Amsterdam' and 'Roses are Red, Violets Are Blue'. Bob Dylan opened our minds in the same way as the Beatles did in the Sixties. OK, he never opened a Thomas Lethaby fete like some of the others, but that wasn't the point. I learnt 'Mr Tambourine Man' word for word and never knew what the fuck it was about. What a great song. That was how much it had all changed in such a short time. From a kid playing Rolling Stones songs to a student of the acoustic guitar.

It was all accelerated one day at East Ham Technical College when I saw an ad for the college folk club. I decided to go. At the Central Hotel in Barking Road, East Ham, I watched my first live, professional folk singer at work, a Scotsman by the name of Alex Campbell. He sang Tom Paxton's 'The Last Thing On My Mind' and his own song 'I've Been On The Road So Long'. It all smacked of that little Northumbrian fishing harbour again. However, my days were numbered in the East End as Glasgow loomed big time. I would spend a chunk of my life there gaining site experience at Babcock's factory in Renfrew. I had just six months to get into my new found social life before I was despatched to Scotland.

I'd become a young man. No more spud guns loaded with dog shit, no more water pistols that shot round corners loaded with fertiliser. I'd started buying second hand books at the East Ham covered market and reading for the first time. I read *The Little Prince* and *The Hobbit*.

Every Tuesday I set off for the Bus Folk Club, situated, not surprisingly, in an old London double-decker that stood in a disused scrap yard off Cooks Road, Stratford. The seats had been taken out, probably stolen judging by the area, and the singer stood with his or her back to the driver's cab. The crowd (crowd??) sat on the floor on old blankets and carpets, the whole place stinking of Yardley talcum powder from the factory close by. Upstairs they served hot oxtail soup as we all froze and huddled together in the name of folk music.

Joe Stead played the banjo and introduced me to the songs of Rambling Jack Elliot and Woody Guthrie. Guthrie had inspired the traditional music movement of America. Even Bob Dylan sang 'Song For Woody' and Joan Baez and Judy Collins sang his praises too. The songs were of persecution and racial prejudice. I remember 'I Don't Want Your Millions Mister'. Crazy days when you think Joe Stead lived in Kent where there were very few cotton fields, but the songs had great meaning to me just the same. Joe charged four pounds and worked the area regularly. He wasn't the greatest folk singer in the world but he was always around and later became an important agent on the folk scene. Cousin Mick's chords had set me off, and now I was watching every single guitar player I could set my eyes on, even noticing their flaws and making sure I didn't develop the same.

A pub in Barking, the Red Lion, had a small folk club with an unknown regular guest by the name of Paul Simon. Transatlantic Records, the English folk label, had turned him down and so he felt there was little future for him on the British folk scene. He would disappear back to America to seek a deal for his new song 'The Sound of Silence'. He'd found a session singer called Art Garfunkel and in the recording studio they became a duo by the name of Tom and Jerry. He never returned to the Barking folk club so I don't know if it worked out for him, although word has it!! I also watched Julie

Felix there. She had one or two minor hits, I think about visiting a zoo, and I loved the fact she was a descendant from a Red Indian, a rare attribute in Barking. Indians? Yes. Red Indians? Not so many.

As my musical taste buds blossomed and sampled this new found form of music, my Thomas Lethaby school-mates were still hanging out at the Kensington Youth Club in Manor Park, awaiting the new Small Faces or whatever. Of course, that wasn't the poncy Kensington on the other side of the city, but a dive situated in Kensington Avenue, Manor Park. I saw less and less of them as my musical horizons widened. Fewer knocked for me as the months passed and soon I'd become a bit of a recluse. Good friends even blanked me in the street because I'd stopped going to the Kensington and grown my hair into a bushy mess.

I went back once and a bunch of them ganged up and gave me a serious going over in the street outside. I had become an intruder. The bruises were my farewell present and I knew then I was a million miles from East Ham and distancing myself further by the day. The gang were my mates who thought I'd become weird. All those years at Thomas Lethaby counted for nothing. All the penalties I saved in cup games, all the runs I scored for the cricket team, went for nothing. They'd split my eye open, I was various shades of purple from head to toe. Thomas Lethaby, whoever he was, had, at least in my mind, died that night. Were it not for two brothers, Johnny and Richard Gibbs of Mountfield Road, and my brother-in-law Rob, I would have been kicked to pulp and ended up a headline in the East Ham Recorder. Their bravery saved my life. Mind you, at the time I could have done with the press.

But even as a hippie, I never stopped going to Upton Park to cheer on the Hammers. Bobby Moore was playing for England, so were Hurst and Peters. It was a great time for West Ham. They signed a goalkeeper called Bobby Ferguson from Kilmarnock. Part of the deal was that West Ham played a friendly against the Scottish side. Out he came, all in red, at a time when most goalies wore green or yellow polo necks. He looked a ponce. Our new goalkeeper who cost £65,000, a Scottish international. West Ham won 8-0 and Geoff Hurst scored five goals without breaking into a sweat. I was to learn more about business deals later in my life. That was just an early taster.

I started attending evening classes at East Ham Technical College. I studied English Literature at my own expense and enjoyed reading the poetic works of Keats, Crabbe and Thomas (blimey, they sound like a dodgy team of solicitors). I passed my A level and was both delighted and proud of myself. Maybe I would get somewhere in my life after all. Jenny was in that class with me and I went out with her younger sister Roz for a while. They lived in Barking but I can't remember their surname. I only ever got a snog from Roz anyway so it doesn't really count.

I have never seen a single member of the Kensington Youth Club crowd from that day to this, with the exception of one brave soul who dared remind me of the event at a show in Brighton which you will read of later. An East End golden handshake, a proverbial kick in the whatsits. The roadies saw to that and it served him right. Revenge was sweet, even if it had taken twenty-five years.

The British folk scene throbbed and became highly fashionable as the sixties drew to a close, particularly in the bedsit areas of London around Earls Court. We brave ones in the double-decker bus were sadly at the wrong end of town, so I started playing guitar at the Troubadour in Old Brompton Road. Sonja Kristina ran a session there once a week, until she became a rock superstar with Curved Air. She was incredibly beautiful and sang a nice song called 'Little Tim McGuire' by a trendy songwriter, Leon Rosselson. Any girl with long brown hair who owned a white Afghan coat was tasty, Sonja was particularly so. Gordon Giltrap ran another night and a guy called Dave Lipson from Hackney did Sundays. He had a white Afghan too, but he wasn't so tasty.

The big nights were Fridays and Saturdays which were run by Martin Windsor and Redd Sullivan. So many big names started out at the weekend Troubadour sessions. Arlo Guthrie, Al Stewart, John Martyn, David Bowie, and, so I am told, Mark Knopfler of Dire Straits. Folk clubs grew stronger by the day and they were cropping up all over the place, my timing couldn't have been better. It looked like Richard Digance had got something right for the first time in his life. I was hanging out where all the others were hanging out, and I was getting to know many of them fairly well.

Ralph McTell had a number one hit with 'Streets of London'. Peter Sarstedt, a regular at the Central and Eden Kane's brother, had the same with 'Where Do You Go To My Lovely'. David Bowie was running a club at the Three Tuns in Beckenham, Kent and there weren't enough evenings in the week to visit all the new clubs that were popping up everywhere. Barbara Dickson was gigging in London, the sweetest voice you ever did hear. She was to feature quite heavily in my business life in later years.

I'd become friends with a singer, Jenny Beeching, who took me around in her Morris 1000 (I didn't have a car of my own) and I'd also teamed up with Roger Moss, now a commercial photographer in Cornwall, to form a duo called New Mythology. We were both big fans of the Incredible String Band. We played every song they ever wrote, until one day, we performed at the Starting Gate in Wood Green, London, my first ever self-penned song 'Symphony of Sadness'. It was a pathetic song that began: 'Is it sadness that makes the sky turn blue or is it only when I think of you. Hours pass by slow today, I can't believe that you went away. Come back baby, you've done me wrong, as you can tell by the words of this song'. Oh dear, how pathetic, but we all have to start somewhere. No, it wasn't pathetic, it was shit. Fair dos, I was only secondary modern and had only recently started reading books let alone writing poetry.

New Mythology, Roger and myself had our first big paid gig at Rush Green College in Dagenham, Essex. It was supporting T. Rex, who John Peel had been raving about for months. Roger and I were booked for eight pounds, which we were to invest in new John Alvey Turner guitar strings, a complete luxury during such skint times. Dagenham was a long way offshore to the hippie duo that had worked primarily at the Electric Garden and the Roundhouse in London and on the John Peel show on the radio. Marc Bolan asked me if they could go on stage before us as they had to train it back to town. We agreed. New Mythology never made it but at least we were supported by Marc Bolan!! Can't be bad. People forget how Bolan popularised the acoustic guitar before going electric. In his own way he was a folkie too, along with the rest of us. He died some years later in a tragic road accident in Barnes. He'd been through the folk scene, the rock scene and pioneered glam rock. Many underestimate the strengths of Marc Bolan. He was a visionary of the highest order. He became a passage of folklore himself. He would ride a white swan forever.

I'd become a particularly good friend of songwriter Al Stewart, although I lost track of him when he went to America and recorded his platinum album *Year of the Cat*. We had a great reunion in 1998 at the Brook, a pub gig in Southampton, where I became his support act for the night. We talked of these old times for hours. It was as though thirty years hadn't really passed, and as I write this it still seems incredible it was over a quarter of a century ago. I started a small club of my own in the basement of an art gallery in East Ham, called the Eyes of Time, on 11th November 1969 and Al came along free of charge. He'd left a band called Piccadilly Line and his debut album on CBS *Bedsitter Images* was doing really well.

They were exciting times but I was broke. I took a job at A.F. Bulgin in Barking as a draughtsman. Each lunchtime I ran home and practised my guitar. Musically, things were going well, I was learning more and more guitar music by following John Renbourn, of Pentangle fame, around the clubs, sitting in the front row, studying his finger-work, but Scotland, and my apprenticeship with Babcock and Wilcox, eventually called. The six-month threat had arrived and I didn't want to go. I'd met a nurse at the London Hospital in Whitechapel called Sandy Mogford. She came from Folkestone and we were big pals, but the northbound A1 beckoned, and up to Scotland I went. The journey took two and a half days in a van owned by another apprentice, Dennis Thys, and his girlfriend Bobby (Roberta), whom I was to share a flat with in Minard Road, Shawlands, a southern district of Glasgow.

We stopped overnight at Scarborough and I met a girl called Linda from Leeds who was also sleeping rough in the castle grounds. We wrote to each other for a couple of months and then the Seahouses thing happened again. I trained it down to Leeds to see her. Her parents were appalled by this longhaired streak of piss and she disowned me. Déjà vu. Now that was a brilliant album, was it not? Their house, was a very very fine house. It's just that her mum didn't particularly want me in it.

I hated Scotland, Scotland hated me and I missed Sandy. She'd already packed me in by this time but I missed her just the same. I suffered from those dreadful crampy pains in the guts that arrive when you're packed in by someone you cannot live without. Sandy Mogford and I would have married if she'd fancied me, absolutely no doubt about it. In fact, I missed everyone south of the border at this time. I even missed that shit PE teacher Alan King, that's how bad Scotland was for me. I was dreadfully homesick.

The tool-room work at the Renfrew factory was dirty, as were the traps of most of the apprentices, many of whom seemed to play football for Clydebank, and the bus journeys home to 90 Minard Road were long. Dennis and Bobby shagged every single night and they both rolled their own fags with Boars Head pipe tobacco. I kept my plectrums in the used bright yellow tins. I felt lonely and more homesick for London by the day. I wished Sandy and I hadn't split up. I probably would have stayed in London and married the nurse from the London Hospital. I wished Rosie Smith and me hadn't split up, and I wished Margaret and I had been married as well as Christine and me. My head had turned to mush. I looked forward to the folk club night in Montrose Street and I couldn't believe it when I went there one night, only to find my heroes, the Incredible String Band, were performing, along with Alex Campbell, whom I'd seen back in East Ham on that very first visit to a folk club. Such an incredible coincidence.

I met up with another up and coming musician that night, John Martyn, who also loved the String Band. He'd made an album for Island Records, *London Conversation* and he'd come round my flat and teach me various bits on the guitar. One song of his in particular sticks out, 'Fairytale Lullaby'. John also wrote 'May You Never', which became a huge song when Eric Clapton recorded it. We followed Mike Heron and Robin Williamson around until I think the String Band went to America. I had all their albums and so did John. *The Incredible String Band, The Five Thousand Spirits Or The Layers Of The Onion, The Hangman's Beautiful Daughter, Wee Tam And The Big Huge.* I bought them all again recently on compact disc. They were crap! We must have all been on something at the time, and listening to those compact discs, it must have been pretty strong!

John Martyn had a gig at the Rockfield Hotel in Paisley and invited me along. Another life-changing event of Seahouses proportions. Compere was Billy Connolly who was about to team up with Gerry Rafferty, the guy who wrote 'Baker Street', to form a folk duo, the Humblebums. Transatlantic didn't turn those two down, like they did Paul Simon! I saw Billy with another chap called Tam Harvey and they told me and the rest of the small audience about the Dunoon Folk Festival. I rolled up a blanket and set off for Dunoon, a strange Scottish island location full of American sub-mariners at the time. I think back now and I recall the film *Local Hero*.

We all slept on the beach and I was so in awe of Connolly I gave him my mum's best blanket that I'd stolen from Blaney Crescent. Still to this day the rotten bastard has never returned it! John Martyn headed south and made some brilliant albums. I planned to do much the same thing. That summer I returned to London, gave up my engineering apprenticeship at Babcock and Wilcox, and took a moonlighting job with my dad on the ambulances. I was so happy to be back at Blaney

Crescent with mum and dad. I broke all the rules on the ambulances because I had no insurance cards, but I kept out of trouble until I was stopped by the police for driving without due care and attention. I was fined thirty pounds and slung in the job, my faith in British justice totally shattered, which it has more or less remained until this day. My loyalty to my dad and the ambulance service do not allow me to reveal too many details but if you have ever thought that ambulances can do what they want on our roads, even with a very sick passenger, then think again.

I teamed up again with Roger Moss but I had a desire to turn professional, which didn't appeal to him. I didn't have my driving job anymore and I needed to earn money. One night at the Hampstead Rugby Club Folk Club, in Redhill Street, Camden Town, I sat in awe of a guitar wizard called John O'Connor. To cut a long story short, we teamed up and became a duo known as Pisces. We made our first album for Trailer Records in 1969, produced by Bill Leader, and at long last I was a valuable part of the British folk scene which I loved so much. I wrote most of the album and I'd become a member of the Songwriters' Guild and the Institute of Contemporary Arts.

It wasn't looking too bad. My teenage days had drawn to a close and my mum saved up her wages at Bard Brothers sweet factory, where she worked as a cleaner, to buy me a decent guitar, a Levin Goliath which I'd seen John James use. It cost £78, an awful lot of money.

My god, I really wish she could read this book, she'd be so proud. She heard me as an embryonic radio presenter and heard others, like Basil Brush and Bernard Braden, recite the scripts I'd written for them, but that was about all. She always told me I'd do well, and sometimes in my darkest hours I never believed her. This is her book really, a confirmation that she was right all along.

Richard Digance began his recording career in 1968. His first collection of demos, eight in all, were recorded at the BBC Radiophonic Workshop, Delware Road, London, in July and August 1968, in the very studios where they invented and recorded the sound effects for Doctor Who. *Richard was smuggled in by his friend David Cain, a resident composer and music producer with the BBC. David worked with the Early Music Consort and composed the music for the radio adaptation of Tolkien's* The Hobbit. *For a couple of years Richard and David were best of pals and there's no doubt that David Cain educated Richard in the various fields of music he specialised in. It was David Cain who also taught Richard his basic recording studio techniques.*

While Richard lived at home, he would often spend weekends at the Maida Vale flat of David and his wife Marianne, until they split. First they became teachers in Cockermouth in the Lake District, then David moved to France and Marianne settled in the Lake District.

With David Cain's recording finesse, Richard composed a musical and poetry opera with a friend, Michael Porter, a poet from Wanstead. It was called And As Winter Faded, it was launched at the General Havelock in Ilford and actually sold out. It was a collection of poems by Michael and songs with Richard playing along to pre-recorded tapes. It was, in Richard's own words, crap but quite innovative for its time. The next time Richard mimed was on London Weekend Television when he bluffed his way unconvincingly through a pre-recorded version of his song 'Tony Hancock'.

Richard's next set of recordings were on a Grundig two-track machine at home, writing and recording songs in preparation for the new album. From there, some seven months later, he made his first album with Pisces at the Livingston Studios in Barnet, a sixteen-track studio in a converted church. The Grundig two-track cost £28. Tape was supplied free of charge by David Cain.

After more demos to try and secure a record deal upon embarking on his solo career, he worked at John O'Connor's eight-track studio in Hainault, Essex, and upon joining Transatlantic, he recorded at Chipping Norton Studios in Oxfordshire, where for his first album, he shared recording session time with the Bay City Rollers. He didn't have his own studio facility until 1978, when he built an eight-track studio of his own in a spare bedroom of his first house in Reading.

The musicians who worked on Richard's albums are a Who's Who in themselves. Jon Lord of Deep Purple, Barrie Barlow and David Palmer of Jethro Tull, Alvin Lee, Geoff Whitehorn of Roger Chapman's Family. Tim Hinkley who played keyboards with the Rolling Stones. Michael Chapman. Rick Kemp who played bass with Mick Ronson. Adrian Shepherd of Bucks Fizz, Nigel Pegrum of Steeleye Span, and the king of George Formby music, Alan Randall. They all played their bit in the making of Digance albums through the years.

Richard now has a 32-track digitised recording studio of his own in a sixteenth-century converted barn in Hampshire. It's never hired out and is only used for his own projects, particularly for sound-tracking the cartoon ideas and adding music and effects by time coders. He still masters in old analogue fashion still to this day, or by DAT mastering or straight onto compact disc. It's all a far cry from the Grundig tape recorder, but one would never have happened without the other. Richard's current state-of-the-art studio cost more to build and design than Richard earned in his first five years as a folk singer.

Chapter Three

Dreams Do Come True

John O'Connor and I rented a flat together at 87 Fairlop Road, Leytonstone. It cost us £14 a week. John earned £11 and I still didn't have a job. It didn't look good! We lived off one loaf of bread and a jar of strawberry jam per week, shared between us as democratically as our stomachs would allow. We specialised in meeting girls who had their own flats with cookers. Some were so ugly they looked like they'd been beaten round the face with a bag of spanners, but if they could cook, John and I were there, snogging them with our eyes closed and our nostrils expanding to the smell of a decent shepherd's pie. We could never look at each other without bursting into fits of laughter, but we really were that hungry. Any port in a storm, but these weren't ports, they were bombsites.

At Hampstead Rugby Club, John met Carol, an American girl who was travelling Europe with her husband Dan. He moved in with them and we used their camper bus for a while and travelled in style. I drove most of the time. They had the back bedroom at Fairlop Road and they shagged all night. It was all too reminiscent of my days in Glasgow with Dennis and Bobby. To redress the balance I spent most of my spare time with Sue Holland from Fanshawe Gardens in Barking. Sue worked for *Reader's Digest* and was the best looking girl in the world. We stayed together until she pissed off to Morocco in a converted ambulance (how apt) with some rich guy and that was the end of that. Christine Lawrence from Vicarage Lane School would never have done that! We had a mutual respect far beyond that. Such a shame she never knew.

The flat at Fairlop Road soon became overcrowded as we recruited Tim Greenwood on bass guitar and a driver, Steve Jones, from Aberdare in South Wales. We all had lots of friends at the time and every single night was a party. Pisces became very popular on the London folk club scene and we were working more and more and seeing our friends less and less. John and I started to put on some weight as more food passed between our lips. The pulling was obviously going well. Tim was middle class and he found life at Fairlop Road strange to say the least. He had a girlfriend called Fiona, so did John and I at some time or other. Not Tim's of course, but a Fiona with a cooker.

We played the Cambridge Folk Festival and started making a name on the college circuit, until too many disagreements forced us to sling it all in and pursue solo careers. We made the album and had a bash at a second.

Where are they all now? John O'Connor wrote and played the instruments on a huge single, 'Star-Trekkin', which made him a fortune. He had another hit with 'Arthur Daley He's Alright' which he also composed, played and recorded in his spare bedroom in Ritchings Avenue, Walthamstow, under the name of The Firm. John now lives in Los Angeles. We speak every so often. Tim became a singer on cruise ships as far as I know, but I was never to see him again. His brother, Nick, played bass in the Crazy World of Arthur Brown, and now works in television. Steve Jones went to America with John and works as an electrician. I often go out of my way to pass 87 Fairlop Road. It makes me smile in the same way, once again, as Seahouses does. It looks so 'ordinary' now. But it wasn't. It had some famous visitors in its day, including Rick Wakeman, who was then with the Strawbs, and Gordon Giltrap who wrote that tune for the holiday programme on telly. It had a deep purple sitting room too but I expect that's changed. I enjoyed living in Leytonstone, I just couldn't afford it.

We opened a folk club of our own at the Red Lion in the High Road. Al Stewart came along, once again offering his assistance. Our opening night featured Spencer Davis who had a massive hit with 'Keep On Runnin' and lots turned up. Then came Rab Noakes, now a BBC producer, who was touring and writing songs for Lindisfarne, and then we closed due to lack of public support.

Quite a few folk clubs suffered from poor attendance at various times, none more so than a club I played in Chichester, the very coastal city where the Digances landed from France to escape the Huguenot persecution of the seventeenth century. All clubs started at eight o'clock with the booked singer appearing at nine. I knew something was wrong when the club organiser came and found me in the pub and asked me to join him in the clubroom out the back at eight o'clock. I walked in to receive the paying audience that couldn't wait to hear Richard Digance, and there was absolutely nobody there. Not a sausage!

'What's happening?' I asked.

'I'm starting on time, otherwise people come later and later.'

'But there's nobody here to know you started on time,' I responded.

'Club policy,' he insisted.

And so this idiot went on stage to perform to me and me alone. What was worse was that I had to do the same at half past eight. Even then, I had more than my fair share of chorus songs, and so it was that a pathetic Richard Digance sang twelve songs, all with choruses to this club organiser who joined in with resounding gusto. He clapped profusely at the end of my set and then announced he'd cancelled the raffle, the nasty bastard.

You never know when there's a bad show round the corner. Even as recently as 8th September 1998, I suffered a humiliation in the Welsh town of Barmouth during their festival week. We, tour manager Micky Brown and myself, were met by a stage manager who confided his name was Michael but his friends called him Michelle, and we proceeded onto the stage where there wasn't a single piece of equipment. The show had sold out and the theatre had been renovated and painted, indeed two of the doors were still wet. Micky waited for the woman to arrive who'd organised the show with my manager. When she turned up he asked if she'd received the technical rider, which she had. She then explained she never read things like that because she didn't understand anything electrical. I did the show with no sound or lights to three hundred people and had a sore throat for two weeks.

Michelle, or Michael as I chose to call him as he wasn't any friend of mine, closed the evening by shouting as we departed: 'I bet things like this happen to you all the time.' He was wrong. We returned to the hotel, run by some bible basher, and our support act, Steve Charrett, asked what beer he had behind the bar. Moses produced four cans of lager, and when Micky asked if he sold peanuts we were simply told that food closed at eight o'clock. Barmouth – look at it on a map, it looks so inoffensive. It was the nearest I ever came in my whole career to walking off stage and saying bollocks to it all. I have never been so humiliated. I strained every muscle in my throat and never got a single word of thanks.

By 1970 I had started to hang out at a club in Carnaby Street called the Shakespeare's Head, run by Dave Stringer. He was to become one of my best friends and still is to this day. He is trustee to my children and will always be there whenever I need him and vice versa. He helped Pisces get a few gigs and it was the connection with this well respected folk club that cut a few corners for me. Rod Stewart hung out there on occasions and all the record companies were using the place to showcase their new up and coming singer/songwriters because of its central London location. Barbara Dickson, Elvis Costello, Gerry Rafferty, David Bowie, members of the Bee Gees, Billy Connolly, Jasper Carrott, they all played there at some time or another.

Dave worked for NatWest Bank and then moved to the Woolwich building society. He wore a suit and always carried a briefcase full of every possible cigarette brand. However, his major downfall was that he loved an evening at Fairlop Road and a game of cards. We were into canasta, which took forever, and many's the occasion when he would arrive, booted and suited, from his upstanding office post, sit down and not get up again until seven o'clock the next morning to return to work. He gave away some mortgages in a rotten state on many occasions and I still feel proudly responsible for helping many undeservers to secure a home of their own. It could well have been you.

At a Pisces appearance at the Pied Bull Folk Club, Islington, Dave introduced me to Debbie Whiteman, who I later married at West Ham Registry Office with a congregation of two, my mum and dad. We skipped the karaoke and the 'Birdy Song' at the reception and mum cooked my favourite roast dinner and apple sponge before I nipped off on my wedding night to do a gig in Richmond. We were broke at this time, as were our friends, and we knew very few of them could afford wedding presents so we didn't bother to invite anyone, simple as that really. I never even bought Debbie a ring. I couldn't afford it, and still to this day she wears my mum's old eternity ring which is so precious to both of us. Through my life, Dave Stringer helped me year after year with my financial problems, securing me various mortgages as I climbed the ladder of home ownership. Dave's right up there at the top regarding my list of friends.

In 1970 I also undertook my first 'professional' engagement in my own right. It was on Monday 5th January, at the Rising Sun, a pub in Catford, South London run by Dave Cooper. I was paid £6. On 8th October of the same year, I played at the Three Tuns in Beckenham for David Bowie, and my fee hadn't changed!

Times in Leytonstone were hard. I took a job as a window dresser for Young and Marten in Stratford. What a shit job that was, sticking electric drills and pots of paint in eight different windows. I went in less and less until I was sacked. They also accused me of stealing an extension lead, which hurt my pride greatly. When they advertised in the local paper for my replacement, John O'Connor applied for, and got, the job. Same housekeeping money, different source. We needed the money and it didn't really matter who went out to earn it. Then John tired of the boring job and crap bosses so he went in less and less too. The boss of Young and Martens called around to Fairlop Road to find out why John was not at work one morning, and was more than shocked when his ex-employee, me, answered the door. I asked him in while I woke John up and pulled him off Carol. In the living room he spotted the extension lead. John got the sack without even getting out of the sack. I was reported for stealing the extension lead but I can't really remember who to!

We lived off Carol's money while we tried to build our name. Pisces broke up in 1971 after an unsuccessful attempt at keeping going with Frank McConnell and, in the recording studio, with Paul Karas of Rare Bird. Our second album *Game of Chess* was never released. When Pisces disbanded I returned to Blaney Crescent and mum and dad. I was broke. John stayed on at Fairlop Road for a while until he did a runner. Dave Stringer was the only person who really kept in touch from the Leytonstone brigade so the all-night canasta sessions switched to East Ham with Doris, my mum, cooking Dave a lovely breakfast before he set off for the city.

I'd known Doug Morter for a while. A brilliant guitar player with a rival band, Hunter Muskett. He lived in Prince Regent Lane, funnily enough, where my mum was born, and he often came round to Blaney for a game of Subbuteo. Oh yes, we were that cool. We started working the clubs together but I knew one day Doug would find his rightful place in a band playing electric as opposed to acoustic guitar. He did just that, teaming up, after a stint with the Maddy Prior Band, with Jerry Donahue, an American musician who'd made his name with Fairport Convention. I knew Jerry as he'd played guitar with Joan Armatrading on a tour I supported for. We played backgammon together on the tour bus and he and Doug were complementary guitarists.

Doug and I went night fishing regularly, to South Ockenden carp fishery, together with Michael Moore, another folk singer. We called ourselves the brotherhood because we were inseparable. We were all broke so we never went anywhere, having to make our own social life without spending. We fished, played darts, played darts and fished. We invented our own darts games and organised our own fishing competitions.

We had so many musical aspirations but never enough money to see them through in the recording studio. John O'Connor helped us out on the odd occasion, recording demos in his tiny four-track studio. Four tracks seems ridiculous these days but one must never forget that *Sergeant Pepper*, possibly the greatest album of all time, was recorded by the Beatles on just four tracks. Listening back to those sad demos, perhaps the brotherhood could have done with George Martin too. Years later, on 'Through the Keyhole', a television programme for the BBC, I had to guess George Martin's house. All those damn music stands and I got it wrong. The house where the music room made history, and I never guessed it. Shame on you, Digance. Mind you, it was a great honour to meet George Martin.

Nothing much had changed at Blaney Crescent upon my enforced return, other than the fact that Captain Blaney's war memorial had been removed to make way for car park spaces. Mum and dad couldn't help me financially so I spent most of my time indoors. At least I was the only child living at home, so there was considerably more space than I'd been used to. I was writing more and more songs, and strangely at such a low time, the lyrics started to include traces of humour here and there. Perhaps that story of all comedians being miserable is true after all. I've read the stories of Tony Hancock and Peter Sellers, perhaps there was an element of truth in it.

1934 was when the world first saw
A genius the likes of which we'd never seen before
A television treasure who buckled with the pressure
But when we watch what's on these days we miss him all the more
He said it was so harmful to give blood by the armful
Everyone remembers those immortal words he said
Hancock was the master of taking a disaster
And making it a story that would make you laugh instead.

In 1968 on the 24th June
The final curtain closed on a genius too soon,
But every time we say a pint of blood's an armful
That star up in the sky is shining brighter than the moon.

My brother, Len, had moved to Vancouver, British Columbia, after finishing at Goldsmith's Art College in South London. He'd set up a pottery studio in Greenwich that didn't get off the ground and he'd become disillusioned by the lack of opportunities in Britain. At one time he had a girlfriend, Chris from Scunthorpe, a fellow art student who lived with us at Blaney for a while. Stories tell how they were at it in the college garden shrubbery, stark naked, when their so-called mates took their clothes and hid them, causing an embarrassed brother and his partner to walk back to the college in the nude. They spent the afternoon scanning the lockers with nothing on but grass skid marks. He eventually married Donna and they have a son, Avrom. They lived in Wickham Road, Brockley, South London, and then they'd upped and gone. We lost touch for nearly a quarter of a century, until in 1998, he spotted my website and emailed me. I gave him all the news, including details of the death of our parents, which he didn't know too much about. Enough said, but the years allow us all to forgive and forget and I was pleased to hear from him.

At least his departure had given us more room in the cramped Blaney Crescent flat. The constant visits by my mates were quite demanding on my parents who didn't have the money to feed such a multitude. I decided to leave Blaney Crescent too, for the second time. I headed for the green pastures of Essex. I think my parents were sorry to see me go, as they loved the buzz created when all my mates were round, strumming guitars and telling funny stories. Mum in particular was there, joining in and laughing. But I did understand the financial strain and an opportunity to move on had arisen.

My first roadie Richard Cole – he who joined Micky Walker and me on our fishing excursions with Leander Angling Club, and lived upstairs from the Digance family at 41, indeed the same Richard Cole who'd entered the rhubarb business with me and Margaret Duly – introduced me to his friend, Jazz Summers, and I rented a room in his house at 456 Upper Brentwood Road, Gidea Park, after a few weeks at Pettits Lane South in nearby Harold Hill. I never had the money to pay the rent but Jazz never really minded. He was to become my best friend for a long time. I had taken a job at the People's Dispensary for Sick Animals in Redbridge, driving once more, as a mobile dispensary and ambulance driver, but I didn't have a car to get to work! Jazz would lend me his MG sports car, until one day the brakes failed and I smashed into the car in front on the Eastern Avenue. I had no insurance and Jazz had no car!

He played drums in a pub band, smoked Embassy and shagged mercilessly. Our time together was nothing short of wonderful. We had everything in common. He worked as chief radiographer at Oldchurch Hospital and then North Middlesex Hospital near Tottenham, and sometimes I worked there in the dark room. Jazz knew I was desperate for work and thus offered to ring round the clubs and find me some. It was on the hospital's phone and Jazz had his own office where he could shut the door to prying eyes. It was a cost-effective agreement and very fulfilling for me, knowing I was being unofficially sponsored by the National Health after my dad had put in so many years with the ambulance service for crap money and I'd come a cropper for jumping a set of lights in Barking.

Things were starting to roll. We immediately put my fee up to £8, we were that bullish, and I started touring the country in his knackered Hillman Imp that had no driver's window. One night-journey home from Hull in freezing fog was particularly memorable, when I climbed out of the car to get warm. Another of our good mates, Ralph Bernard, a journalist on the *Stratford Express*, gave me more press than I ever deserved and soon my name grew in the East End. Somehow, things were definitely beginning to fall into place. The folk scene was quite trendy and I think the people of the East End of London wanted their own scene apart from that on the other side of town.

The three of us would drink in the Squirrels pub in Gidea Park and discuss our plans for the future. We were so excited and we spoke of nothing else, unless a few girls wandered in and then it was a case of fuck the future. Ralph wanted to work for LBC and get into radio, Jazz wanted to become my manager. I wanted to get on the concert circuit. All three dreams came true. We started a folk night at the Angel in Ilford, and our biggest attendance was when I did the night myself. This started to tell us all something. I could hardly believe it but was proud just the same. I started hanging out with Ralph's journalist colleague Jenny Dawson, an attractive blonde girl who had a friend, Lisa, whom Ralph was to marry. Jenny packed me up for a lorry driver, and when I asked her why because I didn't understand, she told me he was very articulated.

Jazz got me onto a tour with Steeleye Span. We had to pay for the privilege, a colossal £750 and two full-page ads in the *Melody Maker*, but it was worth it. Their manager, Jo Lustig, drove a hard bargain, but that's the way it was to build the name. I had joined Transatlantic

Records some months previously and had recorded my first solo album *England's Green and Pleasant Land*. They paid the £750 and we were on our way. Their previous record advance to me had disappeared to America with the previous manager who got me the deal and I remained totally skint. Ralph busied himself writing my press releases and travelling on the road with me, whilst Jazz spent more and more time in the hospital, behind closed doors, scanning the road atlas and finding new gigs in between photographing dodgy lungs and hip joints. These were truly memorable days that I would never change an inch. The fun boiled over most days, new friends came and went, and none of us gave a stuff about anything.

Jazz had started to expand his management circle. Isla St Clair, who later found fame on 'The Generation Game' with Larry Grayson, came to the house for a while, a duo called Robin and Barry Dransfield joined the stable. Isla St Clair was the best female folk singer in Britain and her looks suggested she would be snapped up for media work, so I wasn't the slightest bit surprised when I saw her opening those doors for Mr Grayson. Mr Summers was fast becoming one of the top agents on the British folk scene, which really didn't say a lot when you looked at the starving emaciated bunch that made up the British folk scene at that time. Most of them had ponced fried breakfasts from my mum at some stage in their career. We stayed together as latter day Musketeers until we inevitably went our different ways. Jazz wanted more than the folk scene. He decided to spread his wings and manage some bands. I told him it was a mistake and to part with me would be the worst decision he would ever make in his life.

Jazz Summers went on to manage Wham, George Michael, Lisa Stansfield and Yazz who recorded 'The Only Way is Up'. A slight misjudgement on my part I feel. Jazz and I speak on occasions and we both hold the fondest of memories of the days in the early 1970s. I'm even mentioned in George Michael's autobiography (page 59) which I take as a great compliment. To have just one friend in life like Jazz Summers would be a bonus to most. I'll never forget our days together. I made four albums for Transatlantic Records during this era before signing a new management deal with Jo Lustig – yes, he who bartered with us for the Steeleye Span tour. He handled Jethro Tull and a former nun called Mary O'Hara who played the harp, wore sunglasses on top of her head and probably never farted. Lustig was a New Yorker who also handled film producer Mel Brooks and he had the right connections for me to move from the folk clubs to the concert circuit as a trusty support act.

That was the game plan, it was what I really wanted to do, and it worked. With the Tull connection I joined Chrysalis Records and recorded an album *Commercial Road* with my additional musicians including Jon Lord of Deep Purple on keyboards and various members of Tull. I remember Jon's fee well. It was a bottle of vodka. During the making of this album in Tull's mobile studio, parked up in drummer Barrie Barlow's garden in Shiplake on Thames, we paused for a cricket match at Mr Lord's house. Alvin Lee was there, together with ex-Beatle George Harrison and Ian Paice of Whitesnake. It was a joy to score eighty runs, to be finally out, caught by Monty Python's Eric Idle, bowled George Harrison. We had a do that evening in the Baskerville Arms, Shiplake, and I bashed out 'Here Comes The Sun' for the jammy bowler. He either wasn't too impressed or didn't hear it! Just imagine nipping into the Baskerville for a quiet pint that night and encountering that bloody lot in the bar. Legends of rock and roll and a struggling folkie.

I suppose I wasn't doing too badly by this time in all honesty. Barrie's house was delightful and had Thames frontage. I often fished in his boathouse, much to the jealous annoyance of angling club members situated on the public towpath on the other bank.

'Lucky bastard.'

'He must have some money.'

I didn't.

Jethro Tull hadn't done too badly though.

Barrie Barlow remains the only Aston Villa supporter I have ever known in real life.

Ralph Bernard didn't do too bad either, considering he supported Leyton Orient who were suffering due to their failure to sign young players from East Ham with broken toes. He eventually got his job at LBC news station, moved to Radio Hallam in Sheffield, and then helped to set up Radio Hereward somewhere near Peterborough. He is now a bigwig at endless radio stations around Britain, having become the boss at GWR Radio and Classic FM. We teamed up often, making radio documentaries together. Indeed, 'Down To Earth', with Arthur Scargill, won us an award as Radio Documentary of the Year, as did 'Dying For A Drink', a documentary about alcoholism, something that Jazz, Ralph and myself had grown to almost specialise in at the Squirrels. But the Three Musketeers had come of age and gone their separate ways. Jazz eventually moved to the South of France and Ralph to Marlborough in Wiltshire. To us all, the heady days at Upper Brentwood Road are nothing more than distant memories.

Ralph Bernard always had funny ideas up his sleeve. Being a journalist, ideas for big stories were always brewing. Sometimes he'd make up stories to fit headlines he'd dreamed up. Council function cuts in the East End. He longed to use his header 'Mayor's balls hang in the balance'. I don't think he ever did. He once told me about an occasion when Stratford council wanted to put up a statue of prison reformer Elizabeth Fry, another fine East Ham girl. For financial reasons that was ditched too. Ralph's header this time was 'Mayor fights erection in street'. I lost track of Ralph when he became a newsreader at Radio Hallam, and we weren't to meet up again for seven years.

My first album, *England's Green and Pleasant Land*, for Transatlantic Records, never did set the world on fire but received some fair reviews. It was finally released after great confusion on 24th March 1974, due to a vinyl shortage. It was pressed in France eventually. At least I'd reached established solo artist status with regular articles in the music papers. The game plan was to get out of the folk clubs and into the concert arena as a support act to many of the rock stars that were touring at the time. The Steeleye Span tour had gone well and I wanted more.

I had started the year before, 1973, with Jethro Tull and then onto Elkie Brooks who was to become one of my greatest friends within the industry. At Elkie's sell-out show at the Dome, Brighton, a gent came to the stage door who claimed to know me. He wanted to meet up with me and wondered if I had a few complimentary tickets for the sell-out show. I remembered his name, one of the Kensington youth club mob. The roadies did me a favour that night and at least I'd got my revenge on one of them. He never got to see the show, and if he had, he'd only have witnessed it with one good eye by the time the boys had finished.

The following years I trudged round Britain with the likes of Joan Armatrading, Supertramp and Tom Jones. I began living the life of a rock and roller and was really enjoying it. Every tour had a story to tell. With Steeleye Span, I remember Peter Knight, the fiddle player, begging a night porter for a cup of coffee in Manchester's Midland Hotel. The porter walked with a limp and was one of the most miserable bastards I'd met since Alan King the PE teacher. He resented getting a coffee for a man in dungarees and sporting a long ponytail. He didn't fight the Germans to wait on such an unappreciative tosser. The coffee eventually arrived, half an hour later. Peter gave the misery £100, which he'd collected from us all in a whip round, and told him to keep the change. I still see the man's face to this day. He hated Pete, but didn't know how to react once he'd received such a huge tip. It was mental confusion the likes of which I had never seen before.

With Elkie, we played football matches, drank all night and if a hotel had a swimming pool, Tim Hinkley, her keyboard player, would always set up a cucumber sandwich regatta, even if some fit bastard was to-ing and fro-ing with ease. Jerome Rinsen, 'Stretch' her drummer, who'd worked with Stevie Wonder, Tim and myself played poker incessantly. I won most of the time and earned more on the coach than I ever did on stage at that time. I bought Debbie a classical guitar and paid all my expenses with the help of my fifty-two friends in four suits. Tom Jones I never met until the final night of the tour at the Royal Albert Hall. We were all summoned to his dressing room where he chatted with Prince Edward. Tom was a charming man, no question about that, and when we finally met he asked if the sales had been OK. I realised later, after a few months touring, he thought I'd been selling the merchandise!

Is it usual to be spoken to like that?

In the words of Tom, it's not unusual.

I bought a VW minibus for £770 and went off, with Ralph's mate Chris, to Belgium for a concert to celebrate us going into the Common Market. It was 5th September 1974 and I was supporting a girl singer, Marian Segal, and the entire tour of Belgium lasted four days. I met Nadine Tronion there and fell hopelessly in love again. I think she thought I was a bit of a dick but it was cool to have an English boyfriend. The one-sided relationship went on for a couple of years before she lost total interest and I faced a huge phone bill from British Telecom. She had the greatest pair God ever made, with of course the exception of Geoff Hurst and Martin Peters, and a stunning slim body. Of course she was taking the piss. Me? What was she doing with me? No idea. After two years I put an envelope with £15 on our mantelpiece. It was the ferry money back to Ostend. Should she ever feel lonely, then she always had a means of getting home to Belgium. Above the fire it was placed, and that night she buggered off. Another romance ground to a halt. At least Christine Lawrence spoke English. She would never have left Reading to return to Sandford Road.

★

And still the supports continued as I proved to be easy, what with just a guitar and a vocal mike. Everyone wanted the easy, life by booking Digance. It had little to do with my talent. I was easy to handle, no drums, no amps, just me and the Levin acoustic. I played at Wembley with Cat Stevens and Gary Numan and my name-dropping press releases (well, I'm sure you are impressed?) led to various mentions and another fiver on the fee.

But it was a trip to America that was to get me thinking and that was where I met a man who took me to the very edge of comedy parameters, Steve Martin. Now that is a name drop. We worked together for a while at the Cellar Door in Georgetown, Washington and without question he would become the biggest influence in my career as a folk comedian. Strangely, we had followed a similar path as we tried to make it. We were both writers, Steve for the Smothers Brothers, who branched out with a blend of music and comedy, and myself with Bernard Braden on the BBC. We were both trying to break in a similar fashion. Despite his fame through so many classic films like *Three Amigos*, *Trains*, *Planes and Automobiles*, *Dirty Rotten Scoundrels* and *The Jerk* (my favourite), he remains the greatest banjo player I've ever seen. He just had to become big, he was a genius. Taking the audience into the street to show them how to steal a car, audience participation the likes of which I had never seen before.

My eyes were finally opened to how I could break in England. Audience participation! No-one had heard of Steve Martin in England at the time and I make no excuses for admitting I followed his outrageous path, obviously to a more mediocre success, without anyone knowing where this cheeky cockney had developed the knack of grabbing an audience and getting to work on them. I hereby declare that Steve Martin was the man. My first concert upon my return from America was at the Fairfield Halls in Croydon, and I'm sure I knocked out my standard two-hour show with an American accent!

Oh yes, America. Not the scene of any monumental victory in my career. I'd been signed by Mercury Records in the States, so off I went again for a bit of promotion. I returned to Washington to support Livingston Taylor, the brother of James, supported Billy Swann (who'd enjoyed a number one hit with 'I Can Help') in Atlanta, and even worked with Esther Phillips in Denver, Colorado. Every night I died on my rear end and ended up delivering hired cars until I saved up the flight home. My greatest night in America was playing the Bottom Line in New York as a support to Tom Rush, where I signed the backstage wall next to Bob Dylan and Bruce Springsteen. My final date in America was as support to the Allman Brothers when I returned to Atlanta. I obviously left a great impression, for I never went back to the States for fifteen years, until I played in New Orleans for a bunch of British Ford reps on the legendary Bourbon Street, staying at a hotel adjacent to the house where Tennessee Williams wrote 'A Streetcar Named Desire'. So I never cracked America, but working with Steve Martin I rate as the greatest thing I've ever done professionally. And the timing couldn't have been better. For him alone, I forgive them for dumping all that tea in Boston harbour.

Back in England, Billy Connolly and Jasper Carrott had broken into the big time with mass television exposure. The folk comedian had arrived. Max Boyce had Wales sewn up and Mike Harding had made the Manchester area his own. Later came Fred Wedlock in the West Country and Mike Elliot on Tyneside. Connolly and Harding were good musicians, Max had a band, Carrott I can't recall playing the guitar, although I'm sure he did, but I think for him it was more a prop. The Cambridge Folk Festival loomed and I decided to write an 'anthem' that could be sung and adopted by the audience. I wrote 'Working Class Millionaire', which was to become my most well known song during my days on the folk scene. The whole idea was to become London's version of the other folk comics, and to a degree it worked.

I'd done too many cheap gigs and decided to drop out for a while to build some sort of exclusivity. In 1974, I made my one and only trip to visit my brother in Canada. We spent time visiting Indian reservations in Squamish, BC, and camping in a small national park known as Manning Park, which is actually bigger than Belgium. Imagine being the whistle-blowing parky there? You'd need a new bike every two weeks. That park will be etched on my mind forever. I nearly never made it further than 1974. This time, it wasn't a gang of East End ex school-mates, but a stroppy animal of muscular proportions.

As I slept in a tent outside my brother's caravanette, shouting and screaming awoke me. A brown bear had lolloped into the campsite to up-end the garbage cans for food. With park wardens in pursuit he decided to do a runner and at full speed tripped over the guy ropes of my tent. If that wasn't frightening enough, some stupid bastard was shooting at him. I knew I was a gonner. The only option was how. Being eaten by a bear or shot up the arse by some crazed parky in a lumberjack shirt. We'd caught a few trout earlier in the evening and the smell diverted the bear's attentions from me. They were hanging on a tree branch, ready for a tasty breakfast. My first reaction was 'For fuck's sake take them!'

The brown bear escaped and the shouting grew fainter. My brother slept through it all, something he'd obviously learnt from our dad. He couldn't believe it all the next morning. Various folk had told him of my bravery. Oh yes, I forgot to say, his son was in the tent with me and by all accounts I'd shielded him from the hungry bear. Had I bollocks. I'm surprised I wasn't seen smothering him in tomato ketchup and salad dressing before dangling him outside the tent on a stick.

It was the closest I've ever been to death, possibly excepting the time I jumped, as a non-swimmer, off a lilo in the sea at Clacton, only to discover I was out of my depth. My whole world passed before me, but being seven it was pathetic. I demanded a rerun of the highlights. I flapped about until someone grabbed hold of my trunks and pulled me to safety. Dad was asleep on the beach. I never bothered him, choosing to cough and splutter in privacy further along the shingle. Oh yes, and once I was in an air crash. Not a huge one. It never made 'News At Ten' or anything like that. A tyre burst on landing at New York. We ended up sideways on, looking at the landing lights down the runway from the passenger portholes. It was not a big smash but I shat myself just the same. Anyway, we move on.

During my absence in Canada, my album reached the folk charts and various singers were covering my songs, particularly 'Working Class Millionaire'. It had done me good to stay out of the way for a while and when I returned I undertook my first solo British tour. It began at Sutton and ended at East Ham Town Hall, just a stone's throw from Kensington Youth Club, half a mile from Thomas Lethaby and even closer to Vicarage Lane School and Blaney Crescent. The show completely sold out and I didn't meet up with a single person I knew. It felt strange. I'd become popular with the East End people, accepted as one of their own who'd done well, but totally forgotten by so many friends, class-mates and fellow youth club goers who'd kicked the shit out of me. I bought my first house in Reading, miles and miles away from my roots, but near my mates in Jethro Tull and Deep Purple. No 84 Whitley Wood Lane cost £14,500. Although I had no money I fished on the Thames, played tennis with Barrie Barlow and Ian Paice and went round people's houses for a meal. I'd never done anything like that before. Never taken wine to someone's house. It was all very well, but I missed my roots badly and decided eventually to move back to Debden in Essex.

I'd become a presenter on London's Capital Radio, taking on a new role as disc jockey on their Midnight Special programme. I also qualified as a radio producer. I'd made my first Capital broadcast in 1974 on the Robbie Barrish Show with Wizz Jones, a blues guitarist, and the producer Paul Blencoe remembered me.

Reading was a long drive in to London, three times a week, so Essex beckoned more and more. It all seemed to add up. Debbie and I moved to Fern Cottage, Debden which cost us £45,000. It was a beautiful old wooden-clad cottage backing onto open fields. We rescued two dogs, Russell and Sheba, from Wood Green Animal Rescue and they stayed with us for two more houses, three in Russell's case. It went well at the radio station. I interviewed endless heroes like Joni Mitchell and Arlo Guthrie and my dreams really were starting to come true.

Joni Mitchell's was by far the greatest interview I ever did. Such a diminutive person, such class and poise. I'd only ever seen her from a few rows back at the Royal Festival Hall, and suddenly we're both in the cramped talk studio at Euston Tower. Joni was promoting a new album and was doing the usual tedious rounds of interviews a record company expects of such a star. I'd interviewed Emmylou Harris a few weeks before and didn't really enjoy the restrictions on the questions, even though I adored her music. Joni must have been bored stupid with being asked a million times why she laughed at the end of 'Big Yellow Taxi'. And here was another misinformed radio presenter who didn't know much about his subject matter. Perhaps that's what she thought.

I still have the interview on tape. Four minutes into the interview:

'Joni, when did you learn to drop your top and bottom E strings and play in open tuning?'

'My top and bottom E strings?'

'Yes, and then the fifth string. I watched you D-tune at the Royal Festival Hall and I wondered how you were inspired to play the guitar like this because I'd never seen anyone else use the method before.'

'I've never been asked that question before, Richard. Now let me see. I guess it all started before 'Both Sides Now'. Yes, it came from the blues I guess.'

Joni Mitchell lit up a cigarette. In fact she lit up lots of cigarettes during the interview, which surprised me greatly as she was the best singer in the world.

We went for a coffee together after the taping and she told me how much she enjoyed chatting to someone who knew her music so well. Indeed, after 'Walking In Memphis' on my TV show, Marc Cohn and I decided to do a duet on TV of Joni's 'A Case of You'. A great song, done simply on piano and acoustic guitar. It never happened but we both proved to be dedicated and committed fans of Joni Mitchell.

My weekly income rose from forty pounds a week to three hundred pounds a week and I bought my first brand new car, a Ford!! I remained at Capital Radio for nearly six years. My folk scene days had truly passed and I was settling down to become a radio person. With the producer qualifications I thought about moving to a small station, perhaps in Norfolk or somewhere equally pleasant, becoming a programme controller and fishing and walking the dog at weekends. Then along came Jim Davidson. It all changed. More and more dreams were to come true, as my job at Capital became a nightmare.

Jim Davidson added nothing short of rocket fuel to my career. We first met at a concert at the Victoria Palace in London, at an Ethiopia Aid concert. This was in the days before it was cool to undertake such crusades with mass television exposure and hit records gleaned from such charity work. Jim did charity work. Loads and loads of it. He never made a big deal about it, he just got on and did it. I admired him tremendously for that. It was a side few knew about the wayward nutter.

I'd semi-retired from live work by now as my time was spent searching for the new radio station I would make my home. I was forced back onto the stage because Eric Clapton was on the bill and I wanted to meet him. The year was 1981. Problem was, Eric Clapton didn't really want to meet me – after all, he'd never bloody heard of me so we can't blame him for that one. Jim and I chatted backstage about fishing, and then he sat in with me on my late night radio show, answering phone calls. It was the most hilarious night and the calls came in by the thousand. It was to become a successful live format on British radio, but not many had tried it when Jim and I had a go. Capital's programme controller rang in and asked when we were going to stop talking and play some records. It was at that moment I knew my days at Capital were numbered. I made some clangers there, I accept that, but none were intended.

From the earliest days of his career, Richard has maintained a close relationship with hospital radio broadcasting. He gained his first experience of radio work at East Ham Memorial Hospital, Shrewsbury Road. He acted as a presenter's runner, gathering requests around the wards. After sitting in at Great Ormond Street Hospital in London, he became President of Camelot Hospital Radio in Yeovil, Somerset. Whilst at Capital Radio, he sent the thousands of records he received from record companies to various hospital radio stations around the London area, particularly his native East End.

Strange as it may seem, when he gave up disc jockey work he didn't keep a single record, only the recorded sessions he was so proud of. These included some tapes which became collector's items, particularly those by Otway and Barrett and the late Rory Gallagher, together with the Nick Lowe and Dave Edmunds acoustic set and his interview with Joni Mitchell.

Richard finally qualified as a radio producer in 1982 at Elstree, Hertfordshire. He produced independent programmes for both the BBC and commercial radio and expanded his own recording studio at this time to encompass the composing and taping of incidental and soundtrack music. Before meeting Jim Davidson he was resigned to stage retirement and was writing to radio stations around the country for jobs as an assistant programme controller. He'd been to two interviews but was turned down on both occasions.

Chapter Four

The Continuation of My Radio Career

Without question, the worst mistake I ever made during my radio career at Capital concerned the Carpenters, or more explicitly the sad and untimely death of Karen Carpenter. As I begin to type this tale my toes curl with embarrassment, but it needs to be told because it's an important facet of my leaving the comforts and security of the London radio station to find alternative employment.

A telex (this was before faxes and emails!) flashed its red light at me as I hosted 'Midnight Special'. It was a signal that the message was considered important enough to read out as a newsflash. Although I was never into the Carpenters, apart from that incredible guitar solo in 'Goodbye To Love', I was stunned to discover Karen had passed away.

I hated that telex machine, and particularly the red flashing light. The time of the Falklands War was unbearable. I knew I was never going to be able to pronounce any of the Argentinian generals no matter how hard I tried. I bluffed and bullshitted my way through endless news items, very mindful that British soldiers were being killed in conflict whilst I was making a perfect arse of myself on air. The public wanted to hear the updates and I learnt very quickly how to do the odd vocal editing job so all such generals were excluded. You could say the generals were generalised.

It still amazes me when I think back to my days at London's Capital Radio, probably the most respected and important commercial radio station in Great Britain. After midnight, when I relieved the presenter Mike Allen from his pursuits at the Best Disco In Town, I was the only bloke in the building, apart from a security guard on the front desk who spent most of the night chatting to his girlfriend and scratching his arse. Remember that London was a major target for all kinds of terrorists who would love to have taken over that premier station and have their say to the huge population of England's capital city. And there was just me, and the bloke on the phone. Incredible really. Nothing ever happened except for the one time I was taken hostage by some students during their rag week at Brunel University. It was no big deal, I let them sit in with me and we had a great laugh together. They introduced some of the records and read out the dedications and many say it was the best radio show I ever did. Some of their requests were a little on the bizarre side. I never knew Adolf Hitler lived in Uxbridge. Neither did I know it was in the same house as Mickey Mouse. Capital refused to pay the ransom money, which was eventually paid by a bakery near Ealing.

Mike Allen worked in Studio One and I worked from Studio Two in an area resembling a honeycomb. Mike, who went to LBC and Talk Radio, was a fantastic bloke. He came to Fern Cottage a couple of times, and he always popped his head into Studio Two before leaving for home. We'd have a cup of tea and talk about fishing. When he left I settled down to chat to the late night population of London.

The overnight studio was tiny, about fifteen feet by about six or seven feet. It contained a tiny desk, two tape machines for playing concerts and music sessions, and a wall rack containing numerous radio jingles. Behind the presenter's chair were two boxes containing the chart records, the playlist as it was known. Overnight jocks like me weren't allowed to play the chart stuff because it used up valuable needle-time, which had to be saved for the more important daytime presenters like Grahame Dene and Mike Aspel. That never bothered me, as most of it was crap anyway. I featured obscure blues albums and singer/songwriters who most had never heard of. When I worked with Elton John at the London Palladium at a Prince's Trust concert he told me I was one of his favourite disc jockeys because of the unusual music I played. Francis Rossi of Status Quo paid me the same compliment, indeed Quo covered a Hank Williams country song after hearing the original on my show. So it wasn't all bad. I was getting something right.

The only contact with the outside world was a phone that contained about a dozen lines for phone-ins. We answered the phone ourselves, took weather forecasts ourselves. I made those up because I couldn't see out of any windows and judging by Michael Fish's clangers, most weathermen made them up anyway. I looked out on the main control room where sound engineers helped or 'drove' the

desk for the daytime presenters. Every time I went on air I ripped a
photo of someone or other from a newspaper, and each time I spoke,
I spoke to that one stranger as opposed to London town. That made
it informal, friendly and not so nerve-racking for me. It was a tip the
late Roger Scott gave me, and I never once forgot to take my new
friend into the studio with me. I often wonder if Phillip Schofield,
who followed me at the time, thought I was gay, what with all those
pictures of young men on the mixing desk when he took over. Mind
you, he'd be a fine one to talk, pissing about with all those animals in
'Doctor Dolittle'.

Some nights, out of boredom on the four-hour shift, I invented
races for the bread delivery vans going about their business in the
early hours. I'd hired an unknown impressionist, Chris Barrie, who
rose to fame on 'Red Dwarf' and later 'The Brittas Empire', to do
some commentary voices. Chris was brilliant and would do
anything for the meagre thirty quid Capital paid him. We met
whilst filming a pilot for Central Television, 'The Three Busketeers'
with mime artist Adrian Hedley, which never saw the light of day,
and we got on well together. Chris was incredibly creative and I
liked that in a person.
   If I ever said I was hungry on air a tray of cream cakes would
arrive. I once said I was gasping for a fag and eighty Marlboro arrived
from different sources within fifteen minutes. When I said I fancied
a new Rolex I got absolutely sod all. I had a real parity with people I
never knew, that was a strange feeling. It was night-time and it was
as though the rest of London knew nothing about us all as they slept
or shagged through such unsociable hours. We were a sort of club of
around a hundred thousand and some people still talk of those
programmes to me to this day. It was pioneering and incredibly
exciting. I never rehearsed a single word. I never did after that either!
   Play Misty For Me rang true on a number of occasions. London
can be a lonely place and for many such souls I was their friend
through the loneliest of hours, my cockney tones echoing across the
Earls Court flat area and beyond. I was never a Clint Eastwood on
the good-looks stakes but I had women ringing me regularly and I
could hear the sadness and desperation in their voices. I was their
interlink between the bright lights of London town and acute
loneliness. Me! Their interlink! Me who spent two nights a week, on
my own, talking to a fucking wall. One girl sent me a beautiful suede
anorak that must have cost a fortune. I asked Tim Blackmore what

to do and he insisted it was something that happened to all the disc jockeys and I should return it. I was so pissed off. It was a smart bit of clobber.

Reluctantly and with embarrassing trepidation I return to the Carpenters story. I was going to swerve but I knew every reader would notice I hadn't explained my monumental error. Anyway, the night in question the news rang clear from LBC as I pressed the button that instantly switched Capital to the independent news station that was stationed just off Fleet Street in a place called Dr Johnson's Buildings. Karen Carpenter had indeed died and was the header story of all news bulletins.

LBC took the news for three minutes and then handed back to me, at the press of the button once more, to read the weather. I had a brainwave. I thought it right and proper to come out of the weather details with a song by the Carpenters, but I had only three minutes to find the master keys, run down to the library, search through the endless records by artists beginning with C, and run back to the studio. I decided I'd give it a try. Off I ran, making sure I knew the pass numbers to get back in the studio. I sprinted through three corridors, grabbed a Carpenters record and ran as fast as I could back to the studio. The last couple of news items were under way as I shoved on my headphones and cued up the record.

I pressed the button and on came the Capital jingle. I was breathless. I passed on my condolences to all concerned and admitted Karen would be a great loss to the music world and dedicated a song to Carpenters fans around London. I was horrified. What a choice of music!! Karen Carpenter was singing 'I'm on top of the world looking down on creation.' I banged my head on the mixing desk so hard, my headphones fell to the ground, nearly strangling me in the process. I had immediately realised what a stupid thing I'd done, albeit in innocence.

The next day I was hurled before Tony Hale, the big important something or other, and was told to account for my actions. I couldn't believe the bosses at Capital (and believe me there were bloody hundreds of them) would ever think I would be so tasteless at such a sad time. They kept on about the fact I was a comedian and they found my sense of humour unacceptable to their listeners.

As I say, none of it was intended, but nonetheless my days as a London radio presenter were drawing to a close. I was given strange interviews to take on, including two IRA sympathisers after the bombing in Regent's Park. I was refused a Saturday afternoon slot because my voice sounded 'too East End', for heaven's sake. It was supposed to be a local radio station for the city where I was born and I didn't sound right!! I was doing more and more 'insert' interviews for other programmes and more often than not asking questions on subjects or styles of music I knew nothing about. Bob Voice knew my time was up. He was an upbeat manager who wouldn't tolerate the unfair treatment I was receiving.

I took on a new Saturday evening programme called 'RDU2', a quiz for school-kids. I enjoyed that until I was accused of taking the mickey out of Nick Faldo for crying after being fined for slow play at a golf tournament. Sod's Law, his wife at the time, Melanie, was listening and she made an official complaint to the station. Again Tim Blackmore came to my rescue. This time I was to blame and I unreservedly apologised and sent Melanie a bunch of flowers. I was a bit of a loose cannon I suppose, but Tim and Aidan Day stuck with me. I was promoted to 'Sunday Funday' which I co-produced, and went around London on outside broadcasts. But the Capital days were drawing to a close.

To be honest I was losing interest anyway. The good presenters that pioneered the station were departing and I knew I would join them before long.

It had become a difficult time of my life. I loved my radio career so much when I joined, but I couldn't have worked for a bigger bunch of self-opinionated creeps if I'd tried. I joined under Aidan Day and Tim Blackmore, magnificent men. They weren't there long after I signed up. My first producer was Paul Blencoe whom I worked well with. He was replaced by Jon Myer who was in turn replaced by various oddities who didn't like me or the music I stood for. I was at my happiest when I produced the programme myself, which I eventually did. I learnt various recording studio skills both at Capital and Elstree, thus gaining the ability to work a recording studio, something that became rather useful in later years, particularly when I began working on my children's projects such as the Tidings and Snailhouse Rock.

One of the highlights of my Capital days had to be meeting Princess Diana when she visited the studios. Our programme controller, Jo Sandilands, demanded we all be upstanding in our various cubbyholes, and told us that if the Princess chose to visit one of us we were to stand beside her with our hands behind our back.

She chose the office of Jon Myer and myself as one of her stopping off points. Jon pretended to edit a folk programme. The funny line rang true, that royalty think the whole world smells of paint because everything has a quick coat slapped on before their arrival. The radio station was much the same that day, with no piles of records to be seen, no record requests on the backs of postcards and no gaffa tape on the floor. No paper cups or ashtrays, no pictures on the walls or freebie tee shirts lying around.

Diana, being the interested and amiable person she was, asked about editing and donned a pair of headphones and stayed for a while. She was so nice, I would love to have made her a cup of tea. She was enthralled and Jo Sandilands and Tony Hale were totally aghast that she'd stopped to talk to a lowly folk music presenter when other greater luminaries were waiting further down the corridor. Truly, she was even more beautiful in real life. We met again at the London Palladium when I appeared in a Prince's Trust Gala and she asked me if I was still having to edit my programmes or if I'd started getting them right, thus dispensing with editing. No-one around us understood but I loved the remark and we both laughed. She had a radiant smile, which followed her humorous comments. I couldn't believe she remembered me. One minute she was talking to Elton John and Robin Williams and then asking me about the folk programme on Capital Radio. Talk about after the Lord Mayor's Show!

I met her three times during her short life, and I felt devastated when the untimely end occurred in Paris. My good friend Jeff Mitchell had called round for a game of golf and I'd returned from a concert the previous night at the Oxford Apollo. I knew nothing about the car accident and when Jeff broke the news I was genuinely heartbroken. My family was in Disneyland and I sat with Jeff and Debbie's friend Jane Andrews who'd been selling merchandise at Oxford and when they left I felt sick with emptiness. Alone in my house I studied the teletext for hour upon hour, not choosing to believe what had happened. The same emptiness probably hit us all with the murder of Jill Dando, that 'surely-not' feeling of disbelief and hopelessness. Believe what you will, but Princess Diana was a genuinely interesting lady with a magnetic personality.

As the news built through the day, I chose not to disclose the fact to anyone that we'd met a few times. It would have sounded false and a name-drop of immense proportions. My local television station rang and asked for a comment, which I declined. It was big news in

Romsey where I lived, because she'd spent her honeymoon with Charles at Broadlands, home of Lord Mountbatten before he was killed in Ireland. Local papers wanted quotes from celebrities but I still chose to say absolutely nothing. My mind flashed back to the comment about getting the folk programme right. That was enough for me, a memory and a knowing smile to last forever.

On the day of her funeral service in London, I was entertaining the troops in Benbecula in the Outer Hebrides. I couldn't have been further away from the wave of sadness and emotion around Kensington if I'd tried. But I never forgot. As the silence arrived I stood in a rowing boat in the middle of a Scottish loch with Rachel Ivey, our first Tidings vocalist. Rain belted horizontally as I tried in vain to catch a few trout. I was freezing cold and tears streamed down my cheeks. Rachel never knew, nobody knew. The hood of my anorak was over my head to protect me from the biting cold and it served me well as I paid my own respects and said my own farewell in my own way. My mind returned for a final time to my early days at the radio station. I stood in silence for the three minutes, just imagining what was going on so many hundreds of miles away, and realised I was in the right place, lost in my own thoughts. My life had crossed that of a very famous and dearly loved person. Rachel and the gillie respected my moment of detachment.

In February 1999, I took Polly and Rosie to her memorial in the Harrods basement. It was moving. The beautiful woman who'd stood next to me with a pair of 'cans' on, was no more.

'Did you know her, dad?' asked Rosie.

I looked down at Rosie and then at the many people milling around, taking photos of each other and tossing coins in the wishing well. It wasn't the time.

'I didn't really know her darling, but I met her a few times.'

'Was she beautiful?'

'Yes Rosie, she was a Princess.'

'Wow, you knew a real princess?'

'Yes I did.'

'Cool, dad.'

She was right, it was cool.

So many great presenters worked at Capital at that golden time. Michael Aspel, Mike Smith, Kenny Everett, Phillip Schofield, Russell Grant, Alan Freeman, the late Adrian Love, a great bloke who died of a collapsed lung in March 1999. Adrian always compered my shows if

I worked on stage in London. We stayed friends through his days at LBC and beyond to the days in Guildford. Only the good die young again. We all had a bond, and together we put up with probably the rudest, most bloody-minded management team that had ever been amassed since the Nuremburg Trials. I hated just about every one of them, and fortunately they hated me in equal doses. It was mutual. I can assure you all, the Carpenters goof was totally unintentional, and still to this day, that mob would never believe me.

We all went on to greater things where we were all more appreciated, I'm sure. Mike Smith was a friendly guy, always talking about Blue Peter presenter Sarah Green. He married her in the end. Good stuff. Dodgy helicopter pilot though! Smithy and I used to spend hours in the canteen talking about our future plans of breaking into television. We both got there in the end and didn't meet up again until 1996, when we did a TV show in Birmingham with Jimmy Nail. We'd both lived in Romford, Essex. Smithy used to be Noel Edmonds's driver. Yes, the mad driver of the man who drove us all mad, boom boom.

We had great days out, standing on the float as part of the Lord Mayor's Show, going to Dire Straits concerts at Wembley, attending various charity events as a team. We even had a football team, run by Mick Brown. We played at Stamford Bridge for John Dempsey's testimonial, where I played against Portuguese international Eusebio, one of the greatest footballers in the world. I taught him a thing or two. I was in the heart of the defence alongside Jackie Charlton who shouted at me all night. On another occasion we played at Loftus Road, home of Queen's Park Rangers, for the Goaldiggers charity. A bloke called Paul Mariner who played for Arsenal, Ipswich and England floored me on one occasion. On the Astroturf my bones slid along and my skin stayed where it was as the nasty bastard sent me flying, and I suffered the most awful burns that didn't disappear for months. I looked like I'd been given a hell of a love-bite from a pigmy. I told Mariner it was only a charity game and his plain and simple answer was 'Get up, you poof!'

My greatest day at Capital occurred towards the end of the 70s when I compered the Knebworth Festival, starring the Beach Boys, Mike Oldfield, Santana, and Elkie my mate. It rained and it made the programme scheduling difficult because of the electrical equipment. Mike Oldfield wouldn't go on until his crew considered it safe to do so. He was right, his Tubular Bells were in grave danger.

'Do something Digance, we're going live on air,' Tony Hale, strangely not wearing a German SS trench coat, told me as DJ Nicky Horne handed across from the London studio to the muddy fields of Hertfordshire.

'Me?'

'Yes you, you useless bastard. Do something!'

For Tony Hale that was friendly in comparison to the usual verbal abuse he could fling your way.

There were half a million punters in a field, soaked to the bloody skin and I was supposed to do something? I thought about wringing them out like a huge flannel. What else?

The great London radio station stood silent as Capital failed to boom over the giant PA system. Nicky Horne had indeed passed over to us from the dry London studio. Bold as brass, I strolled onto the stage and sang 'Singing In The Rain'. I think every single one of the hundreds of thousands sang along and the sound of that many people clapping and cheering still rings loud in my ears to this day. It was an amazing experience to sit on the side of the stage as the Wilson legends performed their Beach Boys songs. I spoke to their drummer as he took a short break. Not many weeks later he sadly drowned. I met and shook hands with Brian Wilson, the man who John Lennon claimed to be the greatest inspiration of the Beatles. Good vibrations for sure.

I last saw Tony Hale when he became a door to door census-form collector. Imagine his face when I opened the door to my London Docklands flat. We had little to say. I was on television by this time and doing rather well. Once he'd tipped rubbish outside my office door – strangely, the tables were turned as he stood, bedraggled, at my flat's front door in Undine Road by Clippers Quay.

'Of course I'm only doing this as a favour for a good friend,' he embarrassingly insisted. And he was right. He was doing it for himself, and Tony Hale had no greater friend on earth than Tony Hale.

During my last year at the station I had begun working on stage with Jim Davidson. It was hard finding the time to edit my weekly folk programmes, present a night show and tour at the same time. I started taking work home, editing tapes in my small four-track studio, making ident cartridges and planning the records for the following week. On other occasions, when a gig came in too far away from London, I dropped sound engineers fifty quid to stay at the station and play the 'live' tapes I had pre-recorded at home. The weather forecasts were bland to say the least. How would I know what the weather would be like three days before transmission? I used to tell the listeners to look for themselves out of the window to save me the time. Failing that I would tell them it was dark outside and best to stay in and snuggle up to the radio. The only thing that would have blown my scam is if one of the Royal Family had passed away, forcing the station to immediately switch to solemn music. My luck was in. Everyone stayed fit and healthy and my cover was safe. I set up a studio at home with a clock set for midnight until 4am, my slot at Capital, and I could mix and match various shows. Sometimes I sat up all night making these shows. I remember it well, it was around the time my eldest daughter Polly was born. And what a night that was.

The year was 1983. We approached Guy Fawkes Night, 5th November. I'd been giving out the weather warnings all night. Heathrow had closed and Gatwick was about to. The city was in pea-soup chaos. London was shrouded in thick fog when I received a phone call to say that Debbie had gone into labour at the Rosie Maternity Hospital in Cambridge. I had three hours to go to the end of my show and didn't know what to do. To the rescue came Phil Allen, presenter of the early show before Phillip Schofield, who luckily had arrived early to put his show together, something I rarely bothered to do myself. What a deed, the guy sat in for me, thus giving him a five-hour stint in the studio, while I raced down the M11 in pea-soup conditions to be with my wife.

Polly was born some twenty hours later. I went home to feed our dogs, Russell and Sheba, and then collected some things for Debbie before returning to Cambridge. I hadn't slept. The following night I was playing the Festival Theatre, Frome, Somerset and during the song 'Give Us An Old Song Mary', I actually dozed off for a split second, just like we've all done when driving on motorways. Can anyone actually go to sleep whilst singing a song? The answer is yes they can! Normally at my shows it was the audience, but on this one and only occasion it was me! Three cheers for Phil Allen, wherever he may be now.

Polly and Debbie arrived home to our house in Debden, safe and sound, whilst I finished my stage work and also got home from the West Country via a radio show in London. I hadn't slept for three days, just staying awake by the adrenaline surges of both becoming a dad and the buzz of live work. I hadn't called Debbie's mum Rachel to tell her the good news simply because I was too out of it to remember. We all suffer mother-in-law disagreements I'm sure. This was my first.

I felt I'd done so well in my own small way, getting on with my job, getting back to Capital for the folk programme, looking after the dogs and doing two live shows in the meantime. Sadly I hadn't. A couple of days later I was back on the road, working with David Essex in Harrogate and I knew deep down I was portraying the image of an unconcerned father, husband and son-in-law. I felt accused of unconcern and thoughlessness, neither of which was true.

Meeting up with Jim Davidson gave my career the boost it needed at such a low time. I came close to deciding between being less selfish and being at home every night, or going back on the road to try and achieve even greater things the second time around. I knew my commercial radio days were numbered in London. It was all too insecure to turn down the extra income I could generate by joining Jim Davidson. It took a couple of days to reach my decision. I knew I'd already upset various people close to me through my job and I wanted so much to make amends by becoming successful and thereby being financially a little more secure.

And so my Capital Radio career ground to a halt. I never settled in the small Norfolk radio station that I'd craved for a few years previously. I joined Capital in September 1979, my first show on 28th October featured Martin Carthy, one of Britain's leading traditional folk singers and I transmitted my final show on 19th February 1983, featuring the Arizona Smoke Review. Not bad for what started out as a six-week series for folk music enthusiasts. To this day I'm immensely proud of expanding the broadcasting horizons of a music that was considered boring and full of men with pewter tankards and handkerchiefs tied around their knees. Some of those live shows were classics. Musicians performing at their best with no retakes or ego explosions. They just took out their guitars and played songs in the foyer of the building in front of eighty or ninety enthusiasts.

It was a total joy. 16th December 1979, Fiddler's Dram, top of the charts with 'Day Trip To Bangor'. 13th April 1980, a special with blues guitarist and bloody good bloke, Rory Gallagher, formerly of Taste, who died a few years ago. The following week, American legend Tom Paxton, who wrote 'The Last Thing On My Mind'. Two weeks later, the only ever acoustic set by Jethro Tull, including my favourite song of all time, 'Heavy Horses', a brilliant song by Ian Anderson which will one day become a folk song in its own right. 8th June, Denny Laine of the Moody Blues who co-wrote 'Mull of Kintyre' with Paul McCartney. 21st June, the first ever acoustic set by Elkie Brooks, singing the blues like only Elkie could. 'Blueberry Hill' and the like and a duet with me, 'Bring It On Home To Me'. Elkie loved it, it took her back to her jazz days with Humphrey Lyttleton. Loudon Wainwright, Donovan, even Chas and Dave.

I never forgot the contribution the Incredible String Band had made to my interest in music either and I personally delighted in having Robin Williamson on the programme on 1st May 1982. A few weeks later, strangely enough, John Martyn, my Glasgow pal from all those years ago, appeared, and, with Paul Brady, I'd more or less given the listeners of London just about everyone I could think of, with the exception of my other good pal Al Stewart who, during this time, was entrenched in the vineyards of California. So very much achieved and it all came to such a sad end.

I arrived one Friday night to present Midnight Special, only to find my office tipped into the corridor on Tony Hale's instructions. Four years of sacred tapes, letters of thanks and personal items lay in a pile outside my office which had been taken by my successor Nicky Campbell and his producer. I burst into tears as I scanned the master tapes of Tull, Rory Gallagher and the like. For me and Capital Radio, in the words of Don McLean, it was the day the music died. It was all a far cry from the days of laughter with Dave Cash and Kenny Everett, Alan Freeman and Mike Smith, the early pioneers of the London radio monster. In the words of Elkie Brooks, 'These days are gone now.'

I had started at the BBC long before I made the switch across to commercial radio towards the end of 1979. Alan Nixon, a light entertainment producer, called my manager at the time, Jo Lustig. We met in an Italian restaurant in Gloucester Road. Jo left us to it (he always seemed to have an urgent incoming call from America). Nixon wasn't keen on paying for the meal and wine either seeing as he was offering a radio programme. I ended up alone, scraping round my pockets for more money than I knew I had, always an embarrassing thing. A bit like jumping out of a space rocket without a lifeline, you sort of know you're buggered. I wriggled my way out of the problem in my own way. Was it worth it? The answer had to be yes. I did a runner from the restaurant and have never been back to apologise. Who cares, the garlic bread repeated on me anyway.

I joined BBC Radio Two in 1980, on a programme originally titled 'Braden's World' which of course featured television satirist Bernard Braden. Braden had filmed endless television series but he had become a frail man. We gathered for a script meeting at Broadcasting House: Bernard Braden, Ronald Fletcher, Sally Grace, David Timson and myself. I'd never been to such a meeting. I wrote and sang songs. We studied the pilot scripts that had been sent in by various hopefuls. Most were dubious. Bernard Braden made two episodes that were scrapped and he chose not to continue with the series.

Actor Francis Matthews, whom I respected highly, replaced him. He'd played private detective Paul Temple on television. As a team we got on well and rehearsals were easy. The scripts remained dubious with a capital D. They renamed the programme 'Stop The World' and it ran for a fair few years without a single change of cast. Every Thursday evening and Saturday lunchtime it went on air. The ratings were good and I had to write more and more topical songs to keep up with the recordings, which were two programmes every other Thursday at the Paris Theatre in Lower Regent Street.

What an honour to work at the Paris. To tread the very sacred boards of music hall variety where the Goons and Tony Hancock had recorded their immortal works. Huddling into a tiny dressing room no bigger than a bog standard single bedroom, a cast of five and Alan the producer. To sit on old dusty chairs where once Arthur Askey, Frankie Howerd and Leslie Phillips also took their rests in between rehearsals. It had to be the bastion of British comedy, and I was there every other week, in my own right. My working relationship with Alan Nixon lasted seven years. We made endless radio series, I can barely remember them all. 'A Digance Indulgence', 'Digance Does it Locally', 'Animal Alphabet with Peter Goodwright' I seem to recall were all made during the first few years of my radio career. I recall the sleepless nights trying to dream up titles containing the word Digance.

Alan Nixon stayed at my house often. Fern Cottage in Debden stood equidistant between two pubs and Alan was Scottish. Need I say more. We'd often nip to the Plough for a late night script meeting. Now that was a decent local. I met up with Alan during my final year of performing, on 28th June 1999 at the London studios where I used to record my own television shows. He'd become head of Channel Five and I didn't even know. I was really pleased for him, as his apprenticeship in media comedy was certainly as long as mine if not longer.

With Alan flying my flag at the BBC and my involvement with commercial radio, my radio contributions were expanding. Thanks to Ralph Bernard I worked for Radio Hallam in Sheffield on a documentary series 'Dying For A Drink', for which I received my first radio award, then came 'Down To Earth' for the same station, and then the BBC called me into the Pebble Mill studios in Birmingham to write the music for a documentary on Sir Rowland Hill who started the penny post for the Royal Mail. Whilst at Pebble Mill I appeared on a few episodes of the daily television show 'Pebble Mill at One'. Everything seemed to be rosy in the garden. All was going really well until I broke my collarbone in a charity football match. I'd completed my first sessions at Capital, filmed the special for ITV with Chris Barrie, 'The Three Busketeers', and had been commissioned for a second series of 'Stop The World', I'd appeared on Parkinson's chat show singing a song about Tommy Steele and all was rocking and rolling along... And then, before I knew it I was lying in a hospital bed somewhere near Camberley in Surrey with my left shoulder wrapped somewhere around my neck. *Melody Maker* editor, Colin Irwin, and his wife Val, had taken me to the casualty department. I was in great pain. It had taken years to get the breaks and suddenly another kind of break had scuppered all the hard work. All I'd tried to do was head away a corner for the charity football team I played for and I fell badly.

As I lay in the casualty department there was a phone call from worried team captain Johnny Jones, Ralph McTell's tour manager. He was in a flap and Colin Irwin took the call and returned with a smile on his face.

'What's up, Colin?' I asked.

'Johnny Jones just rang. He's worried.'

'Ah, that's nice.'

'No. He's not worried about you. He's worried about them damaging the team shirt because they haven't got any spares.'

'So what?'

'Well, he knows you won't be playing for the rest of the season so he's got to find another number nine. Basically he wants his shirt back.'

Every time I laughed it hurt, but I laughed just the same. Johnny Jones became stage doorman at Wimbledon Theatre, which was when I last met up with him. He'd had a couple of heart attacks and was smoking like a chimney, but we had many laughs together through the years.

The shirt was cut from me with a pair of scissors and I paid for a replacement just to keep Jonesy happy. I bet that wouldn't be expected from David Beckham if he came a cropper and he's much wealthier than me.

Apart from one television appearance in Scotland on 'Andy Stewart and Friends' when I mimed my salmon song, I was out of action for a few months. I only ever saw Andy Stewart on telly on New Year's Eve. I only ever saw him sing when I wore a new jumper or pair of socks. To see this bastion of my youth in real life was outstanding. He was a genuinely funny bloke. It's too easy to dismiss the performers of yesteryear but most of them were true artists in their own right. They never had autocue or even retakes. Everything was filmed live with crossed fingers. Andy Stewart was part of my youth. I shook hands with him when I did his television show and felt very proud to do so. Sod the cynics.

My first book *Animal Alphabet* was selling well, and I was doing my best, sling and all, to appear wherever I could to promote it by interviews in the press or on radio, but television was difficult with just the one arm functioning properly. Most producers who booked me wanted a song, and that was difficult to do. It was like booking Long John Silver for 'Riverdance'. I read a few of the animal poems on regional TV programmes but nothing much until the break knitted back together. The calls from radio producers grew less and less frequent and there were fewer script meetings in my local Essex pub.

All these years on, I remember every contour and beer glass of the Plough in Debden. I remember every face and recall just about every night. I took Dave Peacock of Chas and Dave there once. They were at their greatest height at the time, top of the album charts and a couple of hit records under their belt. Dave, the bass player, leaned against the huge inglenook fireplace of the Plough, puffing a cigar, whilst Debbie and his wife Sue prepared the meal at home. He was wearing a brown pin striped suit, a pair of Doctor Marten's boots, a collarless shirt and a barrow boy cap. Whilst he puffed away he commented: 'The trouble with me Rich, is I can't go anywhere without being recognised.' Still to this day I laugh at lovely Dave. He reciprocated the invitation and so Debbie and I drove the short distance to Hertfordshire where the Peacocks lived. Round and round the narrow lanes we drove, unable to locate the Peacock dwelling. Suddenly, Debbie noticed a pair of tracksuit bottoms hanging from a washing line by a pair of braces. In a matter-of-fact way we knew it was their place. We were right.

Dave plays a good banjo, he'd have loved meeting Steve Martin. Chas Hodges, his partner, could write a great serious song when he had the mind to. Much as I enjoyed their knockabout stuff there was a certain pathos about Chas's serious songwriting which he seldom let show. Chas went into hospital in June 1999 with a nasty throat and when I think of the boozy nights we spent together on the road I could only say there but for the grace of God. Long live Chas and Dave, probably the last of the cockney music hall entertainers.

I wrote and recorded an additional BBC series again relating to *Animal Alphabet* and again produced by Alan Nixon. We made one hundred and twelve radio shows together. It featured my poems and songs from the book, published in November 1980, which were narrated by a number of performers including Hannah Gordon, Windsor Davies, Martin Jarvis, and even the late great cricket commentator Brian Johnson. Michael Joseph published them originally in hardback and Puffin Books released them in paperback, entitled *The Jungle Cup Final and Other Poems*. You'll be lucky to find a copy of either, although still to this day a number of my poems from those books are featured in educational anthologies across America and Canada. Yes, I did write one about a brown bear. The books weren't so much released, they escaped. Just as I had done, from the claws of death, that fateful night in Manning Park, near Vancouver.

The release of my first book took me to new areas of more upmarket media publicity and promotion. I had been invited to the Christmas lunch of my publishers, Michael Joseph, at Bedford Square in London. I felt totally out of my depth and was! I'd only knocked out a book of poems about animals for god's sake. Mind you, I suppose Kipling could have said the same. Now he did write exceedingly good verse.

I chatted with hugely literate bods who knew big words I'd never heard before. I took refuge by the sausage rolls and nodded at a chap who'd had the exact same idea. We introduced ourselves and the man picked up my East End accent straight away and asked me if I supported West Ham United. Suddenly, I was back on familiar territory. His name was Alf Wright and he too was an author with a few sales under his belt. He told me an interesting story of how, for a pseudonym, he'd used the name of his hero as a young football fan of Birmingham City. I wondered how his books were going and he nodded coyly. He'd renewed his publishing deal the same as myself and we were both grateful. We spoke for ages about our mutual love of the game, ignoring the entire Harris Tweed brigade who laughed loudly at the unfunniest of each other's lines. He wished me luck and I wished him the same when we shook hands and went our separate ways. His hero was goalkeeper Jim Herriott. Oh yes, James Herriott sold a few books alright. Of all creatures great and small, I felt about the smallest of all when I twigged whom I'd been speaking to for all those hours by the sausage rolls.

I shall never forget my conversation with Alf Wright for as long as I live. Take people for who they are and not what they are. If ever that was the perfect example. Two guys chatting about footy, blanked by all the literary agents and publishing clerks whose wages were paid by authors' talents and successes. It's that same feeling when you enter the hallowed halls of the BBC. Everyone rushes about and looks very important. It's all daunting stuff until you realise that the BBC makes radio and television programmes and without artists they would be stuffed. I came to realise that, but I'm not sure most of the people at the BBC have ever made the same admission.

I published my first novel *Backwater* with Michael Joseph, and then moved to Macmillan Press for my fourth book *Run Out In The Country.* My editor Alan Samson had moved there and very much like the TV world, he took me and a few of his other authors with him. That was about it really on the author front. I published two other books myself, *Chardock Rangers* and *Remembers and Rhymes* and still to this day have completed manuscripts gathering dust upon my shelf because I cannot be bothered with that dreaded experience of hawking around and endless rejection slips. Perhaps one day but it doesn't seem so important anymore. I wrote a few books and had four published, who would ever have thought that of the secondary modern lad who went for evening classes when he left school to study English Literature? I cannot complain at the lukewarm taste of success I had experienced in the literary world.

Alf Wright remained the only leading author I ever met until I became friends with James Herbert.

I was appearing on the Isle of Man for the Lady Taverners charity in 1987. Rick Wakeman had rung me and asked me to do the favour and I couldn't refuse. We'd known each other from the days at

Fairlop Road when he was keyboards player with the Strawbs. Sitting at my table were comedian Norman Wisdom, a friend, Martin Butler, and two guys I never recognised. One turned out to be James.

Can you imagine my embarrassment when, upon being told he was an author, asking him if he'd 'had any successes'? It was Jim Herriott all over again. Digance never learns his lessons does he? We laughed about it later, but it actually got worse. To his left was another man I'd never met either who claimed to be a songwriter. Now with music I felt my knowledge was deeper and wider. Upon asking him more or less the same question, but relating to songs, he turned out to have written almost every Status Quo hit record they'd ever had, and one of my favourites in particular, 'Living On An Island'. The stranger was Bob Young. He was actually a member of Quo for a while. Jim and Bob became great friends from that night onwards.

I spent a lovely Sunday at Jim's place near Brighton. He'd invited the family for Sunday lunch. Trouble was, he'd also invited Uri Geller. What a stupid choice when there's cutlery lying around all over the place. Because he'd built his name on bending spoons I had my pudding first and sat in the garden with Bob and singer Mike Berry, rather than tackle the main course with my fingers. All the parents who'd brought their children along were double checking they weren't wearing braces on their teeth because old Uri could inflict dreadful damage on such unfortunates. The guitars eventually came out and Jim was soon strumming and showing us why he'd become a successful writer as opposed to a musician. James Herbert and I were born in the same part of London, and we both shared the fondest of memories, but neither of us would go back, well not physically anyway. I revisit my roots every time I walk on stage, and Jim went back to pen '1948'.

Andy Aliffe, a complete lunatic and Paul Simon lookalike, replaced Alan Nixon as my radio producer. Alan left radio to work in television. With Andy I saw out what was to be the rest of my radio career at the BBC. We opened the boundaries, Andy and I. We made some memorable series together and Andy loved recording the shows in front of a live audience, particularly the warm-up part, which he would do himself. In 1996 I recorded my final series for the BBC. The ratings were brilliant, very high and very appreciative.

Obviously by coincidence, the new boss Jim Moir decided I should entertain all the top nobs at a radio awards type of night in

Birmingham free of charge. It happened to be a night I was already working, but Andy rang me and asked me to cancel the date already in the diary and perform for Jim because his boss had insisted. I refused on both counts. I was working and I got paid when I worked, just the same as anyone else in the country and I didn't want to cancel and let anyone down. I never did another series for the BBC ever again to this day. As I say, an absolute coincidence of course.

My radio career with our great institution had drawn to an unexpected close. I never wanted to leave the BBC. All the rumours are true. It actually cost me money to record 'Digance Does It Sportingly', and 'Digance Does It Locally', simply because they were recorded on location. But I still miss it all just the same. I shall forever hear the echoes of Tony Hancock offering to give an armful of blood. I shall forever hear Spike Milligan tell his audience he had to go to Innisfree to see if his vest and pants were dry. I still see the empty Paris Theatre where I began my trade as a comedy writer, where Basil Brush, for whom I scribbled a few words, attacked me as I tried to stroke the furry bastard.

For twenty-three years, almost a quarter of a century, I had worked constantly and continuously on British radio, both commercial and BBC. The research shows I wrote just under nine hundred songs, and enough scripts to write two novels. Twenty-three years from that first meeting in the tiny dressing room of the Paris Theatre. Six hundred hours of recordings all told.

It is incredible for me to feel a tiny, insignificant, forgettable part of the history of British radio comedy at the Paris Theatre. But however small or insignificant, I stood there just the same, on the very same stage as the all-time greats and that's good enough for me. I wonder if someone will say the same about the late Richard Digance in many years to come. I really, really hope so. Cor blimey guv, nearly 'ad me 'ead knocked off by a flying pig just then. In the words of Max Miller, 'Now that's a funny ol' fing if ever there was one.'

As the years passed I kept my hand in at radio presenting, recording Christmas shows for Kevin King at Ocean FM, for Kevin Spector at Kestrel Radio in Basingstoke and for local stations in Somerset. I loved it. For a while I became patron of Camelot Hospital Radio in Yeovil. I was a director of Yeovil Football Club at the time, but I found the usual problem of all chiefs and no Indians – a big problem with football clubs and radio stations throughout the land it would appear – and I subsequently left the board of directors of the football club after a meeting which grew into an argument over what colour toilet paper we should be using.

The up-side of my time at Capital Radio was very, very up. I had never had any money, had no value of money, and never expected to have any money. One day Debbie noticed something very strange in the post. I'd worked at Capital for two years at the time and I'd never really noticed my agent hadn't collected my wages. He paid me monthly and we lived off our sufficient funds in blissful ignorance. The Capital money had been paid by standing order, directly into a bank deposit account I'd completely forgotten about. To this day I cannot recall how it all came about, but it did. We discovered we had about sixteen thousand pounds we never knew we had, and believe me, sixteen grand was a pools win in those heady days.

We celebrated by buying a new house where I could build a small recording studio. To that end we moved to Appletree Cottage in Cherry Green, near Thaxted in Essex. The house cost us £95,000, plus seven grand for a new thatch. Makes you realise how much Bruce Forsyth must have splashed out every year. We had a lovely garden where I shared many of my mum's last Sunday afternoons with her. She died in 1985 and left a huge void. Appletree Cottage would never be the same without mum and me, playing crib or painting watercolours. It had to happen really. The house had to go up for sale. The buzz of Appletree Cottage had gone. We sold up and moved to Lyme Regis in Dorset because we fancied living by the seaside and thought the Essex coast would be too cold.

Halstock, in Lyme Regis, had some sort of religious connection and looked like a vicarage, perched at the top of Clappentail Lane, overlooking Lyme Bay. The views were stunning and a far cry from Captain Blaney's memorial. The five-bedroom house cost £185,000 and we spent eight happy years on the Dorset coast. I was in summer season with Jim Davidson, Polly was a little one, and we sold Appletree Cottage before we could move to Halstock. Usual stuff. Debbie, Polly and the dogs lived in a mobile home for a few weeks as I stayed in my digs in Torquay.

The house was in need of some love and affection and we got to work on that as soon as we moved in. We modernised the bedrooms, built a new kitchen, a billiard room with splendid sea views and a recording studio for my embryonic projects. Polly fitted in well at Charmouth Primary School, despite developing a worrying illness at a young age, and Rosie was born in Exeter in March 1992. Once again when Debbie went into labour I was working labour, this time at the Intercontinental hotel in London, for Allied Dunbar. Now that really was a fearful drive through the night. I arrived at three o'clock in the morning, and after a couple of hours with my girls, I nipped home to feed the dogs, Russell and Sheba, who'd made the trip from Essex to Dorset with us.

It was a wrench to leave Essex, particularly Appletree Cottage where my mum had spent so many blissful weekends before she died in the London Chest Clinic in 1985. We left behind the conifers and various plants she'd brought along over the years. I recall the time Debbie and my parents waved me goodbye as I set off for the Falkland Islands in 1983. I was scared and took one last look back at them and the house, convinced I would never return from such a frightening journey.

Appletree Cottage had gone. But the memories remain as, hopefully, do some mature trees in the back garden with Doris's name etched upon them. At this peculiar time, my final radio series with the BBC was scheduled and recorded, the door was shut, and suddenly, everything seemed to be rapidly changing. That was frightening, not knowing anything else other than what I'd done for so many years. Little chance really of being smuggled back onto the ambulances. They'd all become highly trained paramedics in green dungarees. It was a far cry from rattling down Romford Road on the wrong side of the road.

Early days at Lyme Regis weren't easy. If ever a town didn't take to infiltrators, particularly mouthy, cockney Londoners, it was Lyme Regis. Within a couple of weeks the police had done me. I'm sure you wouldn't be at all surprised to be informed that I sought my revenge.

One day I was perched up a tree cutting down a dangerous hanging branch in my new garden, when Sergeant Brown of Lyme Regis police entered my drive.

'Is the owner of the house around?' he asked flippantly, looking me up and down like a war criminal.

'I am the owner,' I answered proudly. 'You wanna mind your head, mate or this twig is going fall on it,' I suggested.

'You don't look important enough to be the owner.'

'Really?'

'Yes, really.'

'Mind your head, mate, I told you once.'

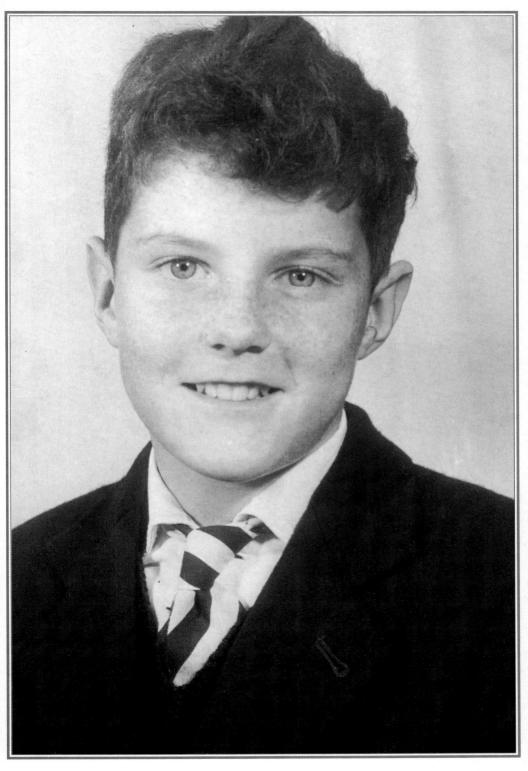

In my first term at Thomas Lethaby Secondary Modern School.

Len and Doris Digance.

The class of '57,
Vicarage Lane Primary School, East Ham.

Vicarage Lane 5-a-side football team:
Richard in goal; Kevin Sullivan; George Hilsdon and John Lacey.

Above: Polly, Rosie and Fozzy Digance.

Left: My wife, Debbie.

Fern Cottage, Debden.

Fozzy, the dog.

With daughter Polly.

Rosie Digance.

My first television series at TVS.

With former hostage John McCarthy.

Left: Meeting the Princess of Wales at Capital Radio with Tony Hale looking on.

Below: With Tidings narrator Susan George.

Singing 'Address Book' with Status Quo.

With business partner
Rod Bransgrove at Sun Studios, Memphis.

In Austria with Reg Parsons on top of the world, but not feeling it.

Left: The green turtle meets the dancers.

Right: Fishing on Ascension Island moments before contracting sunstroke.

Failed goalkeeper with successful goalkeeper Bruce Grobbelaar.

With my good friend, Jim Davidson.

With Jim in Berlin.

Three more good friends:
Jeff Mitchell, Shaun Udal and England cricketer Robin Smith.

An honorary member of Totnes Fire Brigade.

He didn't move.

The bloody branch missed the nasty bastard by inches.

We'd got off to a good start.

As we spoke my dog Russell, a lurcher from Wood Green animal shelter, trotted back home.

'Is that your dog?'

'Yes.'

Russell was the softest dog ever created. He rolled on his back submissively if you called his name. Over he trotted, tail wagging nineteen to the dozen.

'Do you know he nearly caused a multiple pile-up at the top of the lane?'

I looked at the copper in complete bewilderment. There couldn't possibly be a multiple pile-up in Lyme. There weren't enough cars!!

Even Russell looked confused.

If he'd been able to speak there's no doubt he would have told Brown to fuck off, and come to think of it, why I didn't is totally beyond me.

'A multiple pile-up. You must be joking!' I smiled.

'Don't be funny. This is serious. Do you have a licence for this dog, sir?'

Russell went indoors. He'd only been out for a piss. He didn't mean to start all this nonsense and he'd become embarrassed.

I explained we'd just moved into the area and most of our belongings were still in boxes. We had licences for both Russell and Sheba somewhere but I didn't have a clue where they were or what box they were in.

'Produce them at the police station tomorrow between the hours of 5pm and 7pm.'

I was confused.

'Why between 5pm and 7pm?' I asked.

'Because that's when the police station's open tomorrow.'

I noted that if ever I wanted to do a bank raid in Lyme Regis it would be advisable to do it in the morning. You could be on the other side of the world by the time the Lyme police had turned out for the day.

I told Debbie what had happened and she suggested that it would be easier, at 37p a throw, to buy two new ones just to be sure. Next day she took the licences down to the nick at the designated time.

'These won't do. They were bought today and we cautioned you yesterday.'

Debbie explained that we'd taken precautionary measures because we couldn't find the originals and that it was a show of good faith. She was told that it wasn't satisfactory and anything she said would be taken down and used in evidence against her.

'You must be bloody joking?'

'No, madam, this is a serious warning of your rights.'

We were sent a summons to appear at Dorchester Magistrates' Court and as you can imagine I wanted to lynch someone, starting with the idiotic egomaniac Brown and working my way up in status to a police dog.

I spoke to my manager Bob about the situation and then to Jim Davidson and Hale and Pace, who all agreed to partake in a benefit concert at the Royal Albert Hall to pay for my legal costs, which would be minimal, the remaining balance being donated to Guide Dogs for the Blind, of which I'd become a patron. We would make the charity a lot of money and the Dorset police and magistrates would be exposed in all the Sunday papers. I fancied the challenge, to be honest.

I rang Dorchester and visited Herr Brown at Lyme Regis police station warning them all they'd be laughed out of sight once I'd sold the story to the Sunday newspapers. Strangely, Dorchester Magistrates' Court dropped their charges and Sergeant Brown became a laughing stock in the town once I'd told everyone in the pub what had happened. To say Sergeant Brown was annoyed was an understatement. He eventually left the town and moved to Retford in Nottinghamshire. All charges upon my wife were dropped and we paid for a guide dog to be trained as compensation because the concert never took place.

During the following months I was done for speeding at 32 mph and suffered endless grief from the constabulary until I was asked to do a cabaret at their Christmas party. I told them to get stuffed.

My time at Lyme Regis went from bad to worse. We had a pocketful of friends but not that many. I was hugely unpopular and things wouldn't improve.

Phillip Evans, editor of the *Dorset Star*, and a former mayor of the town, had decided to try to build a hospital there. A superb but ambitious idea. I really got on well with Pip. A high percentage of the population were old and the nearest hospital was in Exeter, where Rosie was born. I thought Pip was attempting a great deed and offered my assistance when I read about it in the *Dorset Star*.

We formed a small committee of myself, Pip, John Stamp, Arthur

Larcombe and Keith someone or other from the bank and we set about organising a Lyme Regis week in aid of the new medical centre. We tried to get the whole town involved and to a degree it worked. London Weekend Television came down and filmed the event. In the small Marina Theatre, with a maximum capacity of only two hundred and twenty seats, at the bottom of the town, I organised concerts featuring Jethro, Jim Bowen, Jim Davidson, Brian Conley, Hale and Pace and a 60s disco night with Freddie and the Dreamers. Other friends who turned out included Mike Osman, Hilary O'Neil, Kevin Devane and Dave Lee. All came along free of charge. Jim, trusty Jim, stayed all week, playing cricket, football, working in shops and getting as much publicity and money for us as he possibly could.

We organised a celebrity cricket match and a football match starring Gerry Francis, Phil Parkes, Steve Williams and endless others. Brian Conley played in midfield in his dad's cortina. Jim was to relate the game on BBC television by accusing me of hacking down a seven-year-old lad who had an open goal before him. We were trained hard in the East End, Davidson knew that. It was a splendid week and we raised £34,000 which I handed across to the fund. I was never thanked, no artist was ever thanked, Pip and the committee were never thanked, and David Couzens of the *Lyme News* accused me of wallowing in some sort of ego trip and seeing the world through rose coloured glasses. I was exposed to the Sunday tabloid press for auctioning a five-pound note signed by Great Train Robber Buster Edwards.

I knew Buster worked on a flower stall at Waterloo Station and I'd often nodded his acquaintance the times I went to the television studios on the train. He'd paid his dues and was going straight.

'Hello Richard, how's it going?'

'Not bad Buster. Here, sign this to raise money for a hospital I'm helping to build.'

'Of course I will, but I won't sign it across the Queen's head, that's illegal.'

He was right too.

Various councillors objected to my methods of raising money and then I was in every Sunday paper. I apologised to Buster Edwards for all the bad press and he just shrugged it off.

'No worries.'

'Thanks.'

'Wonder what would happen if they had a heart attack. Would they use your new hospital then?'

A valid point by Mr Edwards. I never went to Buster's funeral but felt very tempted.

And that was the end of Lyme Regis and me. I'd had enough of the place. I loved the town as a town but the people and myself were oil and water. It was time to move on again. Whilst at Charmouth School, I noticed Polly hadn't been invited to any birthday parties and when Debbie and I asked her why, she told us it was because we'd moved into the big house on the top of the hill. I would love to have shown those narrow-minded people of Lyme Regis the war memorial of Captain Michael Flood Blaney and the multitude of council flats that surrounded it. It confirmed a thought I'd had for quite a while, that it was somehow tasteless and unacceptable to become successful in Britain through hard work and dedication. My mum and dad would have been very proud to have seen Halstock and they didn't come any more working class than my parents.

I bought a stretch of the River Yarty, a tributary of the River Axe that flowed through Axminster, and spent many quiet days fishing for trout just south of Stockland. I still own the river today but rarely go there because otters arrived and my children didn't want them disturbed as they reared their young. Well, Polly said they were otters, but I've a funny feeling they were water rats. Never mind.

Meanwhile, it was time to get back on the road for yet another eternal tour, something that had become a twice-yearly routine. This time, some of Lyme's crowd, Dave Street, Jane Perham and Nick Hall, joined the tour selling merchandise and looking after backstage requirements and we had a good time.

When Richard Digance first 'went on the road' it was in a Renault Dauphine which cost £15. The car was dumped on the A4 when the gear stick came off in his hand and he had to catch a train to his gig in Swansea. It was demoralising, as indeed were most of the clubs he worked in and the receptions he received.

Richard Cole became his first roadie, free of charge, and drove a greenish J4 van with a mattress in the back. They fitted a cassette player and toured Wales with just one tape, the Eagles.

Borrowed cars were the order of the day until he bought the VW Camper, HTW 177H, mentioned in the last chapter from Dovercourt, Plaistow. It cost £750, a huge investment at the time. The engine seized and it was taken away for scrap. Richard continued to work the clubs using his dad's Mark Two Ford Consul with the back seat taken out to accommodate the

PA system, a 60 watt Impact rig that was slightly louder than a hooker with laryngitis.

More borrowed cars until Richard bought a Transit van for Pisces and then a Vauxhall Cresta estate when the engine of the Transit blew up. All the bands wandered around Britain in a Transit at that time. So did Pisces for that short while.

Touring wasn't at all luxurious until Richard hired a small fifteen-seater coach from Wakes Coaches of Wincanton for the first time in 1984. The cost of the coach plus driver, Steve Scarsbrook, was £800 per week. One week's hire exceeding the total cost of the VW Camper by fifty pounds. The coach was fitted with tables for playing cards and comfortable seats for sleeping and generally relaxing. Tours usually involved forty-five to fifty shows and the schedules were gruelling. The coach never carried more than half a dozen people. Richard, the tour manager, the driver, the backstage manager, the support act and the merchandise seller.

Richard's own support acts as he toured Britain included Joe Pasquale, Hilary O'Neil, Dave Lee, Mike Osman, Kevin Devane, Steve Charrett, Steve Rawlings and Ian Irving.

The final tours were negotiated in Range Rovers and Mercedes V Class people carriers and the like with all parties making their own way to the concert halls. It was a shame but that was the way the industry had gone, the fun had dwindled and the financial aspect had become more and more important. There was a parallel between show business and football, both had taken a bashing from the wealthy financiers who forgot it was part of leisure and entertainment. It was all far more comfortable in the coach, but never as much fun as the days when the gear sticks came apart.

Chapter Five

With Jim Davidson

I was offered a tour to the Middle East with Jim. I knew nothing about show business at this time, still considering myself a musician of sorts. Jim and his manager Laurie Mansfield travelled first class up the pointed end. I travelled in that bit where you're not supposed to have any legs. I was starting to learn very quickly about pecking orders. The flight to Bahrain took forever and Jim came down the cheap seats to say hello and caught me reading *Angling Times*. It was the start of a great friendship that would continue forever, unless a tasty female came Jim's way and then it was placed on ice for another day. Jim knew many lovely ladies.

I'd removed myself from my career in the radio studios and was back and raring to go for a second run, a second chance that Jim had given me, at live entertainment on stage.

Our first show together at the Club in Bahrain was probably the show that most changed the direction of my career. I observed full-blooded adult comedy dispatched at high speed to an audience that simply lapped it up. Brits working abroad, earning thousands of pounds tightening bolts at oil refineries, laughing themselves stupid. Jim wore a dinner jacket and a bow tie. I felt stupid in my usual pair of jeans and a sports shirt. I was still, in my heart, as I just mentioned, a musician I suppose, but it was Jim who changed all that.

Our tour singalong song in the desert limos was 'Meet Me On The Corner' by Alan Hull of Lindisfarne. Jim used to call me the Lefty because I'd come through the folk clubs, but, secretly, Jim loved the folk music scene himself. I once sang him a song by Australian singer Eric Bogle, 'And The Band Played Waltzing Matilda'. Tears filled Jim's eyes and the following lunchtime he'd learnt the epic war ballad word perfect and sang it to me at the sound check. My dad was a lefty alright but I'm not so sure I was. If I ever had been my experiences at Lyme Regis changed it all anyway. Bollocks to Robin Hood, I'd never have helped men prancing around in bright green tights anyway. I was going to earn some money, as much as I could, and give my family a great lifestyle.

The year was 1983. It had been rather a lean time. The folk scene had more or less crawled back into its pewter tankard shell with its finger in its ear, and the gigs had almost dried up. My third manager Kevin Wyatt Lown, the shortest serving of all, had become interested in video production and studio work by then and quite rightly so. He'd managed Fred Wedlock through his 'Oldest Swinger In Town' phase and really Fred was the last of the commercially successful folk comedians. The folk scene was about to crumble and Wyatt Lown looked towards his future for which I have never blamed him. We'd gone our separate ways the previous year so I was on a sort of free transfer, a sort of Bosman ruling.

The timing couldn't have been better. I hold all previous managers in high regard and Kevin was no exception. He worked from his mum's house in Burden Way, Wanstead when we first met way back in the days of Roger Moss and New Mythology. He became one of the bigger agents on the folk scene and had done well with Fred. He was looking after me for a second time round but things really had changed so much. The small folk clubs had more or less disappeared and making money had become the order of the day. He had smart offices at the Music Works studios near Arsenal football ground but the folk scene was no longer strong enough to support the agents and managers with large turnovers. Something had to give, and it proved to be the agents and the managers. The folk scene remains, cocooned in the music business, wrapped in layers of cotton wool, just strong enough to carry the traditions of folk music as was its original idea. I hope it continues. It's part of our British heritage and much of our history is told through the verses of traditional folk music.

I was hanging on by my fingertips. *Backwater* remained in the bookshops and very few people knew. I'd made an album of the same name that reached number 10 in the *Melody Maker* folk charts on 5th February 1983. Still the novel didn't sell. I had made the retrogressive step back into the folk clubs. There was little doubt that International Artists came along at the right time. How it all came about was quite bizarre.

As Jim, Laurie Mansfield and I drove across the Arabian desert in this stretch limo thing that was bigger than my first house in Reading, straining to the Lindisfarne lyrics, Laurie suggested, on Jim's recommendation, I should go and see him at the London offices of his management company, International Artists, when we returned to England. We three kings had food poisoning at the time because Davidson wanted to stop at a roadside café in the middle of the desert to buy this chicken thing that had been cooked the day of the Mafeking release and had hung in the sun for the years hence. It stank. It fucking stank. Jim had a leg, I think I nibbled nonchalantly at an eye socket. Laurie Mansfield could well have been delirious.

International Artists were big time. If I got with them I'd do well. They had stunning offices in London's Regent Street, opposite Dickens and Jones. They smacked of success. But for the moment, our new arrival, our feathered hitch-hiker smacked of food poisoning. To get Jim to eat anything other than chips was an achievement in itself, but this thing still seemed to be moaning and groaning. Either that or my guts were as it slid down. Laurie called me a doctor when we reached Abu Dhabi and he put my chronic muscle spasms down to too much sun. The dozy bastard had too much sun himself. I'd eaten a bloody dodo.

Middle East tour complete, and system flushed out, I sat in the plush London office foyer at International Artists, overshadowed by a massive painting by Rolf Harris, he who tied down kangaroos for some strange reason or other. I felt full of confidence. A pleasant meeting followed but I soon discovered my social mate Laurie Mansfield to be a very busy man. When I returned home Debbie asked me how it had all gone and I genuinely wasn't too sure.

The following Sunday, at a concert at Wimbledon Theatre, Bob Voice introduced himself to me as my new manager. I'd never met him before and I didn't quite understand. How could he be my new manager? We'd never spoken! It soon became clear. Although Laurie was quite happy for me to join International Artists, he was far too busy to look after me personally so he'd put me with Bob, who'd just joined the company from working with Mike Yarwood. And so began an immensely successful eleven-year relationship that took me all the way through the 1980s. Bob Voice and I were infallible, we decided to take on the world. We even went back to the Middle East a year later and I pretended to be a vegetarian, but I still got the shits.

Bob had been a drummer with a band called Paul Brett's Sage, and he was eager to build his name in management. We were thrown together at an opportune time and it worked. We plotted and planned the Digance television career between us, and always scored heavy brownie points with television producers.

Bob's stable of new artists looked impressive. Hale and Pace, Brian Conley and now Richard Digance. Things moved quickly as I toured Britain with Jim, starting at St George's Hall, Bradford. By the spring of 1984 I'd slotted in comfortably on all Jim's shows. First the Middle East, then Great Britain and then off to the Falkland Islands. It all seemed a far cry from the folk clubs and the supports around England. In June 1984, the entourage gathered at RAF Brize Norton to make the eight thousand-mile trip down to the South Atlantic, stopping at Ascension Island on the way. There were dancers, musicians, a few crew and members of Combined Services Entertainment who put the military shows together.

Ascension Island, used by the Americans as an emergency landing base for the space shuttle, was nothing more than volcanic rock sticking out of the Atlantic in the middle of nowhere, and it was very, very hot. The British forces there were hell bent on giving us a good time and I found it all strange, never having experienced any association with the military since the days I kicked a football against Captain Blaney's war memorial. I didn't even know where the Falklands were, such was my interest in the Falklands war the previous year. In truth, Jim Davidson was right, I was a hippie and anti all sorts of aggression and grief. I thought they were far flung islands off the Scottish coast, accessible only by a bumpy Dan Air experience.

Yes, Jim was right after all. He knew I found it all a bit mind-boggling and, taking me under his wing, we went off together for a quiet fish. The sea was full of grouper fish that could easily be caught on scraps of meat and seeing as the squaddies were preparing a barbecue on the beach for us all, bait wasn't hard to come by. The heat was unbearable, remarkably so as we were on our way to the sub-zero regions of a group of islands near the Antarctic. The fish tugged at our bait and huge specimens were coming to the shore as the rods buckled and bent double with the strain. They were filleted and slung on the barbecue as Jim and I took turns at reeling them in. It was tropical bliss.

I wore a pair of freebie army combat trousers and a tee shirt. As I leaned forward, waiting for the fish to bite, I was blissfully unaware just how strong the sun could be in the equatorial regions. The bare skin between the top of my trousers and the bottom of my tee shirt, just an inch or two, burnt to a frazzle, the scars from which I still bear today. They look like stretch marks. I was in total agony when we boarded the Hercules that would fly us south from Ascension to Port Stanley. There were no seats, only canvas webbing straps tied along the fuselage. They were having a laugh! The whole plane was stacked full of equipment, mail and provisions. Certainly no room for bog standard seating. There was no in-flight movie and the food pack was a white box containing an orange drink, an apple and a Kit Kat and a few other offerings I can't recall. Oh yes, a piece of cheese in a sealed thing I couldn't undo.

My brain went back to my earlier days. The Sunday afternoons at home when the Rossi man's chimes woke up my dad. Those Dairylea cheeses that you always seemed to find on a picnic yet you couldn't break into with a plastic fork. Nobody ever ate them but millions bent them in two and chucked them away, settling for an orange instead. And the cup cakes. Trying to undo the foil wrapper without leaving a piece of chocolate in the corrugated tin foil. My mind was wandering, I was badly burned and my poor body was trying to cool down my blood. I felt awful, and not really ready to witness one of the most frightening moments of my life.

We would refuel in mid-air somewhere near Tristan Da Cunha. Pain, hunger and fear are probably the most dreaded threesome since Freeman, Hardy and Willis. My sunstroke allowed me to sit at the front with the pilot, Peter Harbuck. As we swept southward I saw another Hercules draw close. Now when I say close I mean bloody close. It could only have been a few yards away when it released what appeared to be a large badminton shuttlecock, the wavering object that would lock on to the prod on the front of our plane. It was third time lucky and the relief was immense as the fuel went in for a few endless minutes. Jim videoed the entire exercise. The smell told us how we all felt. Yes, third time lucky. When I asked Peter the pilot how many attempts it usually took before successful engagement he simply told me he had no idea as I'd just witnessed his first attempt at a mid-air refuelling. The smell in the cockpit grew stronger. Thank god he never told us that before we took off from Ascension.

The terrain of Ascension Island is identical to the moon and thus it became the spot where the Americans tested their moon buggy. It has a golf course that has no greens, of which I am proud to say I am a member. And in January 1998 the island would see me realise one of my greatest ambitions when my tour manager Micky Brown and I set off in a rubber dinghy to swim with the dolphins. And these were dolphins in their natural habitat, not circus freaks enslaved in American attractions. They looked us up and down a few times from the corners of their eyes, and then, wow, they started leaping, swimming on their backs and bringing their babies to meet us. It's always difficult to pinpoint one of the greatest moments of your life, but swimming with those magnificent creatures must be close. The blue, clear waters, the natural bird sanctuaries, the undisturbed graves of ancient British mariners who lost their lives to yellow fever after being cast ashore. Some graves were just a matter of feet away from the water's edge, but no sound of the sea could be heard. No seabird flew overhead. In utter silence I read the last scribed thoughts of the ship's surgeon and other crewmembers who'd gone to Ascension Island to die. I actually died myself there too.

Some of the shows on Ascension Island were possibly the worst ever. Someone once had the great idea to entertain the cleaners and janitors who'd arrived from St Helena over the decades. A wonderful idea, but none of them spoke English and it became a tradition that every show that returned from the Falklands via Ascension had to do a performance for them.

With my show it was particularly difficult. Explaining three-wheeler bikes, frozen jubblies and sherbet lemons to an audience whose culture came from poverty, net fishing and slavery, was, to say the least, a bit tricky. One night I spent hours learning Elvis Presley songs and it was a sensible move which saved me additional hours of total embarrassment. They clapped alright. They clapped at anything. If you told them that the mosquito caught in the beam of the follow spot was part of the show, they'd clap. They were proud and polite people, but British comedy? Forget it! But as I say, swimming with the dolphins was worth it.

In 1984 I worked to a totally American audience there. They were even more difficult. They peered at me as if I'd just arrived from space on their sacred shuttle. Once again I went down like a French kiss at a family reunion.

That very trip, my second, to Ascension Island, would provide the backdrop for probably the worst practical joke I ever played on anyone in my whole life!

The vision of Ascension Island is something that never leaves you. The volcanic rock protruding to a lush green mountain in the middle where you'll find monkeys and banana trees. The dolphins and the killer whales gliding fearlessly in their natural environment. The stars in the sky all the wrong way round because of its position.

I was in the company of some good mates. Kevin Devane, one of my best show business friends, Steve Rawlings, Karen Noble, a brilliant singer, tour co-ordinator Dave South whom I'd worked with since my earliest days with Jim Davidson – indeed Dave is married to Jim's cousin Julie. Micky was looking after me and all in all we were a magnificent gang up for a bloody good crack. With us were four of the unfriendliest dancers that the CSE mob could have ever put with us, and not to put too fine a point on it, none of them would threaten Carol Vorderman on the numbers board of 'Countdown' either. Conversation proved to be a waste of time, we discovered that at RAF Brize Norton the day we flew out to the Falklands. They basically went about their business and Sergeant Blue and his army, that's what we strangely called ourselves because we were pissed one night and all wearing something blue, went about theirs. And never the twain would meet until one ridiculous night on Ascension. We'd done the show and by ten o'clock we were on the coach, but not heading back towards our barrack-room accommodation as per the previous night. Tom Spencer of Combined Services Entertainment had told us of the journey of the green turtle, a rare species that swims thousands of miles from Brazil to lay its eggs on Ascension Island and then swims thousands of miles back again. That night we would see some of these wonderful creatures on the sand, actually laying their eggs. It was a sight that even David Attenborough would kill for, an absolute spectacle of wonder, which very few people in the world would ever see.

We couldn't wait. Well, Sergeant Blue's army couldn't wait. The girl dancers weren't that bothered either way but had to go because they were on the same coach as us and it was, after all, my show! Or should I say Sergeant Blue's show! We decided to play the most dreadful of jokes on the dancers, who after a couple of weeks away down in the Falklands and now on the island were pissing everyone off with their stand-offish attitudes and disinterest in anything that didn't mean a part in a West End musical.

That afternoon I had spotted some RAF fire fighters on the runway. They were wearing tin foil fire suits in case of emergency, and it gave me an idea. There were white paper versions of the same thing, which they covered themselves from head to toe in, for possible chemical spillage situations and so on. They were really great guys, the finest and bravest around, and I asked them the favour. I needed four body suits, goggles, face masks and breathing equipment, paper boots and gloves, the lot, all of which was dutifully delivered in secrecy onto the coach whilst the show went ahead in the squaddie theatre.

When we boarded the coach the girls were surprised to learn that to see the green turtles they needed to wear special protective clothing, as the scent emitted by dancers who'd just thrown themselves about for half an hour would prevent the turtles from laying their eggs because of the confusion brought about by the new and unfamiliar female odours. Such strange smells would of course be a threat to the creatures' territories and they would disappear back into the Atlantic Ocean never to return. Such a sad occurrence would of course result in the total extinction of the green turtle and it was something that just couldn't be risked.

Now imagine the scene, it is approaching midnight on a beautiful island in the middle of the ocean, and we are quietly edging along a beach with dim torches in the utter darkness, trying to locate half a dozen turtles the size of tables, that have dug large holes in which to lay their eighty or so eggs the size of table tennis balls. We were to witness the whole incredible event. Mother Nature would put on a show of her own that far surpassed anything we'd done on stage earlier. We found the sand holes and crawled along on our tummies so as not to disturb the turtles that were both laying the eggs and then using their flippers like shovels to cover them up, safe from harm. One noisy intrusion and they would stop laying and leave.

The turtles were exhausted and their job had almost been done. Brazil beckoned and soon they would be gone. What an experience. Our faces, with our chins on the sand, were two or three inches from their shells. No photos, no video cameras, nothing that would disturb the wonderful creatures as they went about their miracles. The white luminous eggs were laid and then buried and the job was done. Only a few of the young would make it to the sea, but somehow the cycle would continue, no matter how adverse the circumstances. And we had seen it with our own eyes.

It was time for the turtles to rest before the long journey home, and enter onto the scene, four astronauts from the coach, dressed from head to toe in white suits. Hiding all around us were the fire fighters who had given us the gear. From each sand dune there was a snigger which the girls never heard beneath all the clothing. We had waited until the turtles' work had been successfully done before exposing them to our own freaks of nature. Up the sand waddled four bodies.

'Where's these turtle things then?' asked one.

'I can't see anything,' yelled another.

The serene beauty of that tropical island was broken, and how. I called the girls over to see the worn out creatures.

'What they doing? Just laying there?'

'Yes.'

'Boring.'

'If you say so.'

'Wanna fag?'

'No thanks.'

'So what happens then?'

'Nothing really, they're just beautiful creatures we thought you may like to see,' I replied.

'Oh yeah, beautiful.'

And so went the conversation. Lying next to me, one of the dancers, dressed in ridiculous paper garments, whispered to me.

'It's a shame ain't it.'

I looked at her and whispered back.

'What's a shame?'

'Lying on a beach like this and the fucking sun ain't out!'

I burst out laughing and ran away from the turtles. Everyone rose to his or her feet and headed back to the coach. Lights were turned on and Sergeant Blue's army was rolling around in utter pain. Those girls looked so stupid, quite befitting the comments I'd heard on the golden sands. When they realised they'd been set up to say they were angry was an understatement. They hated me so much. I don't think they liked me much in the first place, I was a boring old fart they'd never heard of, and they resented being fifth on the bill to Kev, Steve, Karen, and me, none of whom any of them had ever heard of. I think one of them had heard of Stevie Wonder and another knew there was a war in the Falklands some years previously. Their conversations were brisk and mainly to the army boys.

'Got any combats?'

'Got any of them striped jackets for my boyfriend?'

'Bollocks to you then, I'll ask someone else.'

'Got any combats?'

The shows on the Falklands, firstly with Jim Davidson and then in my own right, were sensational. It was a long way and everyone appreciated the effort made by the entertainers to get down there.

The shows were small occasions in the main with some concerts in portakabins to no more than thirty or forty people. We worked our way round the radar stations and far-flung outposts in freezing sub-zero temperatures. The dancers in particular showed their true worth, amongst other things of course, walking across snow-ridden gangways on mountains to reach the various tin venues. Goose Green Social Club, Port Stanley, and all the places I'd heard mentioned on the news by John Nott. And there I was, seeing these tiny airfix kit kind of homes with my own eyes. I even did a stint as a disc jockey on FIBS, the Falkland Islands Broadcasting Service, and I still have this funny feeling I was more appreciated there than I ever was at Capital Radio. Port Stanley was a town of colour, every roof a highly painted offering, which from a distance made the town look like it had been put together by kids at nursery school.

We paid our respects at all the war graves, including Colonel H. Jones of the SAS, who lost his life leading his men at Goose Green, and I sang a hymn at San Carlos Water where two British ships, Antrim and Antelope, were sunk with many lives lost. It was eerie, with the ships' masts protruding from the water like redundant submarine periscopes at low tide. Yet through the adversity of it all came what I described on many occasions as one of my greatest ever performances.

Overlooking San Carlos, known in the war as Kelly's Garden because of its connection with the Irish Rangers, were mountains covered in snow. The boys up on those high altitude bunkers, guarding the Rapier missiles, would miss the show so Jim and I were asked and stupidly agreed to go up the steep inclines in a Volvo BV to say hello. We split the trips with Jim going up one mountain and me up another.

I was convinced nobody would want to meet me as opposed to Jim, he was without any dispute the star of the show and the darling of the forces. I was reluctant to split up like that and see the disappointed faces on the squaddies I met. Luckily for me, it wasn't quite like that. The first sergeant I met came from London and had seen me a few times.

'Have you brought your guitar?' the sergeant asked.

I wasn't actually expecting to play anything. I thought it was nothing more than a short visit. But I was so pleased he recognised me I would have danced the bloody foxtrot if he'd asked me.

'It's in the wagon.'

'Jolly good, I'll tell the boys.'

And off he went.

There was I thinking I'd volunteered for a mountain trek to share a can or two of lager with the chaps. It was pitch black and as cold as I had ever been in my life. My soft contact lenses had frozen to my eyes and I was in pain. I stupidly tried to take the frozen lenses out of my eyes and I scratched both surfaces. It was only the intense cold that subdued the pain. I'd already done the two-hour show in an aircraft hangar and my guitar, or so I thought, had been safely packed away for the night. But it had to come out. There were only eight guys stationed in the bunker, and expecting a show they'd put two rows of four chairs out in their underground haven. Yes, it had to come out. There was a bowl of crisps and a pile of lager cans, oh yes, and sixteen expectant eyes. I couldn't let them down. And I didn't!

To those eight soldiers I did a full two and a half hour show. I still describe the show as my first ever sell-out concert and the greatest performance I have ever given in my life. Twelve years later, there was a knock on my dressing room door at the Prince's Theatre in Clacton, Essex. Before me stood a guy I never recognised. He was tall and looked a bit of a hard nut. I remember thinking that if he was another reprobate from Kensington Youth Club I'd just kiss him and give him a couple of tickets. I remember his words so well:

'No big deal, Rich, just wanted to say thanks mate. I was one of the eight at Kelly's Garden all those years ago.' He shook my hand and with that he disappeared into the audience of hundreds. I've never understood wars, but I'd done my bit for those caught up in such conflicts. I rang Jim and told him. He cheered on the other end of the phone. I almost cried.

'Well done lefty.'

'Thanks mate.'

'Fancy going to Germany?'

'Yes, but don't tell my dad.'

And so we were off again.

Wherever there was trouble in the world Jim would be there. If there wasn't any trouble he was capable of starting some.

I'm coming home back home to you
Tell them all down the old Rose and Crown
There will be some celebrating to do.
I'm coming home back home to you
Tell them all down the old Rose and Crown
I'll soon be in for a few.
I see in your letter it's raining

You say the weather's been bad
But reading between the lines as I do
I see in your letter you're sad.
But it's me that's a million miles from my home
Me that sits here alone
Tell them all down the old Rose and Crown
I'm coming home.

When I attended Jim's London dinner for the British Forces Association in the company of Baroness Margaret Thatcher and Sir Rex Hunt, the whole evening began with Jim explaining to a few thousand people how show business artists travel all over the world to entertain the troops. Big venues and small venues, and the first example Jim gave to that star-studded audience was my tiny bunker show overlooking San Carlos Water. Through adversity comes good. He told them all the squaddies were screaming for an air attack so I'd stop singing.

The military personnel knew I had little interest in warfare. Jim was an authority. One night on HMS Glamorgan we were invited to the officers' mess and as usual I feared them asking me what I thought about this, that and the other because I had very little knowledge or interest. Glamorgan was different, the captain played guitar and between us we did a splendid rendition of 'Duelling Banjos', which I'd played in the dressing room of the Cellar Door in Washington, with Steve Martin, all those years previously. Most of the time I lived in Jim's shadow at such military occasions, but every so often, a little cameo evening occurred, and that was one such without doubt.

Jim Davidson took me to areas of the business I knew nothing about. The left wing musician had met the right wing comedian. Summer seasons at Great Yarmouth and then Torquay. Jim, top of the bill, stayed at a swish hotel. I had digs in a crap house that had no windows and stank of seagull vomit. I lived there for nine weeks. Each afternoon we played pitch and putt and met up for mid-afternoon tea with Jim Bowen at the Torbay Hotel. What a sincere man was the 'Bullseye' king. Our chats were gold dust to this rookie comedian. The two Jims spent hours talking about the art of comedy. Hate or love their comedy styles, their experience was second to none and their generosity was outstanding. I kept my mouth shut most of the time and listened.

I loved Torquay, but my season in Yarmouth, that was a different story. Ten weeks on the Britannia Pier, and it pissed down every single day. Yes, every single bloody day. I lived in a small room that just about housed a single bed, with a television clamped to the wall as there wasn't enough room for a table to rest it upon. Jim and I went fishing together on the Norfolk Broads at Potter Heigham and we were very close pals at this time. We relished the seclusion as we pulled a few tasty roach from the River Yare. Jim is a very normal guy who likes normal things and ladies with big tits. At other times I hung out at the snooker club. It was a terrible down time for me, despite the hanging out with Jim. Smudger, Jim's other guitarist, boarded with a guy from the cast of 'The Diary of Adrian Mole' who later committed suicide.

Debbie brought Polly up to see me and Jim and I took them to the circus. Polly sat on Jim's knee and the pair of them laughed uncontrollably. For those few short minutes, the guy wasn't a show business ogre who attracted tabloid publicity. He'd become a plain, simple bloke who loved the monkeys, dressed up as jockeys, riding on the backs of pigs. Polly loved Jim, who really had become a genuine friend of my family.

Michael Barrymore performed across the road at the Majestic, Chas and Dave were on Wellington Pier and Les Dennis and Roy Walker of 'Catchphrase' were at the ABC in the town centre. We all went down the George for a drink after most shows, except Barrymore who seemed to keep his own station, and we all drank into the early hours. We even formed a football team to play the town for charity. Les Dennis was a classy player, well, we asked a hundred people and they said he was!! Jim and I played in midfield and spent most of the second half drinking lager and looking for an ashtray.

I caught the mumps in Yarmouth and had to return to Essex for treatment. Roy Walker stood in for me. It was a Saturday morning when I knocked on Jim's hotel room door. My neck was huge and I couldn't say a word. Despite a heavy night Jim again showed his friendship and concern by jumping in a cab with me and taking me to the General Hospital in Yarmouth. I was starting to feel a lot of pain. The casualty unit was packed with silly people who'd fallen off ladders and broken their arms playing table tennis. Typical Jim rushed me down to the front of the queue, told the receptionist we had a celebrity auction to do that morning and that I was the auctioneer. The visit would probably have taken two or three hours, we were seen within ten minutes, although Jim nearly blew it when an Indian doctor came out to look down my throat.

'Bloody hell, he wants a doctor not a lion tamer.'

It wasn't racist, it was very tongue in cheek and the whole casualty unit burst into laughter, including the doctor. It was Jim's way of apologising for jumping the queue.

During my second stint in Torquay I moved house to Lyme Regis in Dorset, home of *The French Lieutenant's Woman*. Debbie did all the hard work while I was away on stage duty. I'd always loved the Dorset coastal town and with the development of Stansted Airport, the time had come to move from Appletree Cottage, my second home in Essex. It was situated too close for comfort to Stansted, just a couple of miles from the runway and on the landing flight-path.

At the end of the first summer season I became a studio warm-up act for Des O'Connor's television series. At the end of the second, cars were picking me up to appear on the 'Des O'Connor Show'. What a difference a couple of years makes.

By the time I moved to Lyme I'd been on TV quite a few times. Jim got me my first television special for Thames Television, called 'A Dabble With Digance'. I then moved to TVS after producer John Kaye Cooper spotted me as a TV studio warm-up act for Matthew Kelly. I made my first series for ITV in Southampton, then when John moved to London Weekend Television he took me with him. So most people in Lyme knew who I was. I started drinking at the Black Dog in Uplyme but in the main kept myself to myself. There can surely be no prettier place in Britain than Lyme Regis on a spring morning. We had sea views from our bedroom window and Blaney Crescent seemed an awfully long way away. Every morning Debbie and I had breakfast in bed and stared out across Lyme Bay to Weymouth. It was breathtaking. We had a balcony built from our bedroom which made the panoramic view even more appetising.

I've shared many years with Jim Davidson. By his side in Dundee during one divorce hearing, the only pair of ears that could listen to him so many hundreds of miles from home. I've both watched and read the tabloids as they have undressed him in public. I've seen quotes from Jim that perhaps he would have been better off not to have said. I've seen his wives come and go. In the words of Brian Hanrahan during the Falklands, 'I counted them out and I counted them back in.' Jim is a loveable rogue, always first on the list when there is a charity event. We've more or less been round the world together and every time I see him on television I seem to think of

another mess we two rascals found ourselves in, mainly because of
him! He brought a new dimension to my life. Don't forget I was
nothing much more than a musician when we teamed up.

Both being booed off at Middlesbrough Town Hall, Jim being
stripped at Checkpoint Charlie in Berlin for mooning at Russian
guards from a coach that took us to the Berlin Wall. The two of us at
an afternoon reception in Swindon and realising, despite the fact we
were totally pissed on port, that we had a show that night at Derby
Assembly Rooms, hundreds of miles away. It had passed five o'clock
and we were the wrong side of the country. Jim booked a private
plane, a four-seater jobby, that bashed and bumped its way through
a pea-soup sky with the pilot telling us to watch out for 'the big boys'
as we crossed Heathrow airspace. So what is my favourite Davidson
story? It stands alone as far as I am concerned.

We were together in Doha, part of the United Arab Emirates, and
had finished a show for various Brits in a drink-free zone. So it was
all back to someone's house after the show for drinks and finger
buffet. As is often the case, we were ignored by just about everyone
there. It's strange but it's always the same. People love celebrities
around and when they are around they never know what to say. Jim
and I were intruders into their secret territory and they made it more
than clear they didn't really want us there at all. They all seemed too
full of their own importance and the general feeling was that we'd
gatecrashed a very middle class Tupperware party.

The house, a sprawling Dallas-like residence, belonged to the bank
manager, an employee of Lloyds, whose wife couldn't have been
more self-important or self-opinionated as she told us of the various
servants, maids, cooks and swimming pool attendants she had under
her wing. Bank managers in the Middle East, being a moneyed area,
consider themselves to be made of gold. Her verbal commands made
the Queen look positively nowhere. I would dearly love to name them
here but I honestly can't remember them. They put me off Lloyds
Bank for life.

'Do you know Jasper?' she asked Jim, referring to Brummy comic
Mr Carrott who certainly wasn't Jim's cup of tea at all.

'Jasper who?' replied Jim.

'Jasper Carrott.'

'No, not personally.'

'Now he is funny, don't you think?'

'If you say so.'

'You remind me of him Jim, all those stories.'

'Oh really?'

'But he is so funny. Oh we know the Carrotts very well, we always stay with them when we're in England. Hazel's a love. She shops at Harrods. They're very wealthy you know, the Carrotts. I think they're with Coutts.'

'Is that so?'

She went on and on.

Then she went on and on again.

'Ah, now you must be, now what do you call yourself, the support act?'

'No, I call myself Richard.'

'Do you know Jasper? He's handled show business so well. So wealthy. Mind you, support act eh, oh never mind. Do you like Jasper?'

'So so.'

'Don't you think he's a genius?'

'No.'

I knew Jim, so I equally knew something was going to give. To praise another comedian when you're talking to a comedian, particularly just after a show, is downright stupid and thoughtless, and even more particularly comparing Jasper Carrott with the people's champion of the time, Jim Davidson. She deserved all that was about to come her way. I hated the woman, a jumped-up nobody. To her I wasn't worthy of conversation, being a lowly support act. It was going to snap, just like a huge pink bubble from a penny bubble gum, something was about to explode.

'Would you care for a sausage roll, Jim?'

'No thanks.'

'A piece of cheese?'

'No thanks.'

'Strawberries, fresh from England?'

'No thanks.'

'Is there anything at all I can do for you?'

The place fell silent, one of those odd occasions when everybody, unaccountably, stopped talking at the same time. Jim responded.

'Would you shut up and get your tits out?'

The regal bank manager's wife looked mortified. I laughed myself stupid. Falling backwards and toppling over a settee full of shocked people. She deserved it. We left the party promptly with no one wishing us well. As I look back on my life, I have to say it was one of the funniest occasions I can recall. Jim's timing was perfection personified. Carrott would have needed ten scriptwriters to work that one out. That was probably the difference. We left Doha the next day and flew to Abu Dhabi. I didn't see anyone at the terminal waving us goodbye. We laughed so much.

'But I bet she did have great tits.'

'She did, I saw them!'

'Bollocks!'

Jim would talk about anything to me on a plane because he knew I had a total fear of flying. We took off and flew to Dubai and as we made a wide arc in the sky, the air stewardess explained they weaved around a bit at this point as a few weeks previously a plane had been shot out of the sky by terrorists. I gripped my seat so tightly I bent a metal ashtray in the arm of the seat. Jim gave me a brandy and we carried on laughing about something else. I always said to Jim if I was in a plane crash I wanted to be with him so that I'd make the *Sun* or the *Daily Mirror*.

We used to imagine the comparisons of the headline.

'Jim Davidson killed in plane crash!'

'Plectrum found.'

'Nick Nick comes a cropper in a chopper.'

'Guitar fails to survive big drop.'

I spent nearly five years of my life next to Jim Davidson. Some speak highly of him, some lowly. Whatever one's thoughts, he was the second greatest comedian I ever worked with after Steve Martin and his generosity and kindness was second to none. I therefore considered it a great honour to be the only guest on his BBC television special 'Jim Davidson, The Story So Far'. Thrown together in the Arabian desert all those years ago, I was part of Jim and Jim was part of me.

'Meet me on the corner when the lights are going dim and I'll be there, I promise I'll be there.' The Lindisfarne words I dedicate to Jim Davidson.

My association with Mr Davidson also brought me to the attention of the tabloid press, something I'd managed to avoid up to that point. Perhaps, quite simply, I had never been newsworthy enough to bother with and I hadn't been in the plane crash. With the television series 'Wednesday At Eight', it all changed. Produced by John Kaye Cooper it was a weekday variety show, the like of which the public could well do with today, and I was on every week with Jim, singing a daft song or a poem. It brought total recognition from the public and suddenly my shows were selling out all over the country.

The *Sun* newspaper were running a weekly series, 'Twenty things you didn't know about...' and they decided to feature yours truly. They asked a series of questions that I duly answered and then asked me if I'd been married before. I told them Debbie was my first, or present, wife, and then they asked if I was Debbie's first husband, which I wasn't. She'd been married to Ray Whiteman.

'Did you know him, Richard?'

'Yes, quite well.'

'Was he a friend?'

'They were both friends.'

That Saturday morning we had workmen at Lyme Regis, putting a new kitchen in. I took them mugs of tea and they were all giggling away so I sensed something was afoot.

'Have you seen the *Sun*?'

'No. Why?'

A workman proceeded to turn to the middle pages and there as large as life was the headline:

'Nick Nick's mate Dick nicks best mate's chick.'

I was angry at first, Debbie was totally mortified, but before I could do anything about it I realised that I too had burst out laughing so we took it on the chin.

A couple of weeks later I worked with Kenny Everett and Gloria Hunniford on 'That's Showbusiness', a welcome reunion with my old Capital pal, Mike Smith. I'd been on the show before and been on Gloria's team but never on Kenny's. It all felt very different. Every time I went to say something I was hushed down, so by the end of the show I was mute. The *News of the World* ran a story about how I'd never do another game show because I hated them. There were rumours flying around that I didn't get on with Kenny, which was ridiculous because we'd worked together for five years, also at Capital, and he was a decent enough bloke.

I became more guarded over what I said and to whom, and luckily managed to distract the tabloids away from my direction. I suppose working with Jim it was inevitable but I didn't care much for it. It was the last sort of attention I expected when I set out on the folk scene all those years ago. I wouldn't mind betting I got more press than Captain Blaney. Now he was worthy of a few mentions in my book.

Chapter Six

My Television Career

By 1985 I was becoming an act in my own right but continued working with Jim. He was good both to me and for me. Indeed it was he who, as I mentioned, assured my first TV special with Thames Television, produced by Paul Jackson, and lots more was to follow. My guest was newsreader Carol Barnes who read a spoof news bulletin I'd written.

To chronicle a television career is difficult without reeling off endless appearances and specials that would become a boring read, so let's forget that. It would read as more of an ego trip than part of my life, but needless to say, there was plenty of it. Very briefly, I started at Thames, moved on to Television South before joining London Weekend Television where I stayed for over a decade, unknowingly filming the longest continual series of television specials in the history of British television. I eventually went to Westcountry Television where I enjoyed a kind of freedom I'd never known before at the hands of precious television producers. So that's the ego trip over with, short and sweet. Those that stand out? There's a few.

To stay a favourite with television producers is difficult in Britain, particularly if you're straight, due to that disease in this country of knocking down those who rise to great things. Ian Botham, David Beckham, Steve Davis and Paul Gascoigne in sport, Parkinson, Tarbuck, Selina Scott and countless more in television presenting. Age is a criminal offence in Britain. In America it is respected. That is basically the difference. They come and go as quickly as a curry. Someone said you don't buy a curry, you only rent it for a couple of hours. Television I consider an equal analogy. I rented my television career until someone felt I'd had it long enough and then they took it back. The tabloids make you and massacre you as part of their game plan and the television bosses seem to be guided by them. In a small way I suffered that plight as previously mentioned, but never really worried too much about it. I'd never been a regular London nightclub tripper, so I was considered hugely boring, going grey and not worthy of being a star. I accepted that, being far too busy in my world of concerts, corporate cabarets and writing interests. If I'd built my career on the expectancies of television loyalty I wouldn't have afforded the computer with which I write this story for you.

For years I wrote and starred in endless specials for London Weekend Television, until they decided enough was enough. In all the years, I never received a Christmas card, a congratulatory message, or a phone call when they'd decided to call a halt to my well-received hour specials. They just stopped without notice. LWT top-nobs spent most of their time pampering the egos of their top line Saturday night presenters, no names mentioned, but everyone knows who, and I'm sure we can all estimate the size of such egos. Champagne and flowers in dressing rooms, ensuring the wrong coloured limos weren't sent to their homes – oh, the list is endless and you wouldn't believe me anyway. I simply loved making and writing TV shows and because I asked for nothing I was given nothing.

My sell-by date arrived in 1997 and I was never to hear from anyone at LWT ever again. Some would have scratched their heads and wondered. I never saw the point. I'd been a top-flight comedian for years, selling out concerts around Britain, I knew I'd done something right. No matter how big or small I knew I'd done something right, and I learnt something from Jim about those people. Charity television productions like Red Nose Days and Children In Need passed me by because I never knew or mixed with those who chose to commit to Red Nose Days, some of them for personal exposure and publicity gain. I was never asked to perform at a single solitary event for either charity. Jim taught me never to charge for a charity event. I never did and for that Jim and I stand proud.

I watch the big charity days with disdain, I'm afraid. It is, for so many, an excuse to get on high-rating television programmes. I'd moved out of London, spent eight years in Lyme Regis before moving to Hampshire's New Forest. I was never going to rub shoulders with poncy TV producers and hip celebrities who had all the sway and say for such programmes. It didn't matter. I chose to have a pint with my mates or go for a quiet meal rather than hang out at Stringfellows or Groucho's, begging people to include me on their guest lists for free trips to the Third World. Mind you, let's remind them all that the first ever Ethiopia Aid Concert in Victoria, London starred Eric Clapton, Chas and Dave, Jim Davidson and Richard Digance. You never see those names on Red Nose Day events do you?

Some would say I suffered because of my choice of lifestyle, hopefully others will understand my reasons. I wanted to raise my two daughters, Polly and Rosie, in a world removed from the glitter and glamour of show business. They love the country life of horse riding and dog walking, and I'm pleased about that. It's a long way from Captain Blaney's memorial, indeed Polly and Rosie had never seen the East End of London until February 1999, when I took them to see where their dad was born and where gran was cremated. Strangely, we passed the big white tower block that housed London Weekend Television as we drove along the Thames Embankment on their special trip. They were about as disinterested as I was at seeing the proud standing London Television Studios as they were later re-named. We went to the Natural History Museum on our way home. It somehow had more going for it than a building full of jumped-up insecure television executives who thought they knew what made British viewers laugh. As I say though, some of my shows I recall with immense pride and fondness.

I played guitar duets with Brian May of Queen and the Moody Blues. I joined Status Quo as an honorary member for one special. I asked for Marc Cohn to be on my show and the following Monday the song he wrote and sang, 'Walking In Memphis', was flying high in the charts. Joe Pasquale guested and then toured with me, and many more. Chris De Burgh did a song with me, 'That's What Friends Are For'. Elkie Brooks joined me, as did Buffy St Marie who wrote 'Soldier Blue' and Julia Fordham.

'Julia Fordham? Who's she?' they asked in their ignorance.

'The best female singer/songwriter in Britain,' I replied.

They all agreed she was brilliant after the filming and patted themselves on their backs for thinking of her. Chris De Burgh flew over from Germany at his own expense after I'd contacted him personally. And on and on. Barbara Dickson, Dinah Carroll, Paul Brady, Big Country. They all appeared on my television programmes over the years. Working with them all are the great memories I have. The never-ending phone calls from television people I'd never heard of were the downside. I was too accessible. I could never believe the Barrymores and Cilla Blacks of the world were called day and night by all and sundry being asked what they'd done about finding their guests for the following week. Was it only myself who'd been plagued by researchers who thought working in television was little more than posing in Rohan trousers and bomber tour jackets scrounged off some teenage band of the time? None of them knew a thing about Digance or the sort of guests he required for his 'live' shows. Nobody mimed when I was around. What a weird time. I needed my sanity.

One of my favourite television moments was when I played world champion Steve Davis at snooker. I'd been a great fan and to play him was an honour. I stupidly offered to give him a 40 start. I still see Steve quite often at golf dinners and if there's anyone I know who isn't anything like the image he portrays, it's Steve Davis. Off the table he's a bloody good laugh and a nice guy. That night at Thames Television studios was one of my favourites. The very same Teddington studio the following year allows me to recall my least favourite. Can you imagine 'Celebrity Mastermind'?

I was on the pilot. There was myself, Steve Jones of the 'Pyramid Game', Jeremy Hanley MP and Katie Boyle. I was the only one who wasn't told it was serious. Their specialist subjects ranged from dog handling to politics to Italian cuisine. My selected subject was West Ham half backs between 1955 and 1965. I've never felt such a tit in all my life. Gyles Brandreth, the host, took an instant dislike to me, I scored no points on my specialist subject and not many more on the round about myself!! Brandreth seemed to know an awful lot more about me than I did. Trouble was, his research was bollocks, and each time I corrected him he assured me he could only take the answer that was written on the card. The verbal of the man, no wonder he became a Member of Parliament. One question: Jimmy Greaves joined West Ham in a cash/swap deal for Martin Peters, with which club? It was Spurs. I said Spurs.

'I'm sorry Richard, I can only take what's on the card and it says Tottenham Hotspur.'

If you think that was out of order try this next question:

'West Ham in the 1964 Cup Final against Preston had seven players whose surnames began with B. For one point, can you name them?'

For one poxy point I couldn't actually be that bothered to name them.

One day, out of the blue, my management company, International Artists, sacked me. I regretted it. I thought it strange because I thought management companies worked for artists and not the other way round, but they sacked me nonetheless. Talk about the tail wagging the dog. Bob Voice and I had been through so much together, built our reputations together, but the time had come in Bob's eyes, and that was the end of Richard Digance at Regent Street.

More of this departure when I tell of the Tidings, but I was scared. Not a single concert in the diary. I maintain that Bob Voice was, at the time, the best manager in the country. It was inevitable he would move on to other artists, just like Jazz Summers and Kevin Wyatt Lown before him, but when it happened it was hard to take. Although I had the big house in the country and the Mercedes, I had no work at all. Not a single, solitary date. If I'd been given notice I'd have prepared myself but my dismissal came by letter and that was the end of it. I still don't think it was a personal thing however. Jim, Mike Osman and Dave Lee were all dismissed at the same time. Jim and I received the same standard letter.

Times became very hard indeed. Debbie and I grew our own vegetables on our farm, froze tons of stuff, we stopped going out completely and I suppose I became a bit of an enforced recluse. As a family we spent our evenings doing jigsaw puzzles and watching telly. I worked on local radio stations for anything I could get, sold spare guitars and Debbie's car – whoops, that wasn't too popular I seem to recall. I cashed in various insurance policies and somehow we scraped by without selling up. Times were difficult because I couldn't let on that things had gone pear-shaped. Until now, very few would ever have known.

I met up with Bob Voice again at my fiftieth birthday party, in 1999, and he admitted to me he'd regretted our split and now we are good friends again, which is nice. For a while, another friend, Reg Parsons, tried to take the reins, but it was difficult for him. Reg had experience mainly in corporate entertainment through his company Production Plus. He knew little about touring or television appearances, so although he tried, the working relationship didn't gel in quite the same way as our friendship. We gathered debts that took me personally nearly three years to repay. It was the best thing that ever happened to me. I regained priorities, knew who my friends were, and continued living my quiet life in Hampshire. Brian Shaw, who'd been my tour promoter whilst I was with Bob, rescued me. More of Brian later. He took over my management in July 1996, against the advice of so many who had worked with me until my bubble burst.

With Reg I was able to step up my corporate appearances and get some money circulating again. We went to New Orleans for Fords, and for the same company I found myself in Austria, at the site of a Winter Olympics which I can't remember the name of, let alone spell. It was another night I nearly died. Reg and I loved a drink, so we went on a Schnaps session. Well, it was Austria after all. The drink obviously gave one bravado, particularly when you think back on the energy of Hitler, who was born in the Austrian village in question whose name I forget, and best forgotten too when thinking of their one-time resident.

We drank the stuff all night, with me eventually and cowardly substituting the clear alcohol with water after a tip to the barman, but I'd still had enough to feel dodgy. On the way back to my hotel, which I recall looked like a bloody musical box with miserable people inside, I was sick on some sporty slope or other and the next morning Reg and I made the stupid mistake of going up a huge mountain in a cable car. It was a ridiculous decision which we realised the moment we started rolling, but those cable cars stop for nothing and up we climbed, the air growing thinner and thinner with each passing minute.

We stopped at a log cabin that sold frankfurters and drink. But the problem was not that of hunger, but more the fact we couldn't breathe. A minor point I know. Reg went to the toilet and in Captain Scott tradition, there seemed every chance he would be gone quite some time. He had a good clear-out and returned to the bar feeling worse. He suggested, in the interests of safety, that the slope be closed while his parting motion gathered momentum down the steep gradient. He'd ordered a frankfurter but chose not to indulge when the thing appeared almost raw, seeping red liquid. We went outside and had our photograph taken. I wore a West Ham tracksuit, given to me by my footballer friend Tony Gale. Reg wore a grin that hinted at an attack of piles or similar. I had the photo mounted and it's still on his office wall with the inscription: 'On top of the world but not feeling it, Love, Richard Digance.'

With Reg my only TV was 'Celebrity Squares' with Bob Monkhouse. I met two great guys on that show, another snooker player, Dennis Taylor, and former jockey John Francome. Both, incidentally, are superb after-dinner speakers should you ever get the opportunity to see them. They were normal guys and I enjoyed their company as we chatted together in the canteen. I also enjoyed getting back in front of the camera as I'd missed more and more of the glitter work that had come my way with Bob Voice at International Artists.

My television career had more or less ground to a halt and it remained fairly dormant for a few years. But you hang in there!

In 1997, I was approached by Westcountry Television to film a series, 'Richard Digance, For One Night Only'. I had travelled down to do a song on a chat show hosted by a friend of mine, Nick Owen, and nearly aborted due to a nasty wisdom tooth deciding to speak out for itself. I drove from Leeds where I'd just filmed 'Countdown', to Plymouth where Nick's show was being shot. A bloody long drive with a toothache. I couldn't let Nick down. It was on that show I was seen by the executives of Westcountry and asked to film a series of my own. By accepting this I more or less waved goodbye to any further links with London Weekend Television. Thank god for plain, simple hard working executives at a regional television station that wanted to make good programmes and not piss about.

The first series of 'For One Night Only' produced the highest share of the ratings Westcountry had ever achieved and knocked the BBC for six. I was immensely proud and did a further series for them the following year. Brian Shaw had got to grips with things and settled into my management and things were happening again. He later moved to Hampshire to become managing director of my new company, the Write Good Company.

I'd worked with Brian as a tour promoter, through International Artists, for over ten years and we knew each other well. We shared a fascination for football nostalgia – Brian had to, supporting Burnley as a child. He was top of the tree but had somehow let go of the branches and fallen out during the property market collapse. He needed to rebuild his career and so did I, so it was just as well a chance phone call occurred. He rang me to perform at a dinner for Worcestershire cricketer 'Bumpy' Rhodes in Malvern. We chatted a while and he wondered if he could get me more work. Brian came to my home and within an hour he'd become my new manager. At the time he represented Freddie Starr, Barbara Dickson and Danny LaRue on tour, but didn't actually manage any of them. Together we worked out a secret game-plan which we have adhered to right to this day. What was it? Secret!

Our new family house in Hampshire was coming on well. The builders were busy sorting out the dodgy beams and rotten roof supports. We'd moved to the edge of the New Forest and that's exactly where I'd always wanted to live, it's just that I never realised it until I moved there. Robin Smith's wife Cathy actually found us the house and the deal was done in half an hour. The Lyme Regis saga was way behind us and I only regretted one small thing about leaving the sleepy Dorset resort.

In the back garden, in a wooden summerhouse, I had realised a dream, and I had to leave it behind.

As a child I'd always wanted a train set of my own but Christmases didn't stretch to things like that in those days. Most of my presents related to things for school like football boots or new clothes. Even the dreaded Helix Geometry Set with the two flavoured rubbers and the set of dividers for stabbing the child in front in the back of the head. It was the same for everyone of that generation. Debbie and I agreed it would be a brilliant idea to build a train set of the very period I would have had when a little boy. The signal boxes, the level crossing gates, the steam engines and engine sheds. Although I'd never been a model railway enthusiast, I loved the idea of making hills, rivers and tunnels with cement and stones.

I spent months creating this masterpiece with suspension bridges, waterfalls, roads with AA patrolmen who saluted their members as they drove by. I really went to town, but once it was built it was built. There was nothing else to do. I didn't really want to spend hours watching the bloody trains racing round, I just wanted to make amends for not having a train set as a child. I did that, and in Lyme Regis it remained until we left and I dismantled it and gave the accessories to the children of my tour manager of the time, Mike Rowland. Knowing him, they probably went into a car boot sale the following weekend. The track remained and I hope someone uses it today.

Television had changed in five years, variety had become sparse and I was searching for new challenges. I accepted the invitation to appear on the occasional 'Countdown' programme and the trip up to Leeds the day before Nick's programme at Westcountry was my first appearance on the programme. Being a word game, and me being a word game nutcase, it had been my favourite show for a while and when Richard Whiteley asked me personally to appear, I felt quite flattered and excited. I'd appeared on 'The Richard Whiteley Show' with Vanessa Mae and Curtis Stigers. I told him how much I loved watching 'Countdown', and asked him if he'd get me on. He did. The Channel Four programme had popular and loyal ratings and more people stopped me in the street to talk about my appearances on it than they'd ever done with my own television series for LWT. Strange but true.

'Countdown' gave me the opportunity to get some television exposure without long hours of preparation and with little pressure. I became a frequent guest as the months passed and I looked forward to my drives to the Leeds studios of Yorkshire Television. The film crew were a friendly crowd and I often went up the night before to have a few beers with producer Mark Nyman, who became a personal friend of my family. After the way I'd been treated at LWT, I felt delighted to be of importance once again. The TV shows multiplied as I joined the panel for 'Through The Keyhole' at the same studios and continued and expanded my association with Westcountry Television through Jane McCloskey. 'Countdown' was the first ever programme transmitted by Channel Four, by the way.

Various issues never really added up at LWT. I was never invited to be a guest on the multitude of other LWT productions, and not a single show I filmed was ever repeated. That may not seem such a big deal but one mustn't forget the vast number of repeats that are shown on British television, together with the number of shows they sell to Australia and the States and so on, I was surprised I was never in the frame. I never met a single person from their publicity department. It wasn't meant in any personal way. They were simply absorbed in their prime time scheduling and then taken over by Granada, I think. The regime changed and so did the opportunities.

I took a programme concept to them in July 1986, which I'd been working on for a while. The idea was to present a type of game show involving the more interesting and zany members of the public, as opposed to celebrities, with musical inserts by unknowns, taking a film crew on location. I don't know what happened but the idea was dismissed. I presented the same format again, a while later, to my new producer Mark Robson. Again it was dismissed. I watched Barrymore's public-orientated programmes for London Weekend Television with disbelief. Of course, it isn't for me to suggest his show was anything like my idea. I'm sure as the years have passed and the ideas have disappeared in a haze, I am wrong and there's no comparison between the two formats. There's no doubt that Richard Digance had fallen from favour and none of my ideas mattered anymore at LWT. Michael Barrymore was a far more professional and vibrant presenter than I was anyway, no doubt about that one, so perhaps the format wouldn't have worked with me at the helm. Interesting though, eh?

★

This enforced exile had, without me knowing, been a godsend. During the spare time I'd found in plentiful doses, I'd created a children's television project called the Tidings. I'd presented the first stages to Bob Voice and nothing had happened. I'd presented it again to Reg Parsons and it still hadn't got off the ground. It was the Tidings, the seven little wonders of the world, that would eventually change my world entirely and turn me into a successful businessman and a plc director of a company on the London Stock Exchange.

Chapter Seven

Digance the Crap Businessman

Don't build your hopes up. My career in business didn't start too well. This is not a story like Branson's. My dabbles in business had been nothing short of worthless for more years than I care to remember. I'd set up a record company, Dambuster Records, because I couldn't get a record deal. I'd set up a music publishing company, Pollysongs Music Limited, because I couldn't get a music publishing deal. I'm sure if my sex life had dwindled I would have set up a lousy pimp agency as well. All my business transactions had been taken on in adversity, personal failure and disinterest of others. They had been last resorts to try and keep my name strong. I understood my own motives but it was never a way or reason to start a new business venture. The admission of one's own failings is one thing, to make money out of them as opposed to accepting them is another thing altogether.

I became a director of a corporate entertainment company, Corporaction, with my mate Tony Gale and his teammate at West Ham, goalkeeper Phil Parkes. It would have worked if things had been different, indeed Tony and I discussed going it alone, but he'd been signed by Blackburn Rovers and was enjoying a huge success in the twilight of his career, winning a championship medal under Kenny Dalglish and playing in the Charity Shield Final at Wembley. West Ham had given him away on a free transfer and when Blackburn moved in for him he was training with Barnet reserves. I probably spoke to Tony on the phone longer than any other friend at that time. I felt proud to be the mate he'd confided in through such a troublesome and uncertain time in his football career, and to this day I feel just as proud that I helped write his CV which in turn helped him to become a successful radio and television football analyst. Stranger still that he ended up working for no other than Capital Radio!!

While Tony was still playing at West Ham I'd become a director of Yeovil Town of the GM Conference league. They had sold the famous sloping pitch to Tescos, which probably explains why so many old dears crashed their trolleys into the fruit and veg department. I didn't realise the club were as skint as they were as I was soon paying the players' wages and pumping my own money into the club, much to the disapproval of my wife. I looked behind me in the directors' box one Saturday afternoon during a vital cup match. Two directors were missing and one was listening to a rugby international on a Walkman. It was time to get out, so I did.

Two league clubs and another GM Conference side approached me to join their boards but I declined. I always promised Tony if he'd made it into football management then I'd have loved to be with him but it never arose and so, despite my love of the game, I've since stayed on the perimeter. The strange thing about football directors is that so very few of them have any interest in football. It's a bit like joining a lodge or a Rotary Club to some of them. Yeovil could so easily have reached the Football League but ridiculous deals were done during my time. They played in green and white, the same as Thomas Lethaby Secondary Modern, the school team that dropped me as a goalkeeper. Green obviously wasn't my lucky colour! I heard from their new chief executive, John Fry, some years later in 1999, and he invited me back to the ground as his guest. I was delighted, the silence had been deafening.

I'd been invited to go into a print business with Yeovil's keeper David Fry but I didn't really see the point, nice as Dave was. When I had spare cash I chose to do stupid things like buy rivers and lakes. I still own a few stretches to this day, to remain undisturbed for years and years to come. On my way to Yeovil's Huish Stadium, I crossed a classy trout river that always caught my eye. It was the River Yarty, a tributary of the Axe which flows through Axminster. You may recall I mentioned its lack of use earlier because of the otters. I bought two hundred and eighty-seven yards of it near Stockland and the pleasure of sitting on the old packhorse bridge, staring down at the young playful trout is immense. I visit little these days but it will remain within my family, undisturbed, forever. I also joined a salmon consortium on a river in Strathaine, Scotland, a really stupid thing to do as I love salmon and wouldn't dream of actually catching one and banging it on the bonce with a lump of tubing.

I'd formed a company with Dave Bubb called Overdubb. We tried to sell custom-made music tapes to hotels etc, selling advertising space to make the revenue. It was a brilliant idea. It still is. Tapes on British Rail with adverts, tapes in new cars with advertising space, something Volvo were very interested in. We so nearly got that one away, but we made no money and I pumped more of my own into simply paying Dave's wages and expenses without any company advancement. The company folded when I realised I was spending more time in my recording studio doing demo voice-overs than I was playing music, and that made no sense to my brain whatsoever. Dambuster Records and Overdubb were defunct, Yeovil accepted my resignation and Corporaction had continued in a solo capacity through Phil Parkes. Every business move had died on me. Hardly surprising though, I was fairly useless and quite openly admit that.

I considered buying a hotel in Torquay with some friends I'd made during my summer season there with the obvious consequences. However, I felt more confident about the Tidings project. It proved to be a right hunch for once. Digance, the crap businessman, pre Tidings, I knew would be the shortest chapter in this autobiography, and as you see, I wasn't wrong. Stand back though, the next chapter starts to explain how my business status grew beyond even my wildest dreams.

Chapter Eight

The Tidings

The fact that the Tidings, the Seven Little Wonders of the World, ever reached the attention of the public is, in itself, the eighth big wonder of the world. To have an idea whilst curled up on the settee one cold Boxing Day is one thing, to turn it into a multi-million pound industry in the world of media is another.

This is the story of how my seven little friends from the very edge of Make Believe, big cuddly Blue Bear and myself became known to the children of the world. Through rejection and failure to ridicule, you name it and we suffered it together. At times I could have crawled into those magical holes of Traveller Tiding, particularly when I faced more negative destruction than the Firemads could ever have handed out in the Forest of Lap.

If you've ever felt you had the most incredible idea in the world, and yet resigned yourself to the reality that nobody would listen, then this section of my story will prove one can win through in the end. If you felt you couldn't take on the big guns and win, then maybe this chapter will make you reload your own guns and fire again. I believed I had a possible winner but big guns scared me too. Luckily for me, I had the Seven Little Wonders of the World on my side. Perhaps it was they who tipped the scales in my favour. Through the many dark days of despair, through the endless trips down cul-de-sacs, and beyond the many doubting Thomases and shaking heads, we came through. This is how we did it. You'll see why it became my eighth wonder.

The story of the Tidings story explains how I and my friend and business partner Rod Bransgrove eventually brought success to a project that three of the four high street banks had rejected initially as a negative business proposition. Many problems reared up with alarming regularity and magnitude.

Problem one (and an almost insurmountable problem at that!)

was that no television company, merchandising outfit, publishing or reputable record company would take a flier at a concept such as the Tidings without an assurance that it already had confirmed television backing in the form of a host broadcaster or, failing that, previous transmission. No television company would commit to the project, particularly financially, without seeing the completed product, even though an animation project like the Tidings would cost a few million pounds to produce to finished quality. Problem two: How do you find investors who would pump thousands upon thousands of pounds into a children's television project that had no television ally?

The Catch 22 situation nearly scuppered the project before it ever started, but we beat the system. For three years I became more and more convinced we wouldn't. There can be little doubt that all of us dream of leaving our mark by creating something of great artistic substance. Some ambitious souls aim to write or perform a song or a best-selling novel. More ambitious types long to be stars of the silver screen, whilst others, with slightly lower horizons, wish to delve into the world of amateur dramatics or operatic societies. My dream had always been to create characters that came alive in some shape or form through my very own thoughts and ideas. Little did I really think such extreme ideas and dreams would come true for me.

For every dream there is a need to endure a thousand nightmares before it is realised. The Tidings project contained enough nightmares to keep me screaming and cold sweating forever. There were many times when I decided to sling the whole thing in and call a halt to such a banal exercise. There were times when Rod too wondered what on earth he'd got himself tangled with. But the Seven Little Wonders drove us on, more resolute than ever before. Rod saw it through with me to the television breakthrough, the only work colleague who did.

In the earliest days, I well knew I had little chance of interesting Walt Disney or Warner Brothers, and yet for some strange reason I persisted to the bitter end, and very bitter it became at times.

There were financial considerations in the early days that I found increasingly hard to resolve. Staff salaries, computer equipment and graphics, even enough recording tape to record the first Tidings songs of the project. Despite a most financially rewarding job in show business, I had suffered endless costly Tidings battles with the enemy and my funds therefore weren't quite as large as one would imagine. The bottomless pit had a bottom, and it became shallower and shallower as I paid off my freelance compatriots with what seemed alarming regularity. That aside, the Tidings had to go forward, for they were my salvation on the tempestuous sea of show business, undoubtedly the most insincere and insecure profession ever invented, as indeed I and my Seven Little Wonders of the World were to find out.

Tiny, Twig and Tremble Tiding had become my first three creations from the magical forest. None of them survived long enough to be seen on the small screen. Other prototype Tidings characters and subsidiaries never quite made it to the end of the long road either, yet I remember them all with equal affection. The Ruffs and Scruffs I particularly liked but I could find no place for them within the beautiful Forest of Lap. The final villains had to threaten the well-being of the beautiful trees of the forest, so the arsonist Firemads were inevitable, far more threatening than a gang of threadbare cabin dwellers. The Ruffs and Scruffs, the undesirable neighbours of the Seven Little Wonders, still adorn my office wall. For me, they lived for a while, and then they sadly died. It's the human side of animation.

So many happy songs and enchanting stories later, it's easier to dismiss the many disasters, refusals and disagreements that took place. The endless hours in the recording studio, the hundreds and hundreds of hours inventing, designing and then modifying such delicate characters. It ended up being, collectively, the most consuming of schemes, both in brain cells and time. With the initial concept alone, some sixty original songs were composed and recorded to demo quality, with over four hundred poems, twenty new lyrics to traditional Christmas carols, and of course the stories themselves. Incidental music and demo tapes were pouring from the studio. In two years I wrote thirty-nine Tidings adventures, the bulk equivalent of four full length novels. The greatest element within the whole project was that I loved it. I smiled through the night as they all came alive. I tapped my feet with alarming regularity as another song hit the tape machine. It offered me endless fun with characters I myself had invented. They filled me with pride. Within my brain they were real, and they were darn good company on long winter nights.

However, for long periods nobody showed any real interest in any of them. I devised Tidings for Tots books, another nine volumes in all, an album of songs relating to the disagreements between the Tidings and their environmentally unfriendly neighbours, the Ruffs and the Scruffs, who, as I say, disappeared from the project after the second year of creation.

It is still most bemusing to me that such innocent but caring creatures from a beautifully secret region of the world could ever have affected my life in such a way. To have an idea for a children's project is one thing, but dedicating nearly five years of your life to it is another. To write the story of the story is indeed an exciting project as I recall with this text the many people who were with me on the project before falling by the wayside, one by one, for various reasons, most of which were sadly related to money. It is a testimony of faith and loyalty to those such as Rod who stayed with me until the first days of success. In whatever way they set out their stalls, no matter how big or small, there is a place for them in this story. Everybody connected with the Tidings project, in some shape or form, must have contributed something to its success.

The Tidings have made me many friends since their arrival from the Forest of Lap. They have lost me friends too, although of course they didn't mean to and it certainly wasn't down to them. In their own way they have brought my own life into perspective as I created frosty brains that cared for the environment and conservation of so much. I even educated myself as I studied reference books to find ecological facts. My research confirmed that more areas and animals than we can ever imagine were in need of help. Man has destroyed and decimated mercilessly. I arrogantly but genuinely believed the Tidings could perhaps repair a slice of such wrong-doing by making small children all around the world aware of today's environmental issues and conservation hazards. It is of great relief and pride to me that I have been proven right, in a small way, as children around the world learn how to protect the planet through the songs and stories of my beloved friends from Make Believe. Behind the scenes it proved to be more a case of self preservation and belief. I had more refusals than a pit pony at a gymkhana. But I still believed, just as, deep down, we all still believe in Father Christmas.

So, in the true tradition of all children's stories ... once upon a time. This is how it all began, at the beginning, like all books and egg and spoon races. It was Christmas 1993. I spent the festive period at home in Hampshire, as I always did. The Digance family had settled down for a lazy afternoon in front of the television. Rain poured down outside and the fields around our farm were muddy, windswept and quite uninviting. My late father, Len, snoozed away in the armchair, my wife Debbie cleared away the remains of the cold turkey, jacket potatoes and homemade pickled onions, themselves a success story of their very own, I might add. My eldest daughter Polly and I stared blankly at yet another boring offering on British television. The film was a classic which I have since forgotten. The other channels offered less. Christmas 1993 had been a time for tidings of comfort and joy, the same as any other that I recalled back in Upminster, keeping goal between Uncle Harry and Auntie May's two apple trees.

I remember thinking how nice the word Tidings seemed to be. It sparked the imagination, spreading hints of happiness, somehow something magical. It also portrayed a certain amount of innocence. Good Tidings were offered on Christmas cards too. If Tidings were little creatures, I thought to myself, what wonderful little creatures they would be. As big as the biggest dream perhaps, as wondrous as the most incredible wonder, and as small as the smallest problem. No doubt about it, the Tidings would be loveable, caring things. Furry? Yes, quite possibly furry. Cuddly? Most definitely.

They entered my head one minute and departed the next. Tea had to be made and my daughters' new Christmas presents had to be explained and then played with. Rosie was still a tot, more interested in the wrapping paper than the gift inside. Oh well, many a fine pound note made in the world of gift wrap I wouldn't doubt (there, I've started already!). Our farmhouse had become awash with pens of varying persuasions. Colouring pens, felt tip pens, magic pens, not so magic pens, and my drawing pens. As a family we drew more than most. I'd become a water-colour addict and the Forest of Lap landscape was painted long before I'd invented the definitive characters who would reside within its mass of pine trees.

I'd learnt through watercolour artist Keith Fenwick how to paint snow scenes without using white paint, a small and elementary skill for most painters I cannot deny, but a monumental step for an untrained idiot with a paintbrush, which I'm afraid I was. Yes, there were many attempts at drawing the Forest of Lap. Polly and Rosie both developed an early aptitude for drawing and painting so pens were a safe bet when it came to Christmas shopping for the Digances of all ages and generations. It seemed that the only person in our family that struggled with them was myself.

That afternoon, 26th December 1993, I juggled with the new creatures of my imagination. By evening, when I took on my father at yet another game of snooker, I cared little about potting reds and blacks, and more about my new found friends of fantasy.

We always played the best of three frames. My dad, at well over

eighty years of age, would have had enough by then. Formerly a
marvellous snooker player, he found difficulty in bending his ageing
body over the table until his chin touched the cue. It turned out to
be the very last Christmas spent with my father. I think I knew that
in a strange way. We played hour after hour after hour, talking about
old days in the East End of London. Our snooker parallelled our
corresponding lives. Our breaks were small and I cherished the odd
occasion when I was able to sit in a chair for a few minutes and
picture the earliest of Tidings designs through the sighs of nostalgia.
I popped to the bathroom and noted down a few early ideas for fear
of forgetting them later.

A synopsis of a new novel is sufficient to sway a book publisher,
two pages of descriptive text can assure a commitment for an
established author. I wasn't an established author and this was no
new novel. A demo tape can often prove, to a high flying record
company, that one has composed the new number one. I had no
track record as a successful recording artist either. With an entire
project, ranging from television, video, audio and additional
merchandising products, it was another baptism of fire. Were I
writing a standard comedy script for my former TV company,
London Weekend Television, a few paragraphs would have sufficed to
seal a new television special. I wrote my usual first draft brief in long-
hand as I tend to do, and felt rather pleased with my brainwave. The
Tidings concept consisted of some characters, some pine trees, and
a national competition which would put them on the map. I left my
foolscap pad in the bathroom and finished off the snooker
tournament with my dad.

Late that night I rang my tour manager and confidant Dave Bubb
at his home near Braintree in Essex. Dave spent most of his days
listening to my far-fetched ideas and as I wasn't seeing him until my
next public appearance at a fundraising night for the RSPCA in the
East End of London on 10th January, I called a meeting for the next
day. To avoid disturbing the festivities and the holiday atmosphere at
home I decided we should meet at my London Docklands flat where
most of my constructive ideas were dealt with at that time.

By the time I had driven from my family home in Hampshire to
my flat in Undine Road in my native East End, I had a fair idea what
these little things looked like, and more to the point, what they did.
They'd changed beyond recognition by the time they appeared on
Cartoon Network on 4th January 1999 but I wasn't to know that.
Being Christmas, and remember this started out as a Christmas

project, they would have to come from Lapland, the home of our jovial friend with the white beard, fat tummy and red costume. If not Lapland itself it would be somewhere nearby. But Lapland is real, Father Christmas is real. Stories tell that the great man of folklore once wore a green smock and brown cloak. By all accounts he didn't become red-suited until a famous drink company stepped in with an early form of sponsorship in the 1930s.

So the Tidings lived on the edge of reality and fiction. I imagined such a place and named it the Very Edge of Make Believe, resembling the Scandinavian wonderland of pine trees coated in winter snowflakes, like icing sugar on a birthday cake. Beyond the border of Lapland, towards a land that no-one had ever heard of, let alone travelled to, I claimed a large fictional forest as my very own. This magical kingdom I named the Forest of Lap. You couldn't be much closer to Lapland than that.

The early rough sketches I had made of the Tidings made them look somewhat Nordic, to the extent of perhaps sporting Viking helmets or shields. Dave Bubb would tell me if my ideas were sound. Dave Bubb always did. He was waiting at my flat when I arrived.

It was a crisp day and many families were walking around the area by my London flat known as Clipper's Quay. In years distant the old tea clippers moored up there after their perilous trips from the Indies. The old chimney that sent the smoke of burnt tea chests skyward, still stood proud and erect as a further symbol of bygone days.

Little children clutched new toys and parents wrapped themselves in new scarves and hats. I stared at the toys, thinking perhaps one day they would be taking plush Tidings characters for strolls around the defunct dockyards. If only they knew. I'd had many an idea for a children's project on other occasions, this one had to be something special to raise the eyebrows of a work-mate who'd heard it all before. I had a gut feeling and this time it certainly wasn't a reaction to the homemade pickled onions the previous day. Dave would go for this one.

We sat at a table overlooking the London Marina, drinking tea and coffee, discussing our respective Christmases. It had gone well for both of us and our families. I told Dave he could be in for a busy time if this new idea happened in any shape or form. He made another cup of black coffee with no milk or sugar, an almost pointless beverage I had often surmised, as he became more deeply engrossed in my project. I retained Dave's attention for a considerable time, a proud moment for me. OK, I soon realised the early Tidings looked like the hairy Gonks so popular in the early 1960s. I also realised many others had tried to think up the next Christmas bonanza scheme with little success, but through all the negatives, the positives still outweighed all thoughts of failure. Somebody thought up My Little Pony, someone invented the Ghostbusters and of course the Tellytubbies. Someone had convinced someone else about the impending success of the Simpsons. I had invented the Tidings. They needed developing, but so did the best photographs.

The Tidings weren't Gonks at all. Well, not for long anyway. That became my first amendment. By the end of 27th December, they were foresters from Lap, on the Very Edge of Make Believe; their actual job descriptions of Lumberjacks and Lumberjills were to come to me much later. What did they look like? How did they get around? Nobody knew, for nobody had ever seen them. Their Nordic helmets and shields had disappeared. I wanted non-aggressive, caring creatures. The word used throughout the project was 'soft'. It had to be soft.

Cartoon trends seem to form in the United States and there was a country sick to death of violence and child rage. Soft was the word that echoed across the Atlantic.

They could be whatever I wanted them to be, and behave in whatever manner I wished them to behave in, but with an abundance of softness. The world had tolerated bellyfuls of aggression with various other space age technological projects and cartoon characters, nasty video and computer games that sent shivers down young spines. The time seemed right for a more caring community such as the Tidings to capture the hearts and imaginations of all the children around the world. America was probably ripe for a change. They simply had to be soft. To develop them exactly how I wished gave me an immense feeling of power and control.

Within a few days I had lodged my early thoughts and drawings with Richard Robson, a solicitor in Jewry Street, Winchester. They were signed, sealed and witnessed, and although hardly concrete evidence in the Crown Court, they were a comfort factor to me. As a secondary precaution I lodged more drawings with Kevin Anderson, the manager of NatWest Bank in Welwyn Garden City. Such sealed documents were the basic form of copyright so it seemed the right move to make with a minimum of expense. They remain sealed to this day, although our copyright procedures are somewhat more complex these days. I'm sure it would be interesting to tear open those brown envelopes all these years on. They would make naïve but interesting reading I'm sure, but they will stay forever locked away in the vaults of Robson's office and Anderson's bank.

It all seems so trivial as we discuss Rod Bransgrove's input later in the story. A man who spent sleepless nights ensuring the Tidings concept wouldn't come to any legal harm. The man who later made available the many thousands of pounds we invested in lawyers and copywriters, and there was I, early days, shoving it all in a registered envelope and lodging it down the road for safe keeping. During the Christmas of 1993, I'd never even heard of Rod Bransgrove. He lived a million trillion miles from me, just down the road in Andover.

Dave Bubb agreed I had a winner on my hands. I admit I shared a similar gut feeling. It's quite ironic that seven such loveable little balls of fur could lead me down so many roads of heartache and rejection. But that's exactly what the Seven Little Wonders of the World did. Yet they will remain my best friends for ever and ever.

So what did the Tidings do? Why were they of any significance to the children from all lands? Without even realising at the time that not all children on the planet celebrated Christmas, the Tidings began as yet another Christmas arrival. My enthusiasm couldn't be dampened by religious beliefs or disbelief. I'd seen the massive success of the Snowman in previous years and really thought I could emulate that. The Tidings planted and grew the one real Christmas tree from which Father Christmas would carve his sleigh. Of course, his sleigh had to be lighter than air to carry him and his reindeer over the rooftops of the world to the many girls and boys on such a special day. All believers knew that, but where did that special wood come from? The Tidings nursed that tree through the seasons of the year until the time came to take a top piece and let the carpenters hammer and chisel away. The remainder of the tree would be regrown the following year, and only the Tidings knew of the magical ingredients that made for such a spectacular mode of travel. That's what the Tidings did. That's why they were of such huge significance to the children of the world.

I drew the first draft Nordics very roughly; they were intended to be quite smart but my artistic talents let me down, so Dave Bubb suggested we find a local artist within the area of London's

Docklands who could be commissioned to draw my characters as and when I created them. The costing of such initial artworks was downright prohibitive. I've never understood how artists can look so down on their luck and command the sort of money quoted to me to draw my creations. Plus the demands made upon the writer, keeping the rights on top, plus a percentage commission on all future merchandise and subsidary product. The two artists we approached were never contacted again and I endeavoured to find my own artistic channels to put my ideas onto paper.

I contacted an old friend of mine, Mike Payne. He visited me at my home in the New Forest, from Angmering in West Sussex. He'd become an artist of great repute since appearing on my television show as a tax inspector with the unusual hobby, certainly for such an undesirable, of art. Mike was one of the finest cartoonists in the land. I'd worked with him on many occasions, on a previous children's project 'The Cloud Crowd', the redesigned characters of which were later to be incorporated themselves into the Tidings project and beyond within the catalogue of SKD Media plc, appearing for the first time in 'Traveller Takes a Trip'. We linked up on various television programmes for London Weekend Television, and additionally for a Sussex-based greetings card company, Carte Blanche. Mike worked under the name of Miranda and was unquestionably one of the most successful card artists in Britain too. He created that bear covered in patches.

Steve Haines, the managing director of Carte Blanche, invited me to write copy for Mike's artworks, a job I thoroughly enjoyed. We enjoyed an empathy rarely shared between two people from conflicting areas of creativity. Indeed, when I invented the Cloud Crowd for one of my television shows, I worked extensively with Mike on their designs, eventually inviting him to become a director of the Cloud Crowd Company Ltd., which he accepted. We worked together on the project for two and a half years until we were forced to admit defeat with Cloud Crowd debts of £7,000 and no promises on the horizon.

It's strange to me that these costs were run up to pay those allies on our side in times of difficulty, but business is business and quite rightly so. Our London solicitor, David Landsman, with his office just a pigeon's dump from Trafalgar Square, and our accountant, Robert Symons, were the only two people ever to make money from my first children's project. One looked after the money and the other set up the deal on how the money should be paid, and they were the only two who got anything out of it. Robert is still my personal accountant to this day and has fended off endless visits from Mike Payne's former workmates at the Revenue on my behalf, so I can't complain. When the company closed, however, Mike relinquished his rights as a goodwill gesture to me, and the Cloud stories gathered dust around their silver linings for many years.

The only other person who had shown any interest in my project was Jazz Summers, my former manager mentioned in earlier pages. He was a good mate and wanted to assist so much with my dream, but like so many hugely successful businessmen he had little time, even to spend in Great Britain it turned out, thanks once again to the Inland Revenue.

The first ever Tiding, its appearance a million miles from the friendly creatures that abound in the Forest of Lap today, sported a metal Viking's helmet, had a big nose and a black moustache, thus resembling some crazed Mexican in a Western film. He was armed with a vicious looking axe and actually looked more like a World Cup football supporter than a caring friend of the children around the world. Mike Payne would normally have been in a position to give me all the time in the world – he had certainly done so many times in the past for little remuneration – but his drawings, and consequently his time, were in incredible demand so on this occasion he couldn't help and I was on my own. His work load at Carte Blanche had developed into quite phenomenal proportions and I relayed my gratitude even for the short time he uncovered his felt tip pens as a favour to me, well knowing his commitments allowed him no more gratis time.

When Mike told me he had not the time to keep updating my amended Tidings, I understood perfectly and as thanks for his time, I presented him with a signed Tottenham Hotspur football and a ticket to watch England play the Cameroons at Wembley. The screwed up Mexican thug wasn't right and he lived his last days in my waste paper basket alongside various other screwed up objects, like Metropolitan Police parking tickets and offers of barbecues from the Docklands Residents Association.

By January 1994, the end of the first year, Dave Bubb was working more or less extensively on the Tidings. He was on my payroll and had very little else to do as I wasn't touring until the spring, and it was he who introduced me to a young artist in Chelmsford, Erika

Platt. I knew it would always be hard to present children's stories in
script form only. I knew children loved pictures, and publishers knew
that too. Any classy potential presentation would need visuals. Suffice
to say at that time I knew little about presentation either. I didn't
realise the importance of a style bible or a presentation document. I
just wrote the stories and hoped. I'd never made it to the next step so
I never knew what the next step entailed.

I did know that we needed to add colourful drawings to bring my
gang to life. I met Erika at the Brentwood Post House, and over a
couple of lagers, she presented her most impressive portfolio. She
listened to my ideas and with Erika's skills the Tidings became softer,
more loveable characters, though they still resembled Nordic freaks.
We exchanged endless phone calls and finally met up again at Palms
Night Club in Hornchurch, Essex. We decided to brainstorm until
we had some semblance of originality in the characters. It was whilst
sitting in the corner of this noisy location on the main Southend
Arterial Road, drinking from a large pot of tea, I saw the vision of a
circular furry friend not unlike planet Earth. Still not quite right or
definitive, but the idea took me further down my eventual trail. On
8th January, Dave drew me a large scale map upon which I added
various landmarks such as the Deer, Nose and Throat Hospital and
other references to Christmas, as at this time the Tidings still seemed
destined to be a Yuletide project and nothing more. He delivered the
rough artwork to Erika and she intricately drew the first ever Forest
of Lap, on the Edge of Make Believe. Once again I lodged my new
designs with my solicitor in Winchester.

By the end of the first phase of Tidings development I had already
invested many thousands of pounds in artworks, additional storylines
and monthly wages to Dave. On Saturday 15th January, I did a
cabaret at the Whitbread Brewery Rooms for Renault Motorsport
Awards. I momentarily forgot about the Tidings as I performed to an
audience which included Damon Hill and the legendary Ayrton
Senna. As I drove home an idea entered my head and on the Sunday
morning I rang a business associate from NatWest Bank in London,
Steve Austin.

I had met Steve at a NatWest training event for which, once again,
I was booked to perform the cabaret, and we'd kept in touch.
Strangely, he lived in Chelmsford, just down the road from Erika. He
seemed to be a big player and I thought he could advise me on where
to go with my newly formed Christmas Tidings competition. I

explained my idea over the phone in the hope of securing financial involvement of some description from NatWest head office. He listened with great interest. The Tidings grew and cared for the one and only real magic tree from which Father Christmas would construct his sleigh each year. What if they planted such a tree in this country, and the public had to find it by means of a grid referenced map? What if under the tree was planted a treasure? This led on to Treasured accounts. I devised the 'The Account That Will Not Cost The Earth'.

Steve appeared much impressed by the treasure hunt, and felt NatWest may well be interested in my additional ideas of banking schemes for young savers. The paying-in books which when used left the pages of a beautiful children's story. The Golden Treasure account – after all, the NatWest piggies had been most successful and had become serious collector's items. Perhaps Tidings treasure chests would become equally desirable one day.

Steve Austin visited the farm with his very attractive girlfriend Lisa, and after several hours of deep and constructive conversation, with me trying to avert my gaze from his attractive partner, we washed down a Chinese with a few bottles of the finest red whilst deciding upon the next step, which I seem to recall was another bottle of red.

Steve Austin had a friend and associate named John Walters, an accountant and insolvency practitioner who lived in Ditchling, West Sussex. Walters, I was assured by Steve, had assisted the record producer Pete Waterman, producer of Kylie Minogue and Jason Donovan, in the purchasing of the much loved steam locomotive, the Flying Scotsman. He was an individual well versed in show business and music publishing jargon, and Steve suggested the three of us meet up at NatWest's plush London offices in Bishopsgate. He assured me that Walters was the right man for the job. At that meeting it was provisionally agreed that Walters, Steve Austin and I would become directors of the recently formed Tidings Trading Company Limited. Although agreed at a meeting, the directorships were not issued at this time.

I caught the rush-hour train from Waterloo, and as it rattled through the sleepy Hampshire towns towards Romsey, I put the finishing touches to the Tidings Christmas competition, well believing that we had the endorsement and blessing of National Westminster Bank. Why not? We'd used their shiny table upon which much smaller and less significant issues such as personal overdrafts had been settled.

That night I decided on the definitive rulings for the treasure hunt, and decided either that night or the next morning to run the idea, for the first time, by Bob Voice. I always had a few dozen innovative ideas on the go every week so I seldom bothered Bob with all of them, mainly because most of them turned out to be rubbish. Besides, he was a busy man, as I mentioned earlier, caring for the careers of Hale and Pace and Brian Conley as well as myself. Brian had worked hard on the Jolson musical which he was later to appear in around the world, and Gareth Hale and Norman Pace were a far more successful act than myself. I accepted all that and at times kept my distance from the busy offices of International Artists so as not to become a nuisance to them. The office mood had changed considerably from the days when Jim and I would sit in Laurie's office cracking jokes about rancid chickens and Lindisfarne songs.

The next day I was working at the Silver Skillet Night Club in Maidenhead and as I needed to speak to Bob regarding get-in times and so on, it seemed the perfect opportunity to let him know about the Tidings too.

As I read the brief presentation document on the phone Bob agreed it was one of the greatest ideas I had ever dreamed up and he immediately fixed me an appointment with Mike Leggo at BBC Television Centre. I had met Mr Leggo when he worked on the TV show 'Noel Edmonds' House Party'. I had the dubious privilege of being Mister Blobby's football manager when he played for Crinkley Bottom Wanderers and we all worked well together both in rehearsals and during the live transmission. So I oozed confidence as I entered the forbidding glass doors that led to the reception area of BBC Television Centre in London's Shepherd's Bush. I wore a suit, a rare occurrence. I meant business. It was 27th January 1994, the appointment had been moved from 2pm to 11.30am. I flew down on the shuttle from Edinburgh where I had been filming 'Win, Lose or Draw' with Shane Ritchie at the Gateway Studios. I agreed to meet Bob Voice in the foyer at 11am and felt rather on edge when he hadn't arrived by our proposed time of meet with Mike Leggo. I nervously left the foyer and walked down to the commissioner's hut by the famous red and white striped barrier, so often seen on 'Blue Peter'. I looked down the long road that led to Shepherd's Bush. I needed to pop to the toilet and so returned to reception. As I did so, Bob alighted from a lift – he had already been with Mike Leggo for some time previous, which totally confused me – and together we made our way to the inner veins of our wonderful entertainment institution.

Mike's office resembled a luxury suite in a hotel, with an anteroom containing comfortable sofas and a table bearing trade magazines. Bob wore jeans and white shirt – nothing wrong with that, we both usually did for such meetings – Mike wore corduroy trousers and a jumper. I felt hugely overdressed in my double-breasted suit with the velvet collar and ticket pocket. My tie marked the benefit year of Hampshire cricketer Chris Smith, a mutual friend of Bob and myself. It was the only tie I owned at the time. It was my friend Paul Terry's year by this time, so at least I knew a new tie was on the way.

I felt silly, but overcame my embarrassment as I unveiled my glorious Tidings to the man who could have introduced them to the great British public there and then, Mike Leggo. Their own television show would have been most welcome, an insert into an existing show would have been considered an achievement too. They could appear on our screens during the build-up to Christmas. Where, oh where, could the one real magic tree be buried? If you have any idea then ring this number etc. etc. Interactive television at its most original, I thought. He seemed interested enough and I felt confident when I left the building. Bob stayed on to discuss other things with Mike and I walked the long road down to the tube station on my own. (I was really looking for a cab but as none came, I refer to it as a walk!)

The next seven days were to encompass some of the greatest lows of my life, causing a depression from which I never thought the little Tidings or myself would ever recover. Those January days of 1994 were cold and forbidding. Everything had been going along nicely, people had smiled at my creations, yet suddenly I and the creatures from the Forest of Lap were divorced from the real world. They lived on the Very Edge of Make Believe and it seemed they were destined to stay there, in blissful anonymity. Leggo hadn't responded. I felt uncertain but even so, mildly confident.

I had become increasingly aware that my synopsis had proven to be insufficient and I worked each evening expanding the characters and their particular functions. Various early Tidings were to fall by the wayside. Tiny and Twig, the little brother and sister, stayed for a while, but Trapper Tiding was the first to go. He worked on releasing poor animals from wicked, painful traps in the forest, until I realised that nobody in the Forest of Lap would be of a mind to trap the poor animals in the snares in the first place. Strange thing, a land of make believe, it's everything you want it to be, and as you plan its very being, you realise the cruelty of the real world in which we live. There was absolutely no need for Trapper Tiding, and neither could I defend Temper Tiding as Tidings would never be renowned for their bad tempers. Still no news, but that was good news we were all told, yes?

As my expectations of a deal with the BBC flourished, I worked hard in creating the first stories of the campaign. I dedicated equal time to the radio series, full knowing I was well respected in that field. If television climbed on board, radio would follow as a matter of course. The weekend passed graciously enough, performing at West Ham United Supporters' Club on Saturday 29th. We bought a guide dog called Tonka with the admission money. It was named after our Scottish international full back and captain of the time, Ray Stewart. After the show I took some friends back to my flat in Undine Road, where it had all begun some weeks previously. We sat around, Angie and Steve Jeffs, some friends from Great Yarmouth, my merchandise seller Jane Perham and her sister Sarah from Lyme Regis, Dave Bubb and myself. We chatted into the night about the Tidings as I convinced both them and myself that it was a foregone conclusion the project would be bigger than *Jungle Book* or any other successful epic of immense proportions.

Orange lights lit the London Marina, the Canary Wharf building overshadowed all like the space shuttle ready for lift-off, a most incredible night sight. The streetlights, through the French windows of the balcony, faintly illuminated the various Tidings drawings and scripts littering the windowsills and tables in my flat. It felt spooky, almost as hesitant as the astronaut's wait in that big silver machine. Something seemed about to be born.

London is a forbidding place at night. It is stark, monstrous and impersonal, a strange base from which to develop the friendly Tidings characters.

February arrived, as cold and chilling as the Forest of Lap itself. Maybe everyone's footprints were blue like our bear, I can't remember! On Tuesday 1st, I called Bob Voice from the St Mary Newington Church Hall, near the Kennington Oval, where I was bogged down in rehearsal for my new play 'Sex, Spangles and Sensible Shoes'. Producer Derek Killeen was overseeing a script run with Michael Melia, formerly Eddie Royal of 'Eastenders'. As the writer I chose not to become involved with the direction and so left the two seasoned professionals to their business. I chose to watch and hopefully learn about theatre production. I found it all interesting but my mind kept diverting to the Forest of Lap.

Mike Leggo was obviously wandering around the hallowed halls with my presentation document under his arm, interesting all and sundry. The previous day, the Monday, I had expected to be offered a Tidings TV show, just like the Muppets, together with a knighthood and the Freedom of the City of London for my new creations, but had heard nothing. I froze as Bob told me the outcome. The British Broadcasting Corporation had passed. They weren't interested. It was as though bereavement had occurred, and in a strange way, I suppose it had.

In almost the words of Don McLean, it was the day the Tidings died.

My guts twisted and spasm pains shot from left to right. When such a rejection occurs, other rejections follow like ripples on a rain puddle. I felt stripped of all allies. If the BBC weren't interested, then what was the point of carrying on. It had knocked the stuffing out of everyone, not least of all myself. The bubble had to burst and it did. The Tidings were dead! It made rehearsals difficult as I stared with glazed expression at my conscientious cast, putting my written words to the test. My phone conversation with Bob lasted no longer than five or ten minutes, but its aftermath lingered for hours. I just couldn't believe it. The Tidings, dead?? Maybe so, but not buried! Long live the Tidings! I never really bothered Bob with the project again. In fact, we never spoke about it again until he came along to my fiftieth birthday party some five years later.

The Tidings had come and gone. Besides, I had a play I had written and its promotion needed all my attentions for a couple of weeks. It opened on 14th February at the Key Theatre in Peterborough and I had to make myself available for interviews and personal appearances. The production, well received by both public and press, turned out to be a godsend, taking my mind off my huge disappointment. With the exception of a little songwriting nothing happened with the Tidings project until 22nd February, when it was back to the first floor of NatWest House in London for a meeting with Steve Austin and a guy named Mark Mayhew. I still pinned my hopes on a NatWest involvement and I felt excited, perhaps desperate to get things on a roll again. Mayhew was an hour late, promised us twenty minutes of his valuable time, he waxed lyrical about my project and then left with his left ear glued to a mobile phone.

I never heard from Mark Mayhew again. I wasn't sure what he did, or who he was, and I am to this day none the wiser. He wrote down 'The account that will not cost the earth' when I mentioned it, but other than that reacted little. I left the meeting in Broadgate to rendezvous with *Sun* television journalist Garry Bushell at Foyles bookshop in the Charing Cross Road. We made off for a guitar shop and played some guitars. Nice guy Garry, loves his old music hall songs and is quite an authority. Over a coffee we sat down and put together an interview for the *Sun* newspaper. When he asked of my future plans I felt inclined to reveal my Tidings to the unsuspecting public, but they still weren't really going anywhere so I declined at the last moment.

For a few days I tried little stories out on my daughter and she'd smiled sweetly as she entered the land of zz's, but my only response elsewhere was that many had worked on ideas for children and it had to be the most swamped market in the media industry. Everybody told me that. Incessantly, and they were probably right, but Polly, Rosie later on, and I thought otherwise. There's not a huge chance of winning the National Lottery, but it doesn't stop any of us having a bash, does it? I happened to vehemently believe in what I'd created and for me that was the clearance of the first hurdle.

I was probably right, however, not to confide in members of our national press at such an early stage of the proceedings. Polly and Rosie were delighted that Trapper Tiding had been removed from the plot. Stories involving animal discomfort were not welcome in our Hampshire home surrounded by foxes, badgers and moles. Even the pheasants knew our land acted as a safe house as the shotgun pellets, echoing in the distance, flew through the air each Sunday morning. Goodbye Trapper Tiding, retire in peace. Temper Tiding was surprisingly not annoyed at being dropped either. It had been nice creating him but even nicer scratching through his character reference with a felt tip pen. Goodbye Temper Tiding too.

The next day, 23rd February, I was filming for Anglia Television at the Gordon Craig Theatre in Stevenage. Again a media journalist asked what the future held, what I was working on, and again the Tidings missed out on a mention. I was kicking myself at losing out on all these golden opportunities. What if a big producer was sitting having his tea whilst watching the telly? Tidings? They sound interesting. Think I'll put a few million into them. Oh, if only.

I realised then that an injection of good luck and hard work was critical or my creations would be dead and buried forever. Most creators would give their right arm to plug their project on television. Twice in two days I'd had the opportunity and twice in two days I declined. It had become obvious my heartfelt emotions were disintegrating. Surely someone, somewhere, believed as I believed. Fortunately, Steve Austin did. We spoke on the phone sometimes five or six times a day. He quizzed the people at McDonalds and Wimpy. Steve believed as much as I believed. But the doors just wouldn't open for him. As I drove home from Stevenage, down the A1M, the theme tune came to me. I'd been trying to spell the Tidings word in the opening song, but it was easier for youngsters to just sing:

We're the Tidings,
We're the Tidings.
The Seven Little Wonders of the World.

I must have sung the tune to myself a hundred times. That evening I went into my recording studio at home and put down the first Tidings track before it left my brain, as tunes have a tendency to do. Once more the Forest of Lap bubbled with life. That's how it was at that time. Sometimes I found it all so enchanting, at other times, downright frustrating. The 23rd was enchanting, and the next day just happened to be my birthday. With the birthday cards arrived Erika's redrawing of the Forest of Lap. It was brilliant and again my hopes rose.

My wife Debbie, comedian Mike Osman, and two friends, Pete and Yvonne Brown from Woolston, met up for a celebration at Stanley's Casino in Southampton. Mike, a long standing friend from our days together at Her Majesty's Theatre and the Piccadilly Theatre, listened enthusiastically as I gave a progress report. The project had set me back a serious amount of money but it still remained my hobby and all pastimes cost money. You try and buy a Penny Black for twopence! Anyway, we cut my birthday cake, sang our hearts out and I got pissed. Jim Davidson joined us later. Another year older and deeper in debt. There wasn't a bank in the land interested in lending money at this stage of the project.

Saturday 27th February, it was back to London Weekend Television for the filming of 'An Audience With Bob Monkhouse'. A limousine collected me, making me feel important. Bob Voice was there. We'd hardly spoken since the fateful meeting at the BBC. I sensed a successful business relationship spanning a decade was drawing to a close, and if I ever needed confirmation, my cold welcome at the television studios that night was it. Bob and I had been best of friends for ages, we'd fished and played golf together, we'd more or less lived our lives, and built our dreams, together. I can't recall what went wrong, but that night was confirmation that something had.

I spent the evening talking to my pal Garry Bushell again, and for me it was also a reunion with comedian Bobby Davro; we'd been at TVS together before both being 'transferred' to London Weekend Television with the aforementioned John Kaye Cooper. On a personal, non-professional basis I began to reveal the plot to Bushell. Garry, a writer himself, found the whole Tidings concept of interest, and as I explained the format, I felt excited once again myself. There was a bit of a buzz again.

Because my own television shows were filmed on location I wasn't to return to the London Weekend Television studio until 28th June 1999, when I filmed a show 'The Big Stage' for Channel Five. It was by this time the London Studios and it felt weird, chatting to Cannon and Ball and feeling a complete stranger to the television industry at performance level. I chose to do the show because the presenter, Bradley Walsh, was a big mate and I was a big fan. For me, he is the funniest comedian in Britain. He is a nutter and very likeable as a bloke too. The producer was my old producer, Mark Robson, the lighting director was my old lighting director, Brian Pearce, and the script associate was my old radio script associate, Charlie Adams. Time had passed on and it was all confirmation of my decision to leave the sharp end of the business, in front of the camera.

To keep my mental ball rolling at the time I composed two more songs, 'The Tidings Anthem' and 'Christmas Tidings'. Neither were to feature in the finished project, although I kept the title of the latter. It took me two days to record demos of them in my studio with additional vocals from my daughter Polly and her friend Lauren Birchall. I used all the tracks, trying to give an example of how such simple children's songs could be effective with a lavish and sophisticated production, something that our musical arranger Chris Winter was to confirm later when we made the final recordings of the first collection of songs. There were acoustic guitars strumming away, keyboards, percussion, including the statutory sleigh bells, and various other stringed instruments. It sounded bloody impressive, even if I say so myself. And just the three of us in my home studio. I did the necessary paperwork and registered the songs with both the Performing Right Society and the Mechanical Copyright Protection Society through my own publishing company, Pollysongs Music Limited. I knew many months of composing lay before me, it was with great relief I'd kicked the project back into life.

Within eighteen months I'd composed and recorded forty-eight Tidings songs in all. Recording costs alone would have amounted to a serious investment, exceeding fifty or sixty thousand pounds, had I used an independent recording facility. My own studio and the knowledge I had gained at Capital Radio as a radio producer were both invaluable items and an integral part of keeping the financial aspect of the Tidings project sensible. I played all the instruments, and the girls and I laid down the Tidings vocals between us. It was immense fun, and once again I believed in what I had created. In the later words of Sunny Tiding, was there anybody out there? Harking back on those sessions, take heed of this warning if you should ever enter the same market place. Make sure you record instrumental versions of all your songs in preparation for international sales. You can save yourself about three years of haggling and endless clause clipping in contracts.

Up and down on the helter skelter of life. Steve Haines, the managing director of Carte Blanche greetings cards, whom I mentioned earlier, visited my house on 2nd March. It was a sunny day and we chatted in the conservatory. I showed him art designs for cards and my initial storylines over a couple of cans of lager. I knew Steve could do nothing, merchandise wise, until the product had established itself, but I hadn't been given a no. It was Catch 22 all over again, and yet not quite. Steve firmly believed there was a future for the furry characters, and assured me of any assistance, should it be required. I never heard from Steve Haines again. March turned out to be a strange time in the life of the Tidings and their creator. Dave Bubb had left my employment, a sad loss as Dave had worked on and off with me for ten years. We'd shared many failures together.

Martin Butler, who rented the second bedroom in my London flat, moved his business from London to Manchester, so he too flew the Undine Road nest. The Tidings' very first office was no more. The windowsills where my furry friends paraded in the orange light of the Marina were empty. That showcase for my earliest creations was no

longer mine. I wonder if the present inhabitants know the importance
of their windowsills? The value of their former sitting tenants? One
step forward and two back, the Forest of Lap disappeared further into
the world of Make Believe. Perhaps it belonged there after all, never
to be disturbed by the likes of me. A sad time.

I left for Austria with my new tour manager, Mark Holmes, on a
five day corporate trip for Ford Motor Company. I don't recall the
exact venue but there was plenty of snow and it was very bumpy,
answers on a postcard please! Feeling as I did, I suppose under
normal circumstances I would have stayed on a few extra days to get
my head together but a very important duty called at the Royal
Lancaster Hotel in London on the Saturday, 19th March. Tony Gale
had his testimonial dinner, and I was guest of honour. Debbie and I
sat at the top table and all my claret and blue heroes were dotted
around the ballroom. My speech was greeted with a standing ovation
and I felt a million dollars in front of my heroes. I had a few beers
with Ian Bishop, another great guy, and David Burrows who went to
Everton, and prepared myself to go home the next morning in a state
of alcoholic disrepair.

Steve Austin and John Walters had gatecrashed Tony's dinner to
tell me the speaker at the function they were attending,
coincidentally just down the road, hadn't shown. Would I speak? For
the sake of the Tidings I had little choice, but I felt used. They were
standing either side of me at the top table, in full view of Tony's
guests. I felt mortifyingly embarrassed. Debbie was rightly furious
when I disappeared for over an hour and a half to perform at some
rich guy's birthday whom I never even knew. I questioned the actions
of Steve Austin and John Walters that night, to say nothing of my
own, but funnily enough, when we met again on the 30th in
Broadgate, the evening wasn't even mentioned. Debbie had an
insight into their characters that night. I had been used. I apologised
to Tony Gale by phone.

Next day, back to London for an appearance on Cilla Black's 'Surprise
Surprise'. I sat backstage with the Bee Gees. They never spoke or
nodded to me and vice versa. The place was packed with personal
roadies, personal assistants and any others who could be personal. I
was a big Bee Gees fan, still am.

When I was small
And Christmas trees were tall.

Brilliant words. Simple in the extreme.

I decided to stay over in town for the night and so I checked into the Tower Hotel, by Tower Bridge. It gave me a few hours to myself in a hotel room, a chance to spend some solitary quality writing hours with my Tidings stories. I rewrote the competition rules once again. I'd gone through it a hundred times in my brain. I decided the one and only real magic Christmas tree would be planted in Nottingham. It seemed as good a place as any, after all, Sherwood Forest was a damn big place, a world famous location, and the options were plentiful. The Bee Gees' song with a lyric about Christmas trees being tall when they were small, rang again and again through my head, subconsciously convincing me a Christmas single was one way of breaking the Catch 22 situation. Shame they never spoke or nodded to me. Susan George, the internationally renowned actress and I very nearly went to record in their studio in Florida but various things got in the way and it never happened. There was a time, with Susan's input, it looked like heavyweights like the Bee Gees may well have become interested in my project. But no! Not quite!

A record would create interest in my project, even if it were simply a media hit, a media hit being a song that doesn't particularly sell well, but is played often on the radio stations. To that end, Jazz Summers accepted my invitation to meet up with Walters and Austin. He took the trouble to fly in from his home in the South of France just to do so. Austin and Walters complained about his lateness. I felt an abruptness I'd never felt before and it brought on uneasiness. The whole Tony Gale fiasco was ringing in my head once more. Debbie had been right all along. Attitude problems were on the rise. They thought he wouldn't turn up at all, but I knew Jazz wouldn't let me down, we'd been through too much together during our show business apprenticeships. I also knew, even with the power afforded him by the success of George Michael and Andrew Ridgley, he could do very little about the timetables of Air France. We were joined at the meeting by Lady Alexander, wife of the NatWest boss, who smiled appreciatively at the little characters spread out before her on the highly polished table. My Tidings and I were starting to feel rather important. Perhaps NatWest were about to take a punt. Did they bollocks. Maybe the treasure hunt would occur at Christmas 1994. Would it bollocks.

I was impressed with John Walters' organisational qualities. He had books for this and files for that. He told lots of jokes and appeared a most jovial character. I choose not to discredit any personalities who at some time or other believed in what I believed in regarding the success of the Tidings venture. Walters and his later behaviour could easily be an exception to this, but he worked hard for so many months in helping my project reach fruition. His wheels fell off somewhere down the track. Not so much a derailment, more a head-on crash.

Steve Austin and Lisa visited the farm again on 2nd March. Debbie cooked dinner as Steve broke the news to me that NatWest weren't interested in coming on board with the Tidings after all. A feeling of shock is an understatement. First the BBC and now NatWest. My two big players on whom I'd pinned so much hope had opted out. We had spoken of hundreds of thousands of pounds of capital investment for creative development, Steve himself mentioned four hundred thousand, and suddenly, the big zero. Ever been there? For me it was a kick in the proverbials number five. I couldn't eat. I was a dreadful host.

I thought my presentation to Mayhew and his sidekick had been exemplary. I had obviously been proven wrong. I certainly now knew whoever Mayhew was, he was a more important chap than I had envisaged or given him credit for. I had his business card pinned to my notice board until the typing of this paragraph. Rod Bransgrove once described banks to me as places that lent money to those who didn't need it. How right!

The next morning I felt empty inside, and it wasn't simply because I hadn't eaten. That gut feeling when Rosie Smith and Sandy Mogford packed me up came back to haunt me. That feeling of loneliness when Nadine Tronion buggered off back to Belgium with not so much as a farewell, had returned. The moment when I realised I'd never asked Christine Lawrence out, let alone asked her to marry me. All those dreadful butterflies had returned to kick dance their way around my stomach. I was appearing at the Mayflower Theatre, Southampton, with Jim Davidson and Bucks Fizz and so once again I was able to throw myself into my work and momentarily forget about yet another catastrophic disappointment. Jim, Mike Osman and myself went to Stanley's Casino, scene of my previous birthday party. These two friends were always great company and I needed cheering up after such a setback. I cannot remember how much we lost between us but it didn't really matter. I'd lost substantially more that weekend. A whole bloody forest.

On 13th April 1994, I did a live interview with Pat Marsh on BBC Radio Kent. His researcher Della Mason had briefed me before we went on air, warning me that Pat would ask what I had coming up in future and so therefore to have some answers ready. This local radio interview was to be the turning point for the Tidings. It was time to bring them out into the open and talk about them. To be proud and to start letting the public know they'd be hearing about the Tidings in the not too distant future.

Pat is one of our best local radio presenters and I always enjoy our banter. After many laughs and a plug for the Casino Club in Rochester where I was to appear the following Saturday, I told the people of Kent about my beloved project. I needed to talk about it to convince myself it could, yet again, rise from the ashes of oblivion. The interview did me the power of good and for the next few days I worked tirelessly on the story of Tinsel Tiding, a subsidiary storyline to the main plot. It felt a little like coming out of the closet (not that I would know) or declaring a secret affair. At last, my Tidings project had gone public in a sense, to the good people of Kent.

Through my career in comedy I knew so many people in the media and the press, I knew I had the contacts if the first big break would happen. Indeed on the 23rd of the month I became a journalist in my own right, as I covered the West Ham and Liverpool game at Upton Park for the *Sunday Express*. Ian Rush scored through a mistake by my good mate Tony and my boys lost. I gave my *Sunday Express* 'man of the match' award to Ian Bishop to cheer him up after his fifty-fourth minute substitution. It really had been one hell of a crap week apart from the Radio Kent episode. Strangely enough, I did a corporate event for NatWest Bank at the Copthorne Hotel near Gatwick Airport the next day. Yes, NatWest Bank, the very people I had in mind when creating and expanding the early Tidings concept. All the important nobs were there, but I just couldn't summon the necessary enthusiasm to confront any of them with my new ideas for forward development. Once bitten and all that. I think mentally I closed the book on NatWest when they closed the book on me. They had been a challenge and they had won!

From a man of the press I became a man hounded by the press in a matter of days. I had been playing golf at Ferndown golf course near Bournemouth for my good pal Paul Terry, who had been awarded a benefit year with Hampshire. Paul broke his arm playing for England in his first Test match. People felt so sorry for him. I always said about Paul Terry that I missed his England cricket career because I was opening a Wagon Wheel at the time. So he broke his arm on England duty. It didn't bloody stop Horatio Nelson did it?

My other big mate at Hampshire, Shaun Udal, who'd just made the England squad himself and was about to tour Australia with our boys, was playing snooker together with Northampton and England rugby player Matt Dawson and having a good laugh and a few beers. In strolls Mr Big Time, I'm a Renault rep on expenses. He decided he would make up the foursome and interrupted our game. Shaun, Matty and I were tolerant, we were good mates and didn't feel in aggressive mood. But every time I played a shot and didn't pot a ball, he would say:

'No wonder you're a comedian. You ought to play snooker on stage, it's funnier than your jokes.'

I expected the tough rugby player to turn on him but Matt kept his cool and chalked his cue. Suddenly Shaun dashed across from the bulk end, knocked this rep for six and we carried on playing with this arsehole stretched across the floor in a state of me-no-remember-nothing-John. Shaun shouted down to him:

'That's for taking the piss out of my friend.'

The guy never heard him. He was out cold.

The following week the *Sun* newspaper was onto it. Renault-face had reported the actions to the tabloid and we were in possible trouble. I played golf with Shaun the following Wednesday at Stoneham golf club near Southampton, and coincidentally his phone rang. It was the *Sun*. Did he have a comment to make on helping Richard Digance and Matt Dawson mug, abuse and accost a harmless rep from Renault who was staying at the hotel minding his own business.

Shaun was worried, he'd just made the England squad.

'What do I do, Rich?'

'Tell them to fuck off.'

'Richard said fuck off.'

That was the end of my good television reviews until the autumn.

By the end of April the Tidings were flagging. I still believed there to be a place for their softness and their caring attributes, but nobody seemed to share this belief. Still no television interest, and with no television interest there was no other interest either. All thoughts about my Seven Little Wonders ceased as I went into television production for a new show for Michael Hurll Television called 'Digance on Sport'. It was filmed at White Hart Lane, home of

Tottenham Hotspur Football Club and starred many of my good friends: Mike Osman, Garry Bushell, Robin Smith and my favourite singer Julia Fordham whom I longed to live on a desert island with. Julia Fordham was my original choice to sing my 'Christmas Tidings' song, but I think it was a devious move on my part to get her into a recording studio with no windows. She'd recorded a song 'Love Moves in Mysterious Ways' for the film *The Butcher's Wife* and her voice contained the right ingredients for my haunting song. It was never to be. I was perplexed somewhat to be told on meeting Julia for the first time that she once sang as a young fourteen-year-old at one of my folk club gigs at the Railway Folk Club in Southsea run by Sooty Broughton. She'd been a floor singer at one of my gigs? That meant she knew who I was? I was deeply chuffed. Julia Fordham I had admired for many years.

We left London the next day to appear in Osman's Golf Day at Meon Valley Golf Club, a difficult game to play when all you can see before you is the face of tasty Julia Fordham. It was in aid of Wessex Heartbeat, and followed by the Lakeside Club at Camberley where I did a late night cabaret spot. Bradley Walsh, a high ranking comic within the industry, popped in to say hello. Once again, my confidence was rebuilding in preparation for the next smack round the face in the Forest of Lap. I'd taken quite a bit of lucrative nightclub work around the country to sponsor my business plans. It was the only way it could be done. Banks still weren't interested at this time. Newmarket, where I seemed particularly tall walking down the High Street, before realising that most of the time it was populated by jockeys and horse trainers. The Starlight Suite at Enfield football stadium, probably my favourite nightclub venue. The Lakeside at Camberley. I was doing the rounds. I'd even made it to the East End's own Circus Tavern, a place I never thought I'd work myself when seeing some of the old legends of comedy and music there as a lad out with his workmates.

It wasn't until the 25th May I was able to focus once more upon the Tidings and their problems. Steve Austin and John Walters called a meeting at my house. Walters produced reams of official paperwork but the Tidings themselves were still no further than the starting blocks. Directorships and royalties, financial considerations, personal gains and assurances. I knew it all had to be considered but I thought it was all premature. There was an awful lot more creative work to be written and conceived before we considered the dishing out of the profits thereof, in my opinion. To counteract my disillusionment I wrote two full length stories that week which were never to be used. They were, however, mighty therapeutic. The first was an explanation of how Titch and Toddler Tiding, two now obsolete characters, came to be in possession of the muslin bag containing the sapling of the one real magic Christmas tree, planted each year in the forest by Timber Tiding. The other described the daily deeds of Tinker Tiding, a character who never made it to the quarter-finals really. Tinker was a wheeler dealer. To be honest I could have done with Tinker Tiding in real life. He probably would have handled all those early administration meetings better than me. Poor Tinker, perhaps one day he should reappear.

The following day, I was Scotland bound with my television producer Mark Robson and script associate Alan Wightman, the very man who came up with the idea of the Blue Bear, one of the Tidings' leading characters. I returned two days later, having checked out the venue for my next TV special for ITV, which would be filmed in 'a wee while'.

It was to be Blair Castle in Perthshire, a majestic building, as magical as my own smaller creations. Lord Atholl had his own army. I had mine too, it's just that nobody really wanted to know about them. I recall Mark asking that very question as we roared through Northumberland in a classy British Rail first class compartment. 'I wonder what it's like to have your own army?' he chuckled. Alan tittered too. I knew the answer, it's just that mine had never been to war to show what they were really made of. The show was screened on New Year's Eve and featured Barbara Dickson, Dougie Maclean, and Big Country. It was received well, particularly north of the border.

Saturday 28th, travel weary, we travelled to Ditchling, home of the Walters family. Esme, John's wife, still rates, in Debbie's and my eyes, as one of the friendliest people placed upon Earthy Tiding's planet. She loved the Tidings project and spoke of it often. This night she had the flu and could obviously have done without such a social intrusion. The evening was antagonistic and Debbie knew how uncomfortable I felt in such company. I believe she knew then that the second Tidings team, after myself and Dave Bubb, would disband before too long. In the words of Elvis Costello: 'And I would rather be anywhere else . . .'

On 2nd June I flew to New Orleans for five corporate performances in the Royal Senosta Hotel on the infamous Bourbon Street. I took all my Tidings stories with me and in the home of ragtime, jazz and Tennessee Williams, I produced more stories from the Forest of Lap. I may have discovered a street Tiding named desire whilst staying in Bourbon Street, but I never did. I returned to New Orleans with Rod in April 1999 as a birthday jaunt, and had a great time showing him where an early Tidings adventure reached fruition. In the world of Mardi Gras, Toddler and Titch Tiding were given another plot. Titch wasn't to stay in the frame too long but once again I was on a creative roll. I'd strolled around the sleazy blues clubs by night and wrote 'Monkeys Love Swinging In Trees', a sort of jazzy feel Tidings song that featured in the original story cassette of Panda Tiding.

I returned from Louisiana with great enthusiasm and a fair old suntan. The following Wednesday I spoke for England cricketer David Gower at the Café Royal in Regent Street, London. It seemed very strange to be speaking at the retirement of someone who had to be one of the youngest people in the room. I equated it to turning up to a funeral with chronic chest pains and a shovel.

Long before 'They Think It's All Over', David and I had tried to sort some television work out together. I felt honoured to be asked to speak at such a memorable occasion. He had to be, after all, one of the greatest left handed batsmen of all time. David always showed great interest in my projects and he too thought the Tidings would go places in time. We spoke one evening, on his patio, chatting and staring out over the beautiful high trees towards the New Forest. Gower had done the very thing I so wanted to do: he'd played for England.

I wish I'd played for England like you did
I wish I'd been a quarter good as you
But I was useless and I knew, my highest score was two
But that didn't mean I didn't want to be an international
I wish I'd played for England like you did
I wish I'd had a quarter of your skill
I wish for just an hour, I'd been David Gower
But I never was and never ever will.

I wish I'd been the captain of my country
I would have been the proudest man alive
And hit a century that would have done for me

All the things you did
I so wanted as a kid
Special dreams that never did come true
But David I wish that I'd been you.

The filming of that television special, by this time, was complete. Everyone seemed to enjoy a song I sang with Dougie Maclean called 'Caledonia'. Dougie had been a friend for years, with Debbie and I staying for a while in his crofter's cottage, on the banks of Loch Butterstone. He did well with the writing of the film music for *The Last of the Mohicans.* For me, 'Caledonia' was the greatest song Dougie ever wrote. Rock fans may well remember the Frankie Miller version, which charted.

I felt very proud of that New Year show and on the way home from Scotland I stopped off at a summer garden party for my friend and play director Derek Killeen at the Key Theatre in Peterborough. Since he had directed 'Sex, Spangles and Sensible Shoes', I was more than delighted to return a favour. Derek knew about my creative dreams and had gone with me on my first play. When I told him about the Tidings he suggested we should give the first children's theatre production a run at the Key Theatre. My ego had been boosted and once again I could relax into the world of Make Believe. I had completed most of my heavy work schedule for the year so I attended a few Hampshire cricket matches and shared a few beers with Gower, Smith, Udal and my other pals in the team.

By November I'd decided to attack from a different angle, resorting again to my original Cloud Crowd characters. Perhaps through them I could treat the Tidings as a second phase of a children's television project. The general bickering was getting me down, so I'd decided to go it alone mentally in trying to keep everything buoyant on the creative side. On 8th November I met with Anne Wood, creator of Rosie and Jim, Tots TV series, and much later, a prominent figure in the Tellytubbies' success. We met through Yorkshire Television producer Ian Bolt. The initial meet was at Pinewood Studios with Reg Parsons and later at the Landmark Hotel in the West End of London. Later that evening, as I flew off to Jersey from Southampton, continuing my long tour, I believed I'd managed to steer the ship back onto an even keel. Anne showed great interest in my work, although sadly, I was never to hear from her again either. Don't really know what happened there.

My British tour finished on the 14th December. I went away to

Bowood Golf and Country Club for a couple of days with Robin Smith. He was having a tough time with the managers of the England cricket team and he needed the break too. We both drank too much vintage port and he nearly killed me in a particularly strange attempt at driving a car over a sand bunker. Also in attendance was Mike Dyer, the Havant solicitor who was to become my legal representative, both with my activities during the contractual agreements with Sleepy Kids plc which took SKD Media onto the Stock Exchange, and also as company secretary of the Write Good Company, my own media and leisure based company.

A whole year had passed and we hadn't progressed at all, apart from endless documents of officialdom and equally endless meetings concerning the legalities and personal percentage splits. Nobody seemed interested in the Tidings themselves anymore. It was so demoralising. As I sat down for my annual cold turkey and jacket potato on Boxing Day, recalling indeed that was how it all started, I really believed the whole exercise had been an awful lot of work, heartache and expense for absolutely nothing. Again, the television screen was littered with second rate programming schedules and so deep down I knew there had to be a place for my Seven Little Wonders of the World. It was their first anniversary and I quietly wished them well as I raised a glass in their honour. If I thought 1994 would turn out to be a strange page within my book, then I hadn't allowed for the occurrences of 1995.

We had a lovely Christmas at home. New Year's Eve was spent with a few neighbours and my good friend Jeff Mitchell, a Southampton hairdresser.

'Auld Lang Syne' rang out as I saw my own TV special ring in the New Year on ITV. A weird experience as I sat in my own living room with my own friends. Within days I was back working at the Central TV studios in Nottingham for Bob Monkhouse's 'Celebrity Squares'. Yes, Nottingham where I would plant the one real magic tree. The next day, back to London, 'Talking Telephone Numbers', and a reunion with my old Capital workmate Phillip Schofield. The show was for a younger audience, some of whom would love to have heard a Tidings song perhaps. Instead I did a poem about the World's Worst Magician. It could so easily have yet again been an opportunity to give the little ones an airing. Once again, I declined, the time was still not right.

★

Tidings work began in earnest on 12th January 1995 with news that we had interest from Reed International Publishers, the publishers of Thomas the Tank Engine. I was reliably informed that both Fiona Hardwick and Penny Morris were impressed with my presentation document and suggested I visit them at the Earl's Court Toy Fair on 31st January. It was a pleasant meeting which led me nowhere. It was the first occasion I heard a phrase which would haunt me for the next few years of my life: 'Get it on television and let us know how it's going.'

It was Fiona who gave me some constructive criticism regarding modern trends relating to equality and equal opportunity. Scruffy individuals were not necessarily villains as I mentioned in a previous chapter. That evening at the Swallow International Hotel, I sat up all night, removing the Ruffs and Scruffs from the Forest of Lap script. Fiona Hardwick was absolutely right and strangely I enjoyed some creative criticism instead of the usual business suggestions of others.

I had decided 1995 would be the year to start dropping hints about my new creation. Time to expose. A year had passed with little or no effect, another could quite easily pass in much the same way. The next morning I was in BBC Broadcasting House recording a documentary about singer Elkie Brooks whom I'd worked with for over four years. After a coffee with producer Alan Roberts, I worked my way through the maze of corridors and windows, to the offices of Andy Aliffe a senior producer at BBC, Light Entertainment. He'd been my producer for several years on radio, and he knew I had something on the go. It was time to reveal my plans. I mentioned what the Tidings were and what they did, and left a pilot radio script with Andy.

On Tuesday 14th February, Steve Austin resigned his directorship from the Tidings Trading Company. I'm not too sure what led to such a definite decision, but within days I strangely received various documentation from Walters declaring a new set-up, although I would eventually become the only remaining and original director of the Tidings Trading Company when we began our acquisitional plans. Walters came to my house and ran through different papers with Debbie and myself. Jazz Summers never took up his directorship which John Walters had been in the process of drawing up. I would have welcomed his allied backing for sure but proceedings dragged on and on and I presume Jazz lost interest.

An earlier decision by Walters to quell the involvement in the company of another associate of mine, David Stringer, should certainly have told me something. But it didn't. Even to this day I don't know what it all should have told me. With confused brain and endless messages on my answerphone I decided the time had come to get away for a while. I'd lost Dave, Jazz and Steve Austin, in a relatively short period of time. I felt I desperately needed to remove myself from over-dominant people who needed answers before they'd asked the questions.

On 26th February, I flew off to La Manga, Spain, for a week's golfing. The warm air and superb atmosphere allowed me to think straight, even if it didn't allow me to hit a ball straight. If the Tidings were ever to happen, I needed to start again. I'd made them pink furry balls and blue furry balls, depending upon their sex. That theory had to go. They would have looked fine dangling from cots but there had to be far more substance to carry them through animation and incredible adventures.

Robin Lyons of Siriol was later to give me great advice about animation stories. It was simple: 'Invent a character, drop them in the shit and then get them out of it.' Absolutely right.

Upon my return to England, every existing story was scrapped. I decided to start again. To have one final effort at succeeding with my project. Yes, every single story was binned once they'd been logged with two solicitors, Mike Dyer and Richard Robson of Warner Richardson. Even the Christmas story had to be placed on ice as I searched for a less seasonal role for them. The festive sales campaign was only a couple of weeks but there were fifty-two weeks in the year.

It's strange to think that, after all that work, nothing of the original Tidings concept still exists today in its original form. All that damn work!

I flew to Bangkok on 16th March, to entertain ICL's hardest workers and clients enjoying a week in Thailand. By day I sat by the swimming pool in the grounds of the Shangri La Hotel, piecing together my new Tidings stories and personalities for a fresh assault upon my return to England. The corporate entertainment company that took me out there, Mainstream from Manchester, didn't want me seen around as I was a surprise, so I sat nonchalantly by the pool in my baseball cap and shades.

I didn't let the Tidings down with my workload, or my results. Glad Tiding, a mature housekeeper, was deleted from the equation as I took Fiona Hardwick's advice on board. Stereotyped ageing females were no longer politically correct, no longer acceptable. The children I wrote for would know nothing of all that as they grew older anyway. Trooper Tiding came and went, as did Thumper Tiding. Tidings wouldn't have short tempers, unlike those who were trying to release them to an unsuspecting public.

I'd worked my proverbial balls off in Bangkok. My Tidings file bulged at the seams as I gave the new stories yet another once over on the long flight home. I chatted with snooker star James Wattana for a while, as I took a break from my existence within the Forest of Lap. I don't think we understood each other too well but at least I got his autograph! Bastard didn't even ask me for mine. I think Jimmy White beat him the following week!

Extensive travelling brought about through my comedy engagements gave me endless hours of solitude on the road. During such long hours on my own I lived with the dream of children's projects. They made me laugh, and at times they made me very angry when I couldn't get the characters to express themselves in the way I knew they could.

On 6th April, a train to Gleneagles in Scotland and back the next day, gave me over twenty hours of solid writing commitment. During this return journey to Scotland I decided to find a willing personal assistant and to chase up the planning permission to build a new recording studio at my farm. Yes, no more pissing about, it was time for action. I spoke to John Robinson of Test Valley Planning Department and I put the word out to a few friends that I wished to find an assistant who didn't care what hours they worked or where they went. I waited anxiously for quite a while.

I refused to talk Tidings during my spring tour which took me to 29th May when it finished at Queens Theatre, Hornchurch. I had little else on for a month or two, I had ample time to re-edit my presentation documents, prepare my copyright bibles, and update my business investment proposal booklets. I completed thirty-five Tidings nursery rhymes which were later ditched when the targeted age of the project fell to three years and upwards, or pre-school as it's known in the business. The nursery rhymes were a little on the cheeky side to be honest, and no child in the world of that age would have ever understood them anyway so there seemed no point in going with them.

I interviewed Samantha Wake at La Parisienne in Romsey. We both had a draughting and drawing office background and we understood each other from the first discussions. I'd others to interview, particularly someone who'd worked with me before in the entertainment industry who I obviously cannot name. She was far more experienced than Samantha and already knew all my idiosyncrasies, how I changed my mind at the last moment, how I dropped one topic to work on another as soon as an idea entered my head, probably the most common and most irritating failing of any creative writer.

Miss X worked in London for an agent and was considering a move to the New Forest to work with me as she had done before. It may sound idyllic but it's not if you're a London party animal. Miss X was thinking long and hard, we'd worked together for years and the chemistry was superb. However, I also knew Sam fancied the job. I knew it would fire her belly, so against better professional judgement, I went with my own personal hunch and Sam joined the team on Monday 31st July, with absolutely no experience, as a personal assistant to a precocious creative bod.

Her first role was to accompany me to Dean Court, home of Bournemouth Football Club. They were playing my beloved West Ham in a pre-season friendly. I assured her that the job would get better. She smiled politely and I think, all things being equal, it did improve. It was the start of a tremendous business partnership which carried my projects forward far quicker than ever before. Sam and I got on well, even on her first day she sat in a private box full of West Ham supporters, shouting for Bournemouth. I appreciated her individuality and to a lesser degree her stubbornness.

We also made each other laugh, a vitally important ingredient so often missing between boss and staff. I said to her that evening, in the pouring rain: 'I've had you working with me for a day now and for most of that time I've been damp.'

Sam laughed and I knew she was the right choice.

I had interviewed four candidates in all, but I knew from our earliest conversations at the Romsey restaurant I'd made the right decision. As the business plans grew and grew and other schemes shadowed my Seven Little Wonders, it was a gratifying thing to have a personal assistant by my side, working the most unsociable of hours for something she'd never even heard of until a few weeks previously. The Tidings were growing closer to me. With Sam's help the presentations were classier, the storybooks were upgraded, and the early illustrations were carefully photographed and copied. In a nutshell, the project seemed to develop some sort of creative organisation.

They were difficult times to believe in the concept, often too dark to see light at the end of the tunnel, but between us, Sam and I believed. It's hard to explain the importance of a good member of staff, how they spur you on, particularly in adversity. Sam Wake and I sometimes erupted like volcanoes, exploded rage, but most of the time we offered a tranquil base for the Tidings, safe from the harm of all the business transactions. With the formation of The Write Good Company in September 1998 Sam became head of project co-ordination. It would be just reward for so much early dedication to the cause much further down the line.

One day, a stout and confident man strode into town as if on a fine white stallion. His name was David Bainbridge, the first managing director of the Tidings Trading Company Limited. He wore cowboy boots, a suede jacket and a droopy moustache. David had been married to singer Diane Solomon and worked with Reg Parsons at Production Plus. He'd called earlier in the week. I was playing golf and awaited the arrival of my friend Paul Terry to collect me and drive me to Stoneham. Paul's lateness allowed me to speak to David for a good half-hour, and what a good half-hour it turned out to be. I mentioned in previous pages the tenuous link between Bob Voice, Reg Parsons, and the most expensive door stop in the world. David is the final piece of that particular jigsaw puzzle, the one who picked up the Tidings storybook and studied it.

'I'd like a punt at this,' he admitted.

I had nothing to lose. It was going nowhere and had very little future, even though I'd now invested a considerable amount of money in the project, more than I could afford. David Bainbridge tested the water with various contacts he knew in the world of publishing and public Relations. He'd worked with Shirley Bassey and Barry Manilow in the past. He'd never tried representing anything quite as bizarre as the Tidings though. His enthusiasm both surprised and lifted me. At long last, someone else who believed in what Sam Wake and I believed in. His enthusiasm reminded me of Steve Austin. But would it work this time?

As our receptionist Kerenza Hutchings made endless cups of tea, a compulsory extra in any Digance set-up, Sam and I told Bainbridge all about the Forest of Lap. He saw the map of the forest which Erika Platt had drawn up from my earliest of Tidings days in the London flat. He was impressed and we felt we'd sold the Tidings well so, after working hours, Sam and I celebrated with a pint at the Duke's Head in Awbridge, just outside Romsey. That beer garden ended up being one of the most constructive meeting places during this project, not because of the alcoholic intake, that was all very minimal, but because the setting by the River Test was tranquillity at its very best. We met Bobby our printer from Brighton there. David and I eventually met up with Rod Bransgrove there. In that beer garden the future of the Tidings changed. The Duke's Head could be classed as an annexe to our Romsey offices. If you like, the third team structure began to fall into place with David and Sam.

John Walters, dubious of any additional interested parties, demanded an immediate meeting when I told him about David. This meeting took place at my house on 22nd June. The atmosphere could be described as cordial, but there again, so was the Cuba Crisis. Walters and Bainbridge were never destined to become great friends and neither did they. David knew very little of Walters' involvement in the project – at this juncture it was none of David's business anyway – and Walters was showing early signs of possessiveness by appearing quite confused at the presence of my new found partner. I presided over the meeting in a tentative way, aware of John Walters' touchiness and David Bainbridge's bombastic but enthusiastic nature. It was really a case of lighting the touch paper and standing back to wait for the explosion. With Bainbridge I'd inherited someone who artistically and creatively loved the Seven Little Wonders of the World as much as I did.

John Walters informed us of our second office he'd set up in Lewes, near to his house. I didn't quite realise how far down the line he'd gone by securing premises in the main street, and was even more surprised to discover he'd taken on a secretary, Sarah Gibbard, together with his daughter Charlotte as an operative office junior. I panicked about the financial aspect. Quite justifiably, it was later to prove.

The Tidings had chugged along in a small two-roomed office with myself and Sam, and suddenly the thing had a Sussex branch. My greetings card company mothered the project and John Walters secured a small government loan to finance the card company, thus the Tidings too. I trusted John Walters and he proceeded in expanding the Lewes set-up without interruption or involvement from me at Romsey. If you like, the administration moved to Lewes, whilst the creative department stayed in the two rooms at Romsey. It was to become a bitter splintering of power and interests which led us to Queen's Counsel, endless consultations with Mike Dyer, our solicitor, and a financial settlement. It was my first real taste of business reality, a far, far cry from the forest on the edge of Make Believe. This wasn't make believe, this was for real. It was bloody war!

The day after the Bainbridge and Walters meeting at my home, my television producer, Mark Robson, and I went to watch Hampshire play Worcester at Southampton. We were both big fans of Graeme Hick and despite my allegiance to Hampshire, I hoped he'd be on form. He was out for four so Mark and I got pissed. In the marquee I explained to Mark the Tidings'· developments. He'd always been interested in the project, admittedly from a distance, because his good lady Pam worked in children's publishing and could relate to what we were trying to achieve. Mark warned me of the problems in getting involved only with business people who seek end product, when creative teams who take you to end product status are far more viable and justifiable.

Of course, Mark was right. Everyone longs to jump on an original idea and be a part of it. I'd had my fair share of those, it was time to be creative and get writing and composing. Still within the team, I remained the only one who could add the artistic input with Sam working on the presentation thereof. I agreed to send new texts to Mark for his scrutiny as the time had come to try and interest the television broadcasters once more. Mark Robson and I had always got on well and I always respected his opinions and judgements. He assured me that the Tidings would be a brilliant television concept but not for London Weekend Television, who had so few hours in any week. The project needed to go to a midweek television company who had far more airtime to fill. With the BBC and London Weekend Television distant memories, my options were diminishing.

That weekend I sat down to re-evaluate the whole Tidings scenario. I'd been busy writing two new stories of Tinsel Tiding's adventures, culminating in a twenty-page story in rhyme. Of course, Tinsel strands were mined in the Forest of Lap to produce silvery ropes to tie down the one real magic Christmas tree which the Tidings grew every year. I felt more than pleased with myself but I knew things weren't right on the administration side. I chose to ignore the bickerings from Lewes and set about composing twenty Christmas carols from the Forest of Lap. I found this surprisingly easy and on Thursday 29th June, 1995, I was back in the recording studio with the Tidings Christmas Carol collection. The recordings were fine demo standard and mastered onto DAT for top quality. They would be my additional bait when I offered the concept to BBC Radio later in the year.

Apart from one concert at the Pavilion Theatre, Weymouth, all my creative efforts during the summer were channelled in the direction of the Tidings. I developed the Christmas aspect of the story more fully and by Monday 17th July, the carol sessions were complete and the necessary paperwork involving the Performing Right Society and the Mechanical Copyright Protection Society were finalised. I suppose in celebration, the next night we dined out at the Thai restaurant in Romsey, we being myself and my wife Debbie, Robin Smith and his wife Cathy.

Time began to pass quickly. Samantha Wake had only been with me four weeks before I set off on a gruelling British tour. It opened at the Britannia Pier in Yarmouth on 29th July and would take up most of my time until Christmas. On 1st August my touring unit of Sam, Mark Homes and Ralph Cook, together with our receptionist Kerenza, who'd come along on a jolly, visited the Pavilion Theatre in Worthing. After the show we met up with all the Walters family and enjoyed a few drinks at the Beach Hotel. Walters' wife Esme was as funny as ever, we got along very well. The following week in Romsey Sam started placing all my Tidings scribblings onto disk, a monumental task which we still use to this day. Thank God she completed that one!

On 5th September, my house was disrupted by the arrival of a crew from *Hello* magazine. This surely had to be the time to finally divulge the story of the Tidings, but no. Yet again I kept my cool and decided, despite the magnitude and class of the magazine, I didn't have enough to say about the project, so I chose to say nothing.

But the ideas were taking shape now. On Monday 11th September, Sam and I travelled to the Epsom Playhouse Theatre in Surrey, to meet with theatre manager Trevor Mitchell. It was the venue for my second exhibition of watercolour paintings and I was very surprised upon finding that three had already been sold when we arrived for the press opening. Trevor had also gone with the idea of my new play 'Fear of Frying' and because I loved his theatre so much, it seemed to be a natural choice for the venue of the first Tidings Pantomime, to say nothing of the celebrity launch of the Tidings songs and poems. I'd secured definite theatrical interest from Epsom and Peterborough. Slowly but surely the Tidings edged their way along the ledge towards acceptance.

My British tour took hold and my next day off didn't arrive until 11th November when I took Debbie, Polly and Rosie to see 'Riverdance' at Hammersmith Odeon. It was, without doubt, the greatest spectacle I had ever seen and naturally, through my profession, I've seen hundreds of productions. My mind worked overtime as I studied the incredible lighting and the wonderful weaving of Bill Whelan's story. If such a wonderful occasion could be sparked by a river, then an almost equally memorable theatrical event could transpire from the Forest of Lap. 'Riverdance' inspired me, and judging by the standing ovation, it inspired a few thousand others too, though probably in a different way.

The British tour finished at Her Majesty's Theatre in the Haymarket in the heart of London's theatreland. It had always been my dream to play the West End, and I never had. The night was for me an unmitigated disaster. Very few people came along because various promoters, agents, connected with the show, forgot to realise that no show in London, where people have such a vast choice, will sell without publicity or an adequate advertising campaign.

Sam and I chatted into the early hours about how the following year had to change. How possible projects like the Tidings would allow me to cut down on my shattering number of concerts and personal appearances. Sam was right, it had to be done. As Christmas neared, I actually cried on a few occasions, upon the realisation that once again, the public wouldn't know of my Seven Little Wonders of the World from the Forest of Lap. My card company hadn't produced any Christmas cards either. It was all too frustrating for words. David and I also vowed that next year it would happen. It didn't!! But we were getting closer. The hours of dedication? I have not a clue. The personal investment? I choose not to remember. Perhaps one day, you never know! That's all I kept telling myself as I toasted 1996. With David Bainbridge and Samantha Wake I had creative allies. We'd all become friends and it was all lots of fun once again. So Team Three led the project into '96. Don't get bored, there's a few more teams to tell you about yet!

My eldest daughter, Polly, loved the Tidings. She played many of the tunes on her flute. She'd developed to Grade Five on the instrument and it was nice to hear the Tidings ballads come to life on an instrument other than my own acoustic guitar. Her belief in them continued to spark my belief in the success of them too. Her little sister, Rosie, also loved the songs and the stories, particularly 'Twinkle Tiding', a tape narrated by Susan George that she listened to every single night before she went to sleep. Rosie owned the one and only cassette of the original Twinkle Tiding story, a tale conceived long before Twinkle realised that every twinkling star in the sky told an enchanting story of its own. Twinkle never discovered this until 1996. The girls drove me on more than anyone else.

With the pressure of work, a British tour and a new television special to write, I sought the help of my television script associate Alan Wightman. Alan had written many brilliant scripts in the past, and although he admitted to never having written children's material before, he made a fine attempt at a Tidings story. It felt strange seeing a script come in from someone else, the Tidings had been my creation and I almost felt both traitor and betrayed. A strange feeling. Alan and I had worked together on many BBC radio scripts over the years and I thought the least that could happen to the Tidings would be that they would appear on a radio series or two. Alan accepted the challenge and it proved to be a bonus for himself and the Tidings.

His first script came to my house from his home in Newport, South Wales, and although I didn't feel the content was strong enough, there appeared a character whom I found both enchanting and immediately appealing. I told my children about the new character and they both immediately fell in love with Alan's creation. It was Blue Bear. Yes, good old Blue Bear, the coldest animal in the whole world. I rang Alan and congratulated him on his most imaginative creation. He'd never let me down before and this time he'd certainly surpassed himself.

Over the next few months, although great pals, we made a business arrangement through contract which secured Alan a percentage of royalties for the use of his creature in my project. This would eventually transfer to a handsome share dividend within the SKD Media shareholding set-up. We shook hands on the deal and Blue Bear became the narrator of the Tidings stories in the first television series. I had fallen in love with the bear myself. I tested many of my earliest story lines on Alan Wightman who in return offered various suggestions and changes. Knowing such an established writer turned out to be a valuable advantage as I trod the minefield of children's literature, something I'd rarely done before. Script associates are seldom praised for their backroom 'behind the scenes' efforts, but I give full credit here to Alan. He invented the Blue Bear from his very own vantage point beside the Edge of Make Believe. Thankfully for us all, his creation, Blue Bear, fitted perfectly into his new environment in the Forest of Lap.

Alan Wightman signed a writer's royalty agreement with the Tidings Trading Company, and to this day, remains the only writer to have done so. With Alan's character input I was later able to re-angle my writing approach as the Blue Bear seemed a creature most suitable for child adoption. Blue from being the coldest animal in the whole world, as blue as the sky and the bluest felt tip pen, I pictured him being a gift for any child who needed cheering up. In fact, the good tidings brought by the Blue Bear could indeed make children actually feel better. He could care more than any other animal had ever cared. Every under-the-weather child simply had to have a Blue Bear for company, a traditional get well gift. What if the child had already been given one by another well wisher? No problem, there could even be private collections from caring and concerned relatives and friends. No doubt about it, Alan had come up with a real diamond of a character.

Chapter Nine

Goodbye to Mum and Dad

One of the great sadnesses of my life was that my mum was never to see my successes on stage and my dad wouldn't share my final pleasure in seeing me retire from the gruelling schedules of touring and wearing Nancy boy make-up.

It was 19th April 1985 when I was called to the London Chest Clinic in Bow, East London, because Doris wasn't feeling at all well and had been taken in during the night. She'd actually been unwell for some time but our family doctor, Gordon Brill, for whom she worked as a receptionist at the time, couldn't isolate the problem. She'd been backwards and forwards to hospital for tests, the poor old lady was even subjected to treadmills and running machines to find out if her heart and chest were functioning OK. She was sixty-eight years of age and should never have been a victim of such rigorous tests. But subjected she was and her body took a fair old bashing from it.

Mum was a mature art student, specialising in watercolour studies since she was sixty-three. You can imagine what a proud son I was that she'd discovered such a brilliant talent so late in life. She'd even participated in her first art exhibition at Wendons Ambo, a small Essex village, in the Easter of 1983. She was so proud, having entered six paintings that were all fantastic. She sold every one of them for sixty pounds each, an awful lot of money to a receptionist at a doctor's surgery. Three hundred and sixty pounds of utter pride. I admit to buying one myself, which I never confessed to because she would never have taken the money from me. The boat at rest in the bay still hangs in my living room to this day. It's a little faded now from hanging in the sunshine but the memories are as vivid as the day the first brushstrokes were delicately applied. Its current value is one hundred million pounds and it's not for sale at any price.

It's still hard to believe that mum had nothing more than undetected gall-stones which had been causing her such excruciating pain. It had nothing to do with the chest or her heart until the stones disintegrated and infiltrated into her bloodstream, eventually clogging up various important organs. I was with her when she looked through the ward window at the chest clinic and said, 'Richard, the sky looks very blue doesn't it?' It did, and with that she had gone. The monitors screamed and medics raced backwards and forwards but mum didn't really want to know. She'd had enough and was unquestionably at peace.

Her last chore before leaving was to manicure her nails. It was such a beautiful thing for her to do considering her arms were battered black and blue from needles trying to extract blood from weary veins. Mum kept her integrity to the end, something we all hope and pray will happen I suppose. Very corny I know, but the sky clouded over and I left the London Chest Clinic with dad beside me. He hadn't spoken a word, not knowing or ever knowing how to vent his emotions. Jill was in the car park and I broke the news. It was a very sad day.

Mum's funeral was something she would have been proud of. It left the high rise flats at Austin Court with dozens of onlookers, each paying their own quiet tribute to a brilliant woman. She'd worked tirelessly for Muscular Dystrophy Research after a friend of our family's son, John Cordes, contracted the illness and died at the tender age of thirteen. She knew many of the locals from her role in later years as doctor's receptionist and as the entourage turned right and passed the main gates of West Ham United football ground, the cars stopped once more. Many of the players knew mum because Gordon Brill was the club doctor.

Busy Barking Road made way for the procession. It stopped for a while outside the St Bartholomew's Medical Centre where mum had worked until her illness. It was right opposite the East Ham Granada where Jill and I had seen the Beatles. There was no screaming this time, just a mournful glance from the many pedestrians who sympathised with the tragic loss.

By the time we'd reached High Street South and made our way to St Mary's Church, where it all began for me as a choirboy in the early pages of this book, the procession had lengthened with the addition of the doctors and the staff and a few of mum's friends from the art school. I looked behind me from the leading car. It seemed to stretch forever. It didn't but it seemed to. So many people to say goodbye to such an unassuming, quiet friend. I really wish she'd known how many missed her.

I hadn't been in St Mary's for many years. It seemed very small and mum's coffin filled the church. Dad's emotions cracked and I spent the service propping him up with my left arm.

The service included a tape of myself singing mum's favourite song, 'A Nightingale Sang In Berkeley Square', and as expected at these desperate occasions, something went wrong. The tape player didn't switch on and the vicar came across to me as I stood in the front pew, my arm around dad, and he actually asked me if I could nip over and sort out the machinery. I couldn't believe his lack of tact, but I fortunately had Dave Bubb with me who sorted out the situation and Doris's favourite number echoed around the walls of the Norman church.

There was so much to take in as I stood in the church where I'd once been a choirboy, where I dragged at my first fag on my way home from choir practice, and where my sister Jill had married Rob. In that same building I was saying goodbye to my mum and the only thing that concerned the vicar was the poxy tape machine wouldn't work. I stood a stone's throw from Blaney Crescent. Mum and Captain Blaney were probably discussing the demise of that war memorial with Doris no doubt sticking up for me, insisting I'd never used it as a set of goalposts myself, though my friends had.

Dad died at home some ten years later. That was fairly predictable as he never, ever went anywhere except to my house to play snooker or to Jill and Rob's house in Thundersley on a Sunday. Dad's departure was more expected. He really lost the will to do anything once he got back from the Second World War.

I was raking wood shavings in the horses' stables when Debbie dashed across from the house to tell me Rob was at dad's flat. I knew straight away he had died. He'd gone to the bathroom during the night and his neighbours Flo and Don Cain noticed the bathroom light was still on in the morning. Jill and Rob raced to the flat from Thundersley and found dad. I still miss him around the snooker table though. He potted some good balls in his time, and he also played table tennis for Essex.

His death caused me to stop going to West Ham's games as we sat together just to the left of the players' tunnel. The last time was against Sheffield Wednesday, and what a crap game that was. My Christmas present every year to dad was a season ticket and he thoroughly enjoyed being an executive. I have seldom watched the Hammers since. These days, of course, I no longer know the players either and so it all became less of an occasion. I suppose the floodgates opened when Tony left for Blackburn Rovers and various others were doomed to the reserves and eventual retirement.

At dad's funeral I spoke to my sister at great length of how dad's death had brought a vast chapter of my life to an end. Jill felt the same. Her children Rachel and Marcus had been brought up in Essex and for them all the East End was a fading memory. My final link with the East End of London had passed on and my visits to my place of birth would become less and less. I still drive through on occasions but it just isn't the same. The proud flats aren't so proud anymore and the wasteland that became Wembley Stadium with the kick of a tennis ball has gone forever. Richard Digance, the back street international, had retired graciously. No more cup ties over Gooseley Park or alongside the derelict shop of Alf Jinks the butcher. No more close encounters around the washing lines behind the flats at Blaney Crescent.

It's all too ironic that they then decided to pull down Wembley Stadium itself. That was just taking the piss. But watch out for the rhubarb sprouting out along various parts of the M25 motorway. For that you can blame Mr Snow. It was his rhubarb and if he'd let us steal it then it would have been cropped and not a potential road hazard. Dad's life had ended and the last hours we ever spent together were watching Sheffield bloody Wednesday.

Chapter Ten

The Battle of Somewhere Near Hastings

Mum and dad had gone but the business ventures continued with great purpose. Managing director David Bainbridge was piling the hours into our projects with great gusto, as always. In the meantime, Sam Wake and I made our first trip down to see our administration office in Lewes. It seemed to be a tasteful town, quite artistic and a nice setting for artistic ventures. We stayed at the Shelley Hotel and fell over twice in the snow as we skidded downhill, arm in supportive arm, towards our new business address.

We walked into a myriad of computers and additional office equipment, purchased to furnish the card company and the Tidings project. It all seemed super efficient, though somewhat surprising, one had to admit. We both thought we'd entered the wrong office, but no. In Romsey we sat on the floor and often waited for time quotas on our one and only drawing board. In this new Lewes location there were four or five computers, new fax machines and audio copiers, filing systems, boardroom furniture, even a new fridge. It took us both by surprise. The utter size and the vast amounts of money invested were mind-boggling.

At the meeting we met with Neal Reed of Ipswich-based company Fast Forward Productions and I played him a demo of my first ever Tidings tape. This was before Susan George and Robert Powell climbed aboard. I'd narrated the tape myself and used real dolphin and whale cries to enhance the story of how the Tidings would save all that lived in fear of extinction. At the end of the tape everybody coughed and we had a cup of tea.

Neal Reed: 'I think the accompaniment is a little too loud.'

David Bainbridge: 'Me too.'

The tape was never discussed ever again.

David Bainbridge closed a deal with Aston Villa regarding a book I'd
written about them containing original Styx cartoons and we were all
quietly optimistic. Sam had met up with representatives of Essex
Cricket Club and had sold them the idea of an Essex mug containing
a poem about their history. It was the first deal Sam had closed and
she rightly felt most proud. The mugs were produced and sold in the
Essex shop at their cricket ground. On the Tidings front we endured
more administration meetings with minimal creative progress. Our
small business loan was disappearing via wages and equipment at the
Lewes office and I started to panic inwardly. Our mug sales and
football books weren't meeting the financial outgoings at Lewes.

On 27th October, 1995, representatives from Carlton Television
came along to my concert at St Albans Arena as a guest of David
Bainbridge. There was still a hope we could interest a television
company to come on board, because without their investment we felt
impotent. The gathering was more than amicable but they showed no
interest in coming to Romsey and seeing what we had to offer. No
luck again. Still no income.

David was now concentrating on the card company, as every
avenue we had explored with the Tidings project had become a cul-
de-sac. The Fast Forward team came to my concert at Ipswich Corn
Exchange on Wednesday 8th November, and still felt bullish about
their product, but there could be no getting away from the fact that
we needed serious investment to continue. This time, it wouldn't
hopefully be swallowed up with administration equipment, but
actually in creative advancement. We were all down and I seem to
recall that the only highlight of the month was Sam Wake meeting
Gary Lineker in the Metropole Hotel in Birmingham. Sam came
from Leicester. Gary came from Leicester. Sam worked in a market
in Leicester. Gary worked in a market in Leicester. That's all I've ever
really known about Leicester.

On 5th December, a glimmer of hope, a shaft of light at the end of a
long, long tunnel. I attended the BBC Radio Christmas party and
took along a cassette I had made of the 'Christmas Tidings' story. It
was only a demo tape that Susan George had recorded at her house
with David using his portable DAT recorder, but it was good enough
to leave with possible interested parties. I'd taken the tape and edited
it in my own studio, trying to delete a passing plane. Before the
Christmas break I had received a telephone call from the BBC,
asking if I would be prepared to re-record the story and increase the

script to thirty minutes. Two years, almost to the day, and we had our first confirmation of media interest. It's difficult to explain the light-headed feeling, the euphoria of nothing more than a possibility. I felt we'd made an inroad at last.

My final concert of the year was at Barking Assembly Rooms on Saturday 16th December, in aid of the RSPCA East London branch, of which I was president. We had a celebration drink at Palms Hotel in Hornchurch, where I had spent endless hours sweating over Tidings illustrations with Erika Platt, and I received a decanter for my work with the Guide Dogs for the Blind.

Sam and I had our staff Christmas party, just the two of us as we had no other staff, on Wednesday 20th at the Rockingham Arms pub in Wellow, outside Romsey. We had turkey, wine, more wine, and we spoke and wondered of what the New Year would bring. Little did we know! It was to bring confrontation between the Lewes and the Romsey offices, causing irreparable damage to the team. The battle of somewhere near Hastings. David hadn't received his wages for some while and was living from his savings. The finances of the card company, and additionally the Tidings Trading Company, were now controlled from Sussex.

It's very difficult to describe the desolation when I realised the company's bank loan had been spent the way it had on ranks of computers, office equipment, clothing for staff, fridges, and a mountain of stationery. Chairs were re-covered, and to be quite honest, the Lewes office looked affluent and very classy, albeit perhaps a little over-furnished for three workers. Romsey, although Sam had requested computer and scanning facilities that would have helped our creative side, received next to nothing, and before we knew it, the loan had disappeared. Wages were paid at Lewes and not at Romsey. David's salary had slipped to months in arrears, and I was still financing the running of our office through my own funds.

It's not for me to say if money was squandered or not, it's not for me to decide if John Walters and his team had thought through their spending procedures, but the time had come to call it a day. I was never consulted on the hiring of or the expenditure at the Lewes office, nor its staff, so it's difficult to comment and besides, it would be most unfair to cite only my own opinion in a public manner such as this. It is best left unsaid. John Walters insisted through his legal adviser, that he felt he worked in the best interests of the company. I accept his statement unreservedly. David in particular was devastated, having thrown himself into the project throughout 1995.

Although I chose to accept Walters' statement through his solicitors, I had no desire to ever work with him again. The Tidings were fun creatures that had given me great pleasure in creating and progressing. I never wanted them to become part of a legal wrangle, like unwanted children at a divorce hearing. John Walters had worked long and hard on the project and for such duties he must be mentioned with courtesy and respect. I do so.

1996 had started in earnest and I began working on the Cloud Crowd stories, while Sam updated the Susan George and Digance press kits and biographies. Sam compiled some nice artworks incorporating words and photographs as the first stage of a new Tidings Personnel Pack. It looked most impressive.

The Spring Fair started at the NEC Birmingham on Sunday 4th February 1996. Our team were there in force with our own card company stand. Sam and I joined the team from Enfield, where I'd worked the night before. In attendance were John Walters and his Lewes staff, including his daughter, David Bainbridge, Erika Platt, photographer Keith Curtis, and we even had a personal appearance from Susan George and her husband Simon McCorkindale. Susan recorded the first ever Tidings story tape demos for no charge, as well as being featured in the first animation production with Robert Powell.

Through March we worked away at the contacts we'd made from the Fair. We actually secured a contract with a large firm in Ireland, which we toasted with a bottle of Laurent Perrier champagne. We outlined the Tidings campaign to the directors of Universal International, whose boss, Mike Lewis, showed great enthusiasm and indeed rang us many times the next month. We did a full scale creative presentation to his company, including the newly acquired Tidings music tapes, in the hope they would show interest in the 'paper' aspect of Tidings merchandise. Mike oozed enthusiasm and energy and I'm still not too sure why his company's interest waned. Phone calls were no longer returned after our Essex meeting, and once again, the same scenario, the Tidings had made and lost friends in such a short space of time. Back to the time quotas on the solitary drawing board of the Romsey office.

The first Tidings tapes, released by Fast Forward, were to become our perfect way of showing what the Tidings really were. We had signed the Fast Forward/Tidings agreement at the Spring Fair, with press photos of myself and Susan sipping bubbly with Neal Reed, and soon the compact discs were in production with enthusiastic and positive responses from both *Reader's Digest* and Avon Cosmetics. Eight tapes in all, seven stories and a compilation music tape of my songs. We were on our way!

By the time my spring tour had drawn to a close, I felt tired, and in need of some sort of success. My guitar playing fingers were torn to shreds and my brain felt in a similar condition. Even at the Spring Fair, I did corporate work in the evening at Warwick Castle.

I had accelerated work on my second play, 'Fear of Frying', which would eventually open at the Epsom Playhouse in May. During February we checked out contacts we'd made during the Fair. I did a couple of TV appearances, 'Bushell On The Box' on the 22nd and an art pilot on the 29th. March 1996 was the month when the Tidings gathered more momentum and we really started to feel people were sitting up and taking notice.

David achieved our first Tidings success, having closed that recording deal with Fast Forward. This deal brought together a new collection of personnel that would eventually lead the Tidings to their first major advancement. Within days I was in the studio with record producer Chris Winter. Chris lived in Yate, a small town way out west along the M4 motorway. Chris became the musical director for the cassette and compact disc project, having gained experience with Andrew Lloyd Webber and Tim Rice, and also having worked with the London Philharmonic Orchestra he seemed to have the right credentials. One thing I'd noticed with children's animation was the disregard at times for good quality sound recording. None of that with the Tidings – it was, by my wish and design, a music-led concept and the music and additional effects (M/E) had to be of the highest quality to satisfy myself and Chris. This was a positive decision which brought much early praise when we aired our first animation video.

Chris Winter and I worked well together. We had an instant rapport and mutual appreciation. We worked on forty-eight Tidings songs at his studio. Chris owns one of the smallest and yet most friendly studios in the land, clinging precariously onto the side of his house and disguised as a garage for inquisitive neighbours. In that house in Yate, the Tidings audio characters came to life as Chris, David and I spent days and days and days recording the songs and stories. Susan George recorded her stories later and we edited the two voices together.

We stayed at the Cross Keys Hotel and each morning during breakfast, I composed yet more songs for the project as David and I tucked into a Full English. I recall, regarding the story of Traveller Tiding, that we were three songs short as we began our breakfasts, and by the time David's unreliable Jag had spluttered its way to Chris's studio, I'd written 'Shovel and Pick', 'Traveller Travelled' and 'The Very Funny Thing About a Hole'. I scribbled the notations when we arrived and recorded the original acoustic guitar tracks on which Chris would add what I called the fairy dust by mid-day. That was the way it fell together during the good times.

As we ploughed through these arduous sessions, Sam was faxing new lyrics from Romsey, David was working out chords on the piano and I was writing new songs over breakfast. We were timing, editing, retyping scripts as we went along. In all, we used eight reels of Ampex tape for the first recording sessions as we stored the musical works, via Chris's digital system, onto recording tape. Some eleven hours of music in total, and each track started with just my acoustic guitar. I had blisters on my fingers the size of golf balls, and a smile on my face the size of Gleneagles golf course. I was in my element, and so were David and Sam who worked well under pressure the same as I did. I'd spent a total of thirty-nine hours in Chris's studio, double that in my own studio where I was recording additional tracks and effects, together with the early demos of the Tidings Christmas carols. At that time, studio hours were all we knew as we strove to up the creative input and decrease the ridiculous levels of administration input. It worked and Neil Read, the managing director of Fast Forward, was delighted with our finished product. I was too. I felt very proud.

Chris Winter worked a further seven weeks on the multi-tracks adding instruments and sound effects without hindrance. We spoke regularly but I never distracted him with a visit during the delicate phase of deep concentration. His final result was stunning. Still to this day the Tidings tapes for Fast Forward stand up, I think, as works of art, mainly thanks to the skills, experience and downright enthusiasm of Chris Winter. I completed recording with Chris at his Yate studios on 7th March.

We worked on both the card company, which was to become the parent company for the Tidings, and the Tidings Trading Company itself. Sam and I looked at new premises at the Horsefair, Romsey still our offices to this day, and our solicitor Mike Dyer, who remains our Write Good Company company secretary, set the acquisition deal in motion with Walters. Up to this point, we'd had insufficient staff and equipment to make the necessary high quality artworks and master scripts for presentation. At the Horsefair things would change, with more space, natural daylight beaming through the windows, and a table and a couple of chairs to work on as opposed to the floor were useful additions. We sorted the lease and moved in within two months. The building used to belong to an old brewery, probably why I felt so much at home there.

On Friday 15th March, I took Sam to see my friend Joe Pasquale at Salisbury City Hall. Joe and I had become good pals since the days he supported me on tour. He was always going to do well, but we both shared the same reservations about the business and we often spoke to each other about our let downs. Most of the time it was justified. When Joe supported me at Aylesbury Civic, John Kaye Cooper came along to see him and from that show and the ensuing chat in the dressing room afterwards, Joe secured the Royal Variety Performance. Joe was finally on his way, a good few years after his 'New Faces' appearance, and I was very proud to have helped a pal along in such a way.

In April I flew to Cyprus to entertain the troops stationed out there. It was a time to gather my thoughts, to learn the script of my new play which was to open on 8th May, and to spend some time hanging out with a couple of good pals, Ian Irving the comedian, and a brilliant juggler, Steve Rawlings, who'd supported me on one of my tours and who I would later tour the Falkland Islands with.

During that month back home, David Bainbridge saw endless people from the world of animation and publishing, but nobody would commit himself or herself to the Tidings project unless we actually purchased their services, which stretched way beyond our finances. Nobody suggested investment in the concept, and so although interested parties came and went, particularly in the video world, we were unable to interest any sufficiently to force them to open their cheque books in a licensing capacity. Anyone will make a video for you so long as payment is forthcoming. Unfortunately payment wasn't forthcoming because we couldn't afford it.

David travelled the length and breadth of the country. By the end of April 1996, Neal Reed was still the only believer who'd put his money where his mouth was. The compact discs and cassettes were in full production and at last we had something to get excited about. David spied them on display at Harrods, no less, and we all became rather excited. Much of the excitement was probably due to the fact that we had a business colleague that shopped at Harrods!

The late spring of '96 turned out to be a significant milestone. I treated David to an evening out at the Marriott Hotel in Portsmouth. We had worked exceptionally hard on the Tidings and he was staying down in Hampshire in digs. A benefit evening for Robin Smith was taking place and I'd decided to go at the last minute. As always, Robin, David and I drank too much wine as we adjourned to the bar after a complicated after-dinner speech from Henry Blofeld, a cricket commentator, whom I was far too pissed to understand. All my cricketing chums and associates were there, but I stood at the bar chatting to Portsmouth football captain at the time, Martin Allen, whom I'd met during his days at West Ham. We had a mutual friend in Tony Gale.

I was later joined at the bar by some Hampshire cricketers, my good friend Shaun Udal and Paul Terry who was about to emigrate to Australia. In their company stood a certain Rod Bransgrove. We'd met on previous occasions and spoken about music as Rod proved to be an immense Status Quo fan. I'd played with Quo on television and we therefore had common ground. I scrounged a signed tee shirt from the band and had it framed, an item which Rod subsequently bought for Paul Terry's benefit fund.

Rod had succeeded in securing a vast business deal and personal fortune by selling his pharmaceutical company, Imperial, to a larger company, Shire, and had consequently made a considerable amount of money in the process. He shared my distrust of others and still does. People become mesmerised and subsequently magnetically attracted to both show business personalities and millionaires, and indeed who can blame them. He searched for an oasis, a tranquil breathing space from all who surrounded him with sound reasons as to why he should throw his money their way.

Rod's biggest motivation to search for this watering hole was his need to get up in the mornings, a reason for jumping out of bed and stimulating his brain after such a lucrative finale to his previous business exploits. We spoke often of 'fencing' ourselves from situations we found difficult.

The Tidings team prior to that time, David, Debbie Robertson, Lucy Collier and myself, had prepared presentation documents, investment documents and a bible of the characters. The latter acted as a copyright protection and I'd gone to great pains myself to ensure it remained watertight as I developed more characters within the project. We used a bible devised for the Cloud Crowd some years previously by David Landsman of Clintons Solicitors as a guide to our own. To give you an idea, that document alone cost seven thousand pounds. The bible had really been my baby, a confirmation of personalities and colourings of the Little Wonders that wouldn't leave my brain. That document alone numbered over two hundred pages. As a template, we used the Batman film bible, which Bainbridge had acquired from someone, probably Batman himself if I knew David. The job had been originally assigned to Lucy Collier but it proved a daunting, lengthy tome, which needed the full commitment and concentration of the creator.

As we spoke in that Portsmouth hotel it seemed clear to me that Rod sought a challenge, but something with an element of fun and excitement as well. I must be honest and admit to being surprised when Rod rang me on the Friday morning and asked me to put the kettle on as he was on his way to see me. In fact, the distance between our houses meant I wouldn't have time to brew the tea and open a packet of biscuits before he arrived, but within minutes we were seated in a room in my house which my family call 'the orange room'. It's a room of creativity and tranquillity. Most of the updated Tidings stories had been written there. It was as though I'd welcomed Rod into the land on the Edge of Make Believe itself.

Rod knew nothing more than the fact I'd written and developed a children's video and television concept through the previous years. That alone seemed to stir his imagination. I played Rod the Tidings songs and told him of the Forest of Lap. He loved the concept and I felt proud. In fact, so impressed was Rod we agreed to meet after tea to talk further. My first call was to David's house in Hertfordshire. We'd been to the brink of disaster together, particularly in our legal wranglings with John Walters, and I longed to tell him that we'd won over an ally to the cause at long last. He immediately got in his car and drove the two and a half hours to my house, and the three of us met that evening.

Rod impressed me at that meeting. I knew he meant business as much as I did. Between late afternoon and evening he'd taken the three presentation documents home with him, read them from cover to cover and listened to every one of the twenty-eight songs as well as played them to his children, Lucy and Jack. The two little ones loved the Tidings songs as much as Polly and Rosie and the four became our tests for the project throughout, particularly Jack who adored them and sang the songs incessantly.

David's career had always been linked to marketing and production with Barry Manilow and Jive Bunny amongst others, mine had always been a creative crusade, and at last we had a financial expert who could perhaps structure our dreams into realistic business opportunities. We were all very excited and that night, the alternative Three Musketeers provisionally joined forces. Before Rod could come on board officially, we had to pay a settlement fee to John Walters. We did this by all of us forgoing wages and by selling off surplus computers and other endless items of office equipment and furniture which we'd recovered from the Lewes office when it closed down, and once again the Tidings songs echoed loud. We passed on the sticky buns and office treats for a while but we cared not a jot.

Rejuvenated with hope, all the stories were studied and finely tuned and without question we were on our way. Meetings would be brought to order to allow new directorships and financial implications. Rod Bransgrove had finally made it to the forest. His immediate injection of personal money would keep us afloat for a good while. It was a financial injection that grew over the months, but Rod still believed.

A series of board meetings took place. I choose not to give details of the Walters situation as I genuinely feel he had a passion for the Tidings, but I cannot dispute nor ignore his skills of manipulation. David and I were exceedingly battle weary and bruised from endless dealings with solicitors. We concluded business with the man and we never heard from him again. If he'd chosen to make contact, Rod would handle the disputes from thereon in. I'm more than pleased such disputes never occurred and I appreciate Walters' early enthusiasm and miss the fun times with Esme.

Rod Bransgrove chose not to involve himself with the project until we had resolved our Lewes situation, an upstanding measure under the circumstances, but we all found those few weeks frustrating. However, the Tidings had been cleansed and were ready to fight the world with the concept that would not cost the Earth, although I feel that Rod would personally disagree with that one! Walters had gone, and once he had, Rod was on board. Mike Dyer, our solicitor, was to become our company secretary and my accountant, Robert Symons, would audit our accounts. That's how things remained for a year or so. All I had to do was write the songs and stories and come up with more Tidings ideas, storylines and merchandising possibilities. It was a great relief to once again work in a sphere where I felt comfortable and competent.

Bainbridge more or less travelled the world to gather knowledge that he would find of great use as we expanded through 1996 and into 1997. One minute he was bending ears in Los Angeles and New York, the next he was checking out mug designs in Stoke-on-Trent. David's energies knew no bounds. I never followed the progress of Rod or David or anyone else. Indeed, when the Tidings Trading Company waded in to the Stock Exchange, Rod told me to concentrate on what I was good at and leave the business side to him. He would need creative product for the future if his plan were to work. I was the provider of that future creative product. I worked hard on it too, never wanting to let Rod down after all his commitment. I devised Snailhouse Rock, Porky Pine as a television character, a theme park called Another World, the Cloud Crowd was reborn and I also created a rag doll character called Daisy Whoopsy. By the time Rod went to the City, we had sufficient creative product to impress those who had to be impressed.

The first casualty of the new company structure was Lucy Collier. I liked Lucy, a bright bubbly person, and we got on well. Nobody could dispute her work output, but we couldn't justify a position to someone who could not fill our new needs. We were not a big enough company to delegate work that had to be scrutinised and rewritten in Tidings mode. No fault of Lucy's, but it seemed financially sensible for me to create such manuscripts myself, whilst Rod began work on the legislation of all things legal and admin.

I completed the 'Tidings for Tots' book series for the younger ages. Erika Platt had been finalising the illustrations in her Essex art studio while I added more text, but it still wasn't right. I knew it wasn't right. My brief to her had been inefficient due to my uncertainty, and at all meetings David attended, he was told the Tidings seemed a nice idea but they needed more animated content and individuality. All the drawings were static. I spent many days scribbling visuals in a sketch pad, well knowing the comments were justified.

To change my little friends was easier said than done, but I knew they'd have to change to challenge the other children's characters from other countries, particularly America. The decision to lower our target age to three and upwards to perhaps eight, caused me to widen my thinking, one moment writing about the apple core in the centre of the Earth and then devising basic four-line verses for the younger ones. It had become mind-boggling. Poor Erika became more and more confused with each phone call. I admit here I couldn't see the wood for Mr and Mrs Tree and their pals. There was little doubt that the Tidings would become animated cartoon characters before they became book illustrations, and things would change again.

Our guns were loaded and we were ready to go. It had been a long wait, but no longer did anyone care for personal gain or financial reimbursement. The Tidings simply had to break through or there could be no financial rewards. For once our board of directors were as one and the constructive meetings began with a vengeance.

The very first meeting involving the new Tidings team took place in the Romsey office at 11am on Tuesday 11th June. We welcomed the visit of Carol Hehir of the SOS charity. I had dreamt up a 'Tidings Ball' to launch our characters for later in 1997, the day the clocks went forward to be precise. The ending of British Summer Time gained us all an hour. Why? Of course, to enable the Tidings, in that extra magical hour from nowhere, to raise funds for a children's charity. Carol agreed the Blue Bear should become the first SOS VIB (very important bear!) and we should work together in making the Grand Ball a success to be emulated around the country and perhaps become an annual event. So many bullet points had been mentioned, Debbie and I immediately drafted a report of our meeting so we wouldn't forget anything.

I felt excited and at 3pm the same day we were visited by Alistair Clark of Random Harvest Productions. Two meetings in a day? Whatever next? Nobody had visited us before. We bought new coffee mugs and awaited the next arrival. Rod took the meetings in his stride, he'd been there many times before, but remained confused as to why everyone wanted money to become involved. There remained no other personal investors other than Rod himself and 1997 was approaching fast. It came and went and we spent a whole year trying to make sense of the business. David had left us to work on 'The Professionals', but Rod and I could never be labelled as quitters.

Former England cricketer Chris Smith moved into the Horsefair offices to run Rod's other business involving a chain of wine bars and restaurants, and I spent more and more time in my studio, working on the new projects we still believed we would need to bolster the attraction of our company. 1997 was nothing but sheer hard work and a few drinks thrown in for good measure. Rod and I had become firm friends and we are still able to divorce social evenings from heady business days. Not many business partners can boast that one.

Chapter Eleven

Rise and Shine Sleepy Kids

New Year's Eve 1997 was spent at Les Mirabelles, our favourite restaurant, in the New Forest. Rod and Mandy had organised a large table consisting of Debbie and myself, Susan George and Simon McCorkindale, Robin and Cathy Smith, Shaun and Emma Udal and Robin's brother Chris and his wife Julie, and of course my manager Brian and Lisa, who got pregnant that night in our spare room by all accounts. We all heard the shag, as did most of Hampshire, and we're surprised little baby Leila wasn't born with deafness. We knew something was up because the next morning our dog kept licking himself.

We sang our socks off in that restaurant.

> I get knocked down
> But I get up again.

It was good to see Rod letting his hair down, something he was unable to do too often without some sort of catch to a social night out. Bob Terris, owner of Meachers Transport, a Southampton haulage company, had another large gathering in the small but cosy restaurant. We sang 'There's no yellow lorries over here'. Yes, he owns those yellow things that you see so often on the motorway. It isn't funny now but it was then. Then we all became members of the Glitter Gang led by Robin Smith who'd just had news he'd become captain of Hampshire. Rod vowed it would be our year, having had such turmoil the one before. He was to be proven right. We toasted our future and then it was back on the tables for 'Hi Ho Silver Lining'.

Come the New Year of 1998, I took my touring team on a fishing holiday to the Gambia. The tour had been never-ending and we were all in need of some sun. I left Rod to continue the delicate end-dealing with Bainbridge and his associate David Lamping and disappeared for a fortnight in search of barracudas. Rod didn't actually need help anyway, particularly from someone as inadequate in business as myself. There was nothing I could do to help Rod, I'd already buggered up enough business deals as it was.

The travellers consisted of my tour manager Micky Brown, driver Del Smith (the European pike fishing champion by the way), merchandise seller Rachel Ivey and photographer Keith Curtis and it all came about one wet and windy day as we drove through the Essex town of Great Dunmow. I had large blisters on the tips of my fingers from too many gigs and I was at a low ebb. Finger blisters are the one thing I will enjoy never feeling again. The pain is bad when you've been on the road for a couple of months. We'd played the first of two nights at the Sailing Oak club at Braintree, run by Bob Wheatley who ran the Circus Tavern in Purfleet when I was a rookie, and we were driving around killing time. I asked Micky where he thought the hottest place in the world was at that very moment. We both guessed Africa but went into Dalton Travel in the High Street for confirmation. We were right and within half an hour it was booked and we would be on our way from Gatwick. And it was damn hot in Africa, no doubt about it.

Rachel was actually a vocalist Brian Shaw had found through an advert in *The Stage*. A proficient Welsh singer who'd just left drama school in High Wycombe, she'd gained the session job with us, being chosen from over seven hundred hopefuls, and then joined the tour to earn a few extra quid before her next assignment. She was at home when I rang her to tell her she was off to the Gambia. Like most of us really she couldn't believe it.

We eventually lost Rachel from the team when she decided that show business was not for her. I couldn't believe that either, she was a natural talent who would give endless hours in the studio to get things right. When she left I felt devastated, as though a real good friend had disappeared from my life. But these things happen, nonetheless we all often wonder how she is doing and hope at times she misses us as much as we all missed her. Despite the age difference, Rachel and I became good mates and laughed and joked most of the time.

We had plans for Rachel to lead the Christmas Tidings campaign and I admit we had a job finding a replacement. We advertised again in *The Stage* but were disappointed with the response. Everyone sounded like Whitney Houston (if only!!). We eventually found Julie Thompson who'd just qualified at the Paul McCartney music school in Liverpool. Upon my return from the Gambia, Julie would be straight into the studio. Not only did she do the Tidings songs, we were so impressed with her vocals she also did the first set of songs for 'Snailhouse Rock'.

We were all serious anglers apart from Rachel, although she'd had fly fishing lessons on my friend Shaun O'Brien's stretch of the River Dun, a tributary of the Test, while she was down at the recording studio recording Christmas carols for the Tidings. She caught a small trout and nearly died of exaltation. Micky and Del had both fished in Ireland in the European pike championships and Keith had a trout river running through his field at home, so we all sort of knew what we were doing.

The Gambia Experience certainly was just that. The memories are contrasting, with me retaliating against the Larium tablets that were supposed to stop me getting malaria. I would have probably preferred malaria as I negotiated panic attack after panic attack due to the dreadful side effects of those tablets. Then I suffered an enormous gastric reaction to something or other, probably the water or ice cubes or whatever. My arse felt like it was on fire and every groan was met with a violent stomach cramp and a cascade. Tell you what, I never minded fishing in the Gambia but I would never have eaten any of them knowing how much me on my own had polluted their natural habitat.

We had a great break at the Senna Gambia Hotel and when I returned I was ready to get stuck into some serious work for the Tidings team. We went for two weeks, I lost two days somewhere, but that's another story.

Will I ever go back to the Gambia? Only to find my guts. We said our goodbyes to Rachel Ivey at Gatwick and none of us would ever see her again, although I begged her to change her mind.

It was 18th February 1998 when Rod called me into his office and shut the door behind me. It was something he'd never done before. He'd either something very confidential to tell me or he'd turned gay. I sat down and he stared at me for what seemed an eternity. Perhaps he had turned gay. He whispered so none of the office staff would hear the conversation.

Rod's office was tiny and outside sat Collette Timson and Debbie

Ansell. I'd worked upstairs until Chris Smith moved in. I then converted my barn at home into offices and recording studio. I'd never enjoyed office life, and after a devastating point of order that took me to the brink of an industrial tribunal, I pulled away and went my own way. The boardroom where so many Tidings ideas had reached fruition had become an accounts area, and most meetings took place in the broom cupboard where Rod guided operations.

Rod had been scanning the City pages for a few weeks, just wondering if a door was ajar for the Tidings Trading Company to get their feet into. Echoes rarely sounded around the London corridors of power but Rod knew so many influential people. If there were any noises being made, he would hear them. Shire shares were going through the roof and those who'd invested had made nothing short of small fortunes. There was more news, better news, that Rod had to tell me about.

That day I began to learn the skill of big business. If people weren't taking our Tidings project seriously then we'd have to force the issue and become serious ourselves. Expansion by acquisition Rod called it. With only one project at Cannes, we hardly looked big players who just had to be visited by potential buyers. Quite the opposite. So what would happen? The company would try to take over or merge with an existing Stock Exchange listed company that appeared to be in some sort of financial trouble. The accumulated power would save the listed company, thereby elevating ours to City status. It was known as a reverse takeover.

It was difficult to find such a company because of their very status on the Stock Exchange, and were we to find one, the timing would have to be such that we could move in and do the deal before the company went under. It was fearful and most exciting. Rod gave a slight smile when I closed his office door. It meant he'd come up with something – or he'd had too much lager the night before. Being one of the few guys who could drink me under the table it may well have been the latter, but it wasn't. He showed me the share prices in the *Financial Times* and one was sticking out like a sore thumb. It was stuck in the bargain basement department at six pence per share. Rod simply had to make the call. It was what he'd been waiting for.

The Duchess of York had achieved great international success with *Budgie The Little Helicopter*. It had sold around the world on television, video, books and all things additional. It was indeed an accolade for Her Royal Highness that a project had stood up in its own right for as long as it had. Nonetheless it was still the creation of a member of the Royal Family. For various reasons that are none of my business, Sarah Ferguson had undergone a change of image with the people and Budgie seemed to have fallen in proportional altitude. The Duchess of York had been most prolific with her writing and her television series had sustained well around the world. It's all too easy to diminish her hard work because of who she was, she'd put incredible elbow into her project and her public relations campaign with Budgie was relentless and remarkably successful.

The company that made the series was Sleepy Kids plc and they were the very company that Rod had observed for a few days on the money market. His initial call to their managing director, Martin Powell, heralded the beginning of nearly a year of intense negotiation. We began talking to them on 4th March 1998 and the deal was completed on 29th December 1998. With only the Tidings in our possession we looked weak ourselves, and that's where I'm proud to say my own input assisted. As Rod went about the delicate negotiations with Sleepy Kids and the City financiers, my job was to work on new titles to establish our creative strengths and expand our own exciting catalogue. I did just that with 'Snailhouse Rock', Porky Pine, Daisy Whoopsy, the Cloud Crowd, the projects I mentioned earlier, and a collection of Styx cartoons we'd sort of inherited from David Bainbridge's era.

'Snailhouse Rock' was a slightly zany idea I had regarding an utopian dream, the wonderland for the poor old snail. It had often rained cats and dogs, but one day it rained snails. The Rock was a tropical island and the destination of all snails wherever they may be and how slow they may travel. I worked on the songs with two musicians, Beau Dinnage and Matt Payne, a Hampshire pianist and pub entertainer. Beau had the necessary experience and vocals to create that old rock and roll feel the project required. He'd had a minor hit during the sixties with a cover version of the Beatles' 'Maxwell's Silver Hammer', and played bass with Mungo Jerry. The three of us worked tirelessly with Julie Thompson on vocals and produced a tape of moving music which had missed the point with age targeting, and so we had to start again.

Porky Pine I created as a greetings card character in 1995. We called him the squiggle with the giggle and, keeping the same design of his body, I transferred him to other situations and merchandisable projects.

The Cloud Crowd was a leftover from an earlier project also, but I extended them to become a children's weather service for television. It was an innovative idea that all the companies were interested in pursuing.

Rod explained he'd been tailing the progress of Sleepy Kids for some time and that he thought the directors would be interested in a deal which would expand their wealth base and product catalogue. He outlined the confidential game plan and it all looked very good to me. They had interesting product: Budgie, Transylvania Pet Shop, The Disguisables, Potsworth and Co, and Tickling Funster. They also had pending deals with the Horticultural Society for a set of videos and the Prince's Trust relating to something or other. It all looked interesting. We had the Tidings, the Styx cartoons and Rod's excellent CV which was more attractive to Sleepy Kids than anything else. He'd made millions on the Stock Exchange and they wished to do the same. With Rod's track record the deal could be done. So long as it didn't get in the way of our cricket fixtures.

Rod had a team in Andover called the Staggerers, a side I never quite aspired to, not being as heavy a drinker as my pals. We were both followers of the fortunes of Hampshire Cricket Club and good friends with most of the players. Club captain Robin Smith bought shares in our company, as did his fellow England internationals at the time, Alec Stewart, Mike Atherton, Graeme Hick and Gus Fraser. During Robin's benefit year I kept wicket for a celebrity side at Andover. The side included Rory Bremner, probably the most serious cricketer both amateur and professional; commentator Mark Nicholas who used to sing my songs at university when a little youngster; and a neighbour from my days living in Essex, hostage John McCarthy. Mark Nicholas's comment will slay me forever, when he demanded that nobody should allow John McCarthy to go for a piss because he had a dreadful habit of not returning. John took it all in good spirits and having read the book *Somewhere Over The Rainbow* Mark was probably right.

Amid the cricket fixtures Rod worked ridiculous hours to bring the deal to fruition, which finally occurred on 29th December 1998 at the offices of Lawrence Graham in the Strand, London. SKD Media was accepted into the London Stock Exchange and the amalgamation of the two teams, Sleepy Kids plc and the Richard Digance Card Company, along with Cardiff based Siriol Productions, our very own animation studios, fused together SK for

Sleepy Kids and D for Digance. For the first time in my life my name was appearing on the business pages of the *Financial Times* and Moneymail. I was very proud. In the *Sun* too:

Digance saves Budgie from the chopper.

Rod and his partner Jan Mohammed, Mike Heap and I toasted the deal at the Russell Hotel in London, at five o'clock in the morning with a bottle of brandy. That was all the night porter could muster. For six months I was to become a non-executive company director of a listed company and a major shareholder of the new set-up. I resigned my directorship on 1st July 1999 to become creative consultant of SKD Media plc. In no way was the resignation underhand or devious. It removed me from meetings I found tedious and not important to the role I was to play within the company. I could concentrate on new projects without the threat of inside knowledge and other sacred information which the directors were party to. And of course, I had another life to live. It was all very well being creative consultant of a media company mainly specialising in children's products, but Richard Digance had to earn a living and keep his own name alive. My shares were of paper wealth only whilst 'locked in' to the deal and besides, there were other ideas I had which were of no interest to SKD. To expand upon these ideas, and to represent my consultation interests with the major company, during the middle part of 1998, I'd formed The Write Good Company Limited.

It was agreed that all relevant projects, related to the interests of children's media, would be given to SKD Media on a first option basis, but my more diverse business interests also had to be catered for away from SKD who were specialising in growth by acquisition ahead of creativity.

Chapter Twelve

The Write Good Company

The Write Good Company Limited became fully operational on 1st September 1998. I'd spent three months hand-picking my team that would carry the company forward with unique ideas for SKD Media and beyond. I had numerous plans that SKD would have never been interested in, and indeed other ideas which SKD were offered and preferred to pass on, which was fine and as agreed. But my consultation fees were minimal and my living through 1999 remained on the road as a guitar-strumming entertainer.

Robert Symons, my accountant, formed the Write Good Company as suggested by Rod, to work on my personal interests in business. Brian Shaw, my manager, became managing director with twenty per cent share of the company. I retained the other eighty per cent. Mike Dyer, who'd worked with the Tidings in the early days, became company secretary and solicitor and then the staff had to be found.

Samantha Wake rejoined me as project co-ordinator, and after a few hiccups, we were joined by Alison Edwards, who had some experience in hospital and local radio. She passed her interview with flying colours and graduated from an office junior to my personal assistant in four months. Colin Wilson became financial director in June 1999 and with Micky overseeing tour arrangements the office, albeit rather small, was complete. I was amazed how quickly the company grew from such a little acorn to a healthy tree in such a short while. So much so, that it helped me in coming to a decision I'd wanted to arrive at for two or three years. To retire from touring and concentrate on my writing. It was a tough decision to make after thirty years on the road, but I made my final decision on my fiftieth birthday. And what a day that was and if I recall, the night was even better.

The gang at the Write Good Company had planned a party for me at the Mill Arms in Dunbridge, near Romsey, a pub I frequented often. With the exception of one or two, everyone who'd been part of my life in some way for many years turned up. There were eighty-five friends in all. And these were good friends. Jim Davidson had to be there, and was!! There were fellow show business folk, Hampshire cricketers, and friends of long standing. Jeff Mitchell flew over from Bangkok just for the party, Mark Nyman, 'Countdown' producer, drove from Leeds, Mike and Judy Hamon flew over from Jersey where they own the Secret Garden tearooms. Beau Dinnage's band Tramp played and my favourite performer, Chris Luby, was booked as a special treat to me. It was a splendid night. Daughter Polly brought her friend Hannah, Debbie chatted with our old friends from Debden, and face after face came through the door until I thought I was brain dead.

Just when I thought I couldn't take another surprise, Rod made a speech and handed me a piece of paper which I was a little too pissed to understand at the first attempt of slurring. I was talking to ex-manager Bob Voice, whom I hadn't seen for four years, when Micky tell me to read Rod and Mandy's note again. And so began the journey of a lifetime. A gift that a hell of a couple of mates had instigated as a total surprise. I was on my way to a musical trip around Nashville, Memphis and New Orleans, taking in the Grand Ole Opry, Elvis's home at Graceland and the jazz and blues clubs of New Orleans. It was very special. The next day I cried my eyes out. Joe Pasquale rang to apologise for not showing as he was starring in 'The Nurd' and couldn't get away. I told him I was going to the States and Joe said:

'You've got some good friends, Rich.'

'Joe, you're right.'

The trip started in Nashville. Actually no it didn't, it started with a two-man champagne reception at Heathrow – why leave that bit out? We flew first to Chicago and then on to Tennessee. It would be a holiday of a lifetime and a chance to chat to Rod about my future as an entertainer. He'd been saying for two years I should kill it before it killed me, and now the two of us were on the other side of the world with ample time to think about things. It had been a hell of a year. Rod had made me financially secure for life through his company acquisitional skills and I could do whatever I wanted. Rod was the major shareholder of SKD Media plc, and I was second largest. We sat in first class and ploughed our way through a week's *Daily Telegraph* crosswords. Nashville was out of this world and reminded me of what music should be and how it all starts. To stand in Tootsie's bar, where Willie Nelson worked as a barman, where Kris Kristofferson lived upstairs, where Patsy Cline and Dolly Parton were bar staff, all that in a club the size of half a dozen table tennis tables. Everyone starts out somewhere. They were bigger than me and started out in humbler surroundings than mine. So what was the big deal about Richard Digance? There wasn't one. I got up and sang 'American Pie' the first night we were in Nashville, and it wasn't the day the music died at all. It was more the day the new life of Digance started. We saw John Berry at the Wild Horse Saloon, walked into guitar shops the length of a tube train. Into the Gibson coffeehouse for a beer.

'Don't I know you?' I was asked.

'I don't think so,' I replied.

'Yes, you're on television in England.'

'Yes, but now I'm on holiday.'

I was surrounded by true musicians who were the best in the world. I couldn't lick their plectrums and I was recognised for being who I was. I felt stupid in a funny sort of way. Imagine trying to explain to Willie Nelson or the late Roy Orbison that you wrote songs about train spotters and sherbet lemons? I felt confused and crept out of the bar towards isolation once more. Rod freaked out.

'You were recognised in fucking Nashville!'

'Yes Rod, but the waitress came from Manchester.'

'Forget that bit.'

Then it was on to Memphis. The home of the delta blues.

Memphis was a three hour car ride down the main highway and a stop-off for a burger on the way. Rod didn't eat anywhere where they didn't serve Chablis and he was gutted to discover that McDonalds didn't serve house wine. In Memphis I was in my element and I knew my touring days were over. I visited the legendary Sun Studios where Elvis made his first recordings. Four dollars for 'You Ain't Nothing But A Hound Dog'. Session musicians were Jerry Lee Lewis and Roy Orbison. I held the very microphone he used and studied the Studer three-track tape machine which recorded the tapes that almost half the world's population would hear. They were exciting days for sure.

And then to Graceland, where Elvis lived and died. It reminded me of my television show when Marc Cohn launched 'Walking in Memphis'. My god, what a famous song, and it was played everywhere, but aired in England for the first time on my own TV show. What about that? To hear the blues the way B.B. King played it, to hear the street musicians and see the guitars signed by the famous, hanging in the Memphis Hard Rock Café, I was a minnow. I'd done really well, but compared to the big leaguers I was only ever a minnow. Retire, get out.

In 1997 I wrote to Arsenal footballer Lee Dixon for a signed shirt for a sick friend. Lee and I had shared a few laughs together at various football dinners, the last one I did for Paul Merson before he went to Middlesbrough. I've always liked Lee and his deadpan Stoke-on-Trent humour. If you don't get to know him quickly you can take him the wrong way, I suppose we're quite similar in that way. He rang me one night to see if the shirt had arrived, which it had.

'Do I owe you anything?' I asked.

'No, have it on me,' Lee replied.

'Thanks mate, and if ever I can do anything in return,' I responded.

'Well there is one thing.'

'What's that, mate?'

There was a short silence and Lee Dixon answered.

'Please retire?'

We both laughed. Lee had a great 1998 and so did I. It would now seem we both had the same thing in mind at round about the same time.

Rod and I were caught in a minor hurricane in Memphis and sadly we were stranded in a bar called the Otis Bar on the corner of Beale Street, made so famous by Cohn's song. We couldn't leave and after fifty years of alcoholic ignorance I discovered vodka and orange. Rod was so proud of me, slugging away the spirit with such gay abandon, well, we could have died after all in the hurricane. By normal standards, I am a fair drinker, by Rod's I am a Quaker.

Graceland moved us both to tears. Neither of us being great Elvis fans, we never knew how either would react to such a memorial, but moved we most certainly were. The whole thing was done with taste, particularly for America, and I stood a long time at the singer's grave, and strange as it may seem, I realised that whatever it was that sent him to an early grave would never be worth it in his eyes if he were given the chance to reopen them. There was more to life than standing on stage and going to bed at three o'clock in the morning after a long haul along a motorway in the pouring rain. Be it England or America, Chelmsford or California, we'd shared the same jobs, it's just that he was somewhat more successful at it than me. The dangers were still there though. With that, I smiled a goodbye to a legend I never saw, let alone met, and met Rod by the waterfall where he was waiting for me. I simply bought an Elvis mug which I keep my pencils in beside this computer and we were on our way to New Orleans.

It was my second visit to New Orleans and I wasn't disappointed. The trip down the mighty Mississippi is worth the price of the plane itself. It's industrial and real. It's historical and wide, so very wide. They still find cannonballs in the mud from the famous Battle of New Orleans where Packenham said we could take them by surprise. The vibrant French quarter where Tennessee Williams wrote 'A Streetcar Named Desire', the changing face of commercialism, where Preservation Hall stands proud as the bastion of where the whole jazz thing began. Once again like Nashville, a tiny, smoky room hardly big enough to warrant such fame or place in history.

But time had moved on. The day trippers want to see sleazy bars and loud music. The days of jazz are distant and diluted, as indeed are the halcyon days of the British folk scene where it all started for me. There's no point pretending to work a circuit that no longer suits. I never wanted to end up as a club comedian and so it wasn't difficult to decide on my fiftieth birthday to kick the game into touch.

If I ever needed confirmation I was doing the right thing, it came in July 1999, after the final leg of my spring tour, which had been never ending and arduous. I was coughing and spluttering my way through a two hour act every night and a noisy corporate bash had forced me to shout over the rude pissed-up businessmen, causing me to strain my vocal cords. I decided to go for a check-up with my doctor Rosie Parry who wasn't happy and sent me to Salisbury District Hospital for further tests at the Ear Nose and Throat department. The specialist there gave me a good once over and I saw my throat and vocal cords on a video screen. They were clear, if a little swollen, and I was relieved. No nodules, no growths, no sinus problems either, but I'd become 20 per cent deaf.

My life on the road had finally taken its toll and I knew it was time to pack it in. I was discharged from the hospital and went home with mixed feelings, delighted I wasn't plagued with bad throat complications, but somewhat downcast that my ears weren't that great and never would be again. Nobody seemed that concerned, most made jokes, but underneath the smile, I was devastated. All those thousands of shows and my own tiny pair of speakers had blown.

★

I met with Brian Shaw and we decided to make the autumn tour the last. It would allow me to rest my throat and my ears, and to work on my business interests as creative consultant with SKD Media plc and as chairman of the Write Good Company. My various television programming ideas and leisure projects such as the Game Park would at last have my full attention. I would continue to work in television and radio and maybe wipe off the dust from my old guitar for a charity show or similar, but in the fast lane that was it.

And so this book came to be, at a vital transitional phase of my life, when I wanted to be at the riding stables with Rosie more than I wanted to be waking up in a strange hotel room. Where I wanted to offer my help and encouragement to Polly as she entered womanhood at a rate that would have threatened the re-entry procedures of a space module. Fifty years on from Howards Road, Plaistow. It doesn't really seem that long but I suppose my body would disagree. Perhaps one day I'll have the opportunity to write volume two, perhaps I won't. In the words of my characters, the Tidings:

> But only time will tell
> If we are right or wrong
> Yes only time will tell
> If we are weak or strong.
> And will our children say
> We didn't do too well.
> We threw it all away
> Only time will tell.
>
> The ocean and the sea
> Are just like you and me
> They're older every day
> That's why they're turning grey.

I hope you enjoyed reading of all the things I have done in my life as much as I have enjoyed recalling and recounting them for you.

Richard Digance.

Acknowledgements

ALIFFE, Andy
ALLEN, Mike
ALLEN, Phil
ANDREWS, Jane
ARMATRADING, Joan
AUSTIN, Steve
BAINBRIDGE, David
BARLOW, Barrie
BARRIE, Chris
BEE GEES
BEECHING, Jenny
BERNARD, Ralph
BLACKMORE, Tim
BLENCOE, Paul
BOLAN, Marc
BOWIE, David
BRADEN, Bernard
BRADY, Paul
BRANDRETH, Gyles
BRANSGROVE, Rod
BROOKS, Elkie
BROWN, Micky
BROWN, Pete
BUBB, Dave
BULL, Steve
BUSHELL, Garry
CAIN, David
CAIN, Don
CAIN, Flo
CAIN, Marianne
CAMPBELL, Alex
CARNABY, Jackie
CATCHPOLE family
CATER, Andrew
CATER, John
CATER, May and Harry
CAVE, Michael
CHARRETT, Steve

CLAPTON, Eric
CLARKE, Steve
CLATWORTHY family
COHN, Marc
COLE, Richard
COLLIER, Lucy
CONLEY, Brian
CONNOLLY, Billy
COOK, Margaret
COOK, Mick
COOPER, Dave
CARPENTER, Karen
CROCKFORD, Bob
CURTIS, Keith
DAVIDSON, Jim
DAVIS, Spencer
DAVIS, Steve
DAWSON, Jenny
DAWSON, Matt
DAY, Aidan
DEBELL, Leslie
DELL, Denis
DENNIS, Les
DEVANE, Kevin
DIANA, Princess
DICKSON, Barbara
DIGANCE, Avrom
DIGANCE, Debbie
DIGANCE, Doris
DIGANCE, Henry
DIGANCE, John
DIGANCE, Len
DIGANCE, Leonard
DIGANCE, Mary
DIGANCE, Polly
DIGANCE, Rosie
DINNAGE, Beau
DONAHUE, Jerry

OWEN, Nick
PACE, Norman
PAICE, Ian
PALMER, David
PARKES, Phil
PARSONS, Reg
PASQUALE, Joe
PAYNE, Matt
PAYNE, Mike
PEACOCK, Dave
PEART, Brian
PEGRUM, Nigel
PERHAM, Jane
PILKINGTON, Mr
PLATT, Erika
PORTER, Michael
POTTER family
PRIOR, Maddy
RANDALL, Alan
RAWLINGS, Steve
REED, Neal
RENBOURN, John
ROBSON, Mark
ROBSON, Richard
ROSSI, Francis
SANDILANDS, Jo
SARLING, Jimmy
SARSTEDT, Peter
SCHOFIELD, Phillip
SHAW, Brian
SHAW, Lisa
SIERCE family
SMITH, Chris
SMITH, Mike
SMITH, Robin
SMITH, Rosie
SNOW family
SODEAN, Charles
SOWDEN, Trevor
ST CLAIR, Isla
STEAD, Joe
STEWART, Al
STEWART, Andy
STITSON, Percy
STRINGER, Dave
SULLIVAN, Kevin
SULLIVAN, Redd
SUMMERS, Barbara
SUMMERS, Jazz
SWANN, Billy
SYMONS, Robert

TAYLOR, Livingston
TERRY, Paul
THE DREAMERS
THOMPSON, Julie
THYS, Denis
TINHAM, Mrs
TRONION, Nadine
TRUEMAN, Freddie
TUCKER, Raymond
TUNGATE, Jill
TUNGATE, Marcus
TUNGATE, Rachel
TUNGATE, Rob
UDAL, Shaun
VOICE, Bob
WAKE, Samantha
WAKEMAN, Rick
WALKER, Michael
WALKER, Roy
WALSH, Bradley
WALTERS, John
WERNHAM, Vick
WHITEHORN, Geoff
WHITELEY, Richard
WICKHAM family
WIGHTMAN, Alan
WILLIAMS, Colin
WILLIAMS, Dick
WILLIAMS, Keith
WILLIAMS, Winnie
WILSON, Colin
WINDOW, John
WINDSOR, Martin
WINTER, Chris
WOOD, Annie
WYATT-LOWN, Kevin
YOUNG, Bob

He's Not Drowning
He's Waving

Learning, laughter and tears
Living with learning disability

Marlene Spencer

SOLOMANWHITE PUBLICATIONS